《佛光叢書》系列

FO KUANG DHARMA PROPAGATION SERIES

贈閱 For Free Distribution

佛光山溫哥華講堂 Van.IBPS
國際佛光會溫哥華協會 BLIA Van.
6680-8181 Cambie Rd., Richmond, BC, V6X 1J8
Tel: (604) 273-0369 Fax: (604) 273-0256

With Taiwan's President Li Teng-hui, who is Christian, 1993

Parading
alongside
ninent masters
Thailand, 1993

Greeting the Dalai Lama at Hsi Lai Temple, 1989

Ordaining the first-ever Buddhist monastics in Africa, 1994

A Ch'an, Pureland, Esoteric rally in Taiwan

Dusting the world of defilement
(Courtesy of Chen Chih-min)

Fo Kuang Shan by day
...and by night

Ven. Master Hsing Yun leads distinguished guests at the second annual conference of Buddha's Light International Association, Taipei, 1993 (Courtesy of Cheng Cheng-hsun)

Greetings from the young
(Courtesy of Tseng Yao-chih)

Giving the tonsure (Courtesy of Chen Chih-min)

A noted calligraphist
(Courtesy of Chen Chih-min)

Return to the Epoch of the Buddha
(Courtesy of Chen Chih-min)

Presiding over Dharma function
(Courtesy of Chen Chih-min)

With mother again (Courtesy of Fu Chi-ying)

Strolling at Hsi Lai Temple
(Courtesy of Chen Chih-min)

Inspecting the site of Fo Kuang University (Courtesy of Yang Wen-ching)

A portrait in oils by Li Zijian. (Opposite) *Miao-yin ching-kuo* (wondrous cause, pure fruit). Hsing Yun's calligraphy in running script, 1995

妙因淨果

星雲

一九九〇年九月 佛光山

The Biography of Venerable Master Hsing Yun

Handing Down the Light

Original Chinese text by Fu Chi-ying

Translated by Amy Lui-Ma

Hsi Lai University Press

Hacienda Heights, California

ISBN 0-9642612-2-7
Library of Congress Catalog Card 95-79446

Editorial advisor: Venerables Tzu Jung & Yi Kung
Managing editor: Venerable Man Ho
Editor: Edward Little
Production coordinator: Cheng-yung Kuo
May Lui
Proofreaders: Fred Webb, Jeane Tsai
Cover design by Anthony Ma
Cover calligraphy: The characters *ch'uan* (top) by Su Têng-po (1037 - 1101) and *têng* (bottom) by Wang Hsi-chih (303 - 361), both in running script

Printed in Taiwan, R.O.C.

Contents

The master's note	*ix*
Author's note	*xii*
Translator's note	*xvii*
Preface	*xix*
Part I Many, many returns in Buddha karma	*1*
1 To the delight of all Buddhas	*7*
2 Promise on Cloud-dwelling Mountain	*27*
3 Facing the turbulent times	*49*
Part II Crossing the nighted sea, light in hand	*63*
4 The T'ang monk set sail	*73*
5 Ilan, the cradle	*87*
6 Master of innovation	*103*

Part III 'Tis with him perpetual Buddha truth *125*

7 Heading south *133*

8 Epoch of Buddha's Light *151*

9 Dragons and elephants of Buddha gate *169*

10 Traditional monastery, current version *197*

11 Dharma shoud not be separated from worldly awakening *219*

12 Good affinities around the world *243*

Part IV Spreading the Dharma to deliver all beings *267*

13 The baton, its passing and receiving *273*

14 Like clouds and waters *289*

15 Heart for the isle, soul for the mainland *309*

Part V Buddha's Light held high *333*

16 The Dharma coming west *341*

17 Buddha's Light International Association *365*

18 Holding space in an embrace *387*

Part VI Returning on wings of his vows *409*

19 Heart of a child *417*

20 Buddhist path only *449*

21 No regrets whatsoever *465*

Appendix 1 The chronology of Venerable Master Hsing Yun *483*

Appendix 2 Fo Kuang Shan: Distribution of branch temples in Taiwan, 1996 *496*

Global distribution of branch temples, 1996 *498*

Appendix 3 Buddha's Light International Association: Global distribution of chapters, 1996 *500*

Master's note

Having marched through life for close to 70 years, I am but an ordinary monk who deems "preaching the Dharma a daily duty and benefiting all living beings a lifetime career." Whatever transpires in the outer conditions, I have always felt profoundly blessed to be in the favor of the Buddhas from the ten directions and with the affinity of all living beings. With them watching over and caring for me, little by little I have been able to carry out the sacred mission that pertains to a monastic. These past few years, friends have taken such an interest in my life that they have been quite vehement in writing about it. Some of the results are exalting, others critical; some well-intentioned, others without much intention. All of them I invariably choose to regard as references for my practice and mirrors for my doings.

For some time now I have enjoyed the congeniality of those at Commonwealth Publishing Company. A refreshing bunch of idealists, enthusiasts, and professionals under publisher Kao Hsi-chün! When the group came up with the notion of doing my biography, I was only too glad to comply.

Commonwealth's chief editor Fu Chi-ying was the one to author the text. After working closely with her next two years, I was left with no doubt that the task had fallen on the right shoulders. A receptive yet independent thinker, the skilled journalist persisted in taking her subject back in time without appearing to cross-examine me. I have only good things to say about the thoroughness of her research and investigation. The first draft alone struck me as being incredibly complete in its portrayal of my disposition, thinking, and spirituality: the essentials were all there in one articulate flow. I was won over instantly, which was not much of a surprise; so were the senior disciples of Fo Kuang Shan, which, in a way, was a surprise.

Too insignificant are personal footprints along the river of no return that is history. That I am prepared to disclose my life, work, faith, experience, thoughts, and feelings is because, in so doing, Buddhists may be able to draw cross-references for their own cultivation. But most of all, I hope this offering of the records of my inner growth and outer journey should prompt everyone to rise in unison to extinguish the flare of worldly strife, to light in its place the light within each of us, and to create the joyful, harmonious Pureland on earth.

Once again, my thanks to friends at Commonwealth and to Chi-ying for this book. Let me pray that the compassionate light of the Triple Gems be around you, dear readers, and that health in body, mind and propitiousness be yours!

Hsing Yun
Taipei Temple
December 1994

Author's note

From reporter, copy-editor, producer, to chief editor, I have a career that is composed of my favorite thing – words. Since leaving school over ten years ago, daily I count my blessings. But never have I thought of penning a book.

How strange are the causes and conditions taught in Buddhism! How wondrous they are!

I first had a personal interview with Venerable Master Hsing Yun six years ago for *Global View Monthly*. Then, a proposed biographical series featuring contemporary figures at Commonwealth Publishing Company two years ago triggered off unanimous efforts to solicit rights to the biography of the master. As events snowballed, the first-ever chance to author a book fell in my lap! It was not until the master acquiesced and I hastened to ready myself for the task that one innuendo or other came filtering through: for years the project was the most sought-after among those who are by far my superior in learning and writing. But, green as I may be, I happened to be the one with the right causes and conditions.

In the course of the next 600 or so work-days, the master tolerated and commiserated with the worldly, unknowing creature that I am; the inquisitive – at times unrelenting – journalist that I was trained to be, the master accommodated to the fullest and showered with quotable quotes.

In no time did he free me from nagging thoughts of certain restrictions which a biographical project on a living subject might otherwise entail. He showed me trust; he gave me room. I, too, soon found myself in touch with the openness and pureness beneath that towering countenance.

In the following I have shortlisted some of the primary source materials on which I worked:

- 19 personal interviews, each lasting 2-3 hours and resulting in 32 90-minute cassettes
- investigative interviews with 38 relatives, teachers, disciples, devotees, friends, Buddhist scholars, Buddhist and non-

Buddhist personalities, and members of the media

source texts: 19 of the master's titles; the complete lectures in four volumes; the complete diary; letters; notes; newspaper and journal clippings [of his activities] in Taiwan (since 1968), Hong Kong, the United States, and Germany; *Universal Gate* magazine; *Buddha's Light Newsletter*; *Awakening the World*; and major religious references such as *Biographies of the Eminent Masters, The Buddhist Religion and Buddhist Monasteries in Taiwan, The Ch'an School and Tao School,* the *Fo Kuang Encyclopedia*, and others.

To further capture Master Hsing Yun's life and spirituality, I visited Fo Kuang Shan in Kaohsiung, other branch temples, and related organizations many, many times, and traveled to his hometown Chiangtu in Chiangsu, Ch'i-hsia Temple, Nanjing, where he was tonsured, the United States, Hong Kong, and Berlin, Germany. I *hung* around as best I could for his lectures and classes, travels and visits, meetings and conferences, or when he entertained guests and devotees and rejoined loved ones. On one such tour last summer, it seemed that he finally had to say something about my shadowing him. "You sure are getting the *hang* of this!" he laughed.

The illustrious venerable and his phenomenal feats are not for me to affirm. This is not a book about an unreachable legend. I am merely trying to recreate an honest, intact record of this philosopher of life, his words and actions, his thinking and spirit ... overall, just as he is. My touch I want to be light; my expression I hope to be open. May readers not only find a success story but also benefit from the enormity of his wisdom and intensity of his life-force.

Although the protagonist is a Buddhist monastic, I have intended that the religious flavor be somewhat diluted, and, indeed, this is a book for everyone, not just Buddhists. Hoping to interest and inspire, and to ensure readability throughout, a popular approach has been adopted in the general presentation. May readers, too, be led to reflect on their Buddha nature and, ultimately, find the clear, cool source of the river of life.

The text is titled *Handing Down the Light* to represent the Dharma as a light which, when passed onto the hands of Master Hsing Yun, has come to shine across five continents. Further, the light, also representing his aspirations and deeds, shall continue to dispatch messages of compassion, joy, generosity, appreciation, affinity, humility, and gratitude through the defilements both within our minds and without.

The project has, for the past two years, kept me from home and loved ones more often than I would have liked. Gratitude is especially due to my parents, whose love and concern for their daughter, and for their daughter's daughter, seems boundless. Most of all, I must thank my loving husband, without whose support this task would never have come to such a prompt finish.

Last, may I offer this book for the benefit of all sentient beings.

C.Y.F.

Translator's note

Quintessentially this being the narrative of a many-splendored career in religion, translation has been a cross between literature and journalism, with a dash of sinology.

All Chinese names and terms, for the most past, have been romanized according to the Wade-Giles system except for a few established in Pin-yin phonetic systen, like the extremely familiar Beijing and Nanjing, and others. Specifically, the less familiar names of places in China and Taiwan follow Wade-Giles.

All proper names, especially those of places and institutions, have been transliterated, with respective translations given in parentheses unless stated otherwise. Efforts have been made to translate these to enhance textual understanding and to convey an atmospheric feel.

Second and ensuing mentions of a place, institution, or publication without official translation, however, are in roman, which is a slight departure from the regular practice of italicizing titles of publications.

Last, all footnotes have been researched and written expressly for this translation.

A.L.M.

Preface

"Let the blood flow with that of the masses; let the pulse throb with that of the masses!"

Just what is that? ... Some election promise? A bestseller's blurb? A rave review of some rock star's grass-roots appeal? A description of a physician's concern for patients?

None of those.

It is really Venerable Master Hsing Yun's memorandum to disciples for the spreading of the Dharma.

In the warming presence of the pervasive, harmonizing force of humanistic Buddhism and its staunch commitment to render faith, joy, convenience, and hope unto others, who can come away unaffected?

* * *

Up till now, I have yet to find a religion for myself. But then again, to those who have found theirs, I have only admiration. And, I look forward to the day when, quite spontaneously, I shall find mine.

The last couple of years have seen me have the good fortune to be in Master Hsing Yun's company. Each time we met though, I dared not ask him about the Buddhist philosophy but rather let him speak of social trends, everyday relationships, educational systems, media impact, politics between Taiwan and the mainland, and much, much more – all within the domain of *humanistic Buddhism and realistic Buddhism,* the form of Buddhism Hsing Yun advocates. I cannot begin to say how much I have learned from those exchanges except, maybe, that each time I left wondering how students might have benefited from his exhaustive arguments and elucidations if he were an academic.

About the master, I was always an admirer but only knew him through his column in *Global View Monthly* and his diary in *Universal Gate* magazine. While I saluted his philosophy and concepts, I knew next to nothing about what he went through in promoting Buddhism.

Deep down I yearned to know

- how he, with wisdom, makes abstruse doctrines easy and understandable

· how he, with fortitude, makes these doctrines concrete and practicable
· what underlies the competence to run this mammoth organization
· what underlies the nobility to pass on the abbotship and complete Fo Kuang Shan's succession at age 58 – only to carve out another more expansive space for Buddhism
· how he, with the strength of his vows, his causes and conditions, and his virtuous deeds, has projected Buddhism to the corners of the world.

How this happened, at long last, would be told.

* * *

In depicting a character of multiple dimensions such as Master Hsing Yun, no doubt Fu Chi-ying has prevailed.

With a total of 130,000 words in 21 chapters, a clear-cut structure, rounded diction, delightful illustrations, and first-hand reporting and interviews, the author enables those who know and may not know the master to see how he created the symbol of spirituality that is Fo Kuang Shan and his all-pervasive humanistic Buddhism.

The greatness of Master Hsing Yun, as summed up in this biography, is threefold. He is

- a religious reformer of remarkable resolve and practice
- a masterly innovator with the compassion to popularize the Buddhist teachings
- a caring educator who makes religion realistic

His will to reform stems from his determination, his will to innovate from his creativeness, and his will to educate from his compassion. With all three, Hsing Yun is a Buddhist master from whom the world shall benefit and a social educator whose influence reaches far and wide.

* * *

I have always believed that "concepts are capable of redirecting the course of history." Now I believe even more that "religion is capable of redirecting the course of life." What is recorded here about the master are those bits and pieces which, together, form the potent medicine needed to turn lives around.

Humanistic Buddhism and *realistic*

Buddhism, which the master has expended a lifetime in spreading, have not only changed the lives of countless Chinese people but will for certain alter Chinese history one way or another.

As Buddha's Light International Association speedily expands worldwide, Master Hsing Yun has a much longer path to tread and much more Dharma to preach. His wanderings the author has put in these words:

> Every step of his shoes leaves behind
> trails of lotuses;
> The wind under his robe sweeps clean
> [the path to] the Pureland.

With a heart of devotion and compassion, the monk from Yangchou has passed through and now on the tunnel of time. Forty years in Taiwan and now on to create an infinite world of Buddha's Light.

This surely has been a miracle which surmounts even the growth of Taiwan's economy.

Kao Hsi-chün
Taipei
December 1994

Part I

Many, many returns in Buddha karma

A student at Chiao-shan Buddhist College

In his twenties

His birthplace in Chiangtu
(Courtesy of Fu Chi-ying)

Master Hsing Yun with his mother ,
immediate family and disciples, 1989

Ch'i-hsia Temple, where
Hsing Yun was tonsured
(Courtesy of Fu Chi-ying)

Venerable Master Chih K'ai (second from left)
and teachers at Ch'i hsia

Madam Li speaking to devotees
at Fo Kuang Shan

Chapter 1

To the delight of all Buddhas

'*T*is the vernal month of March. The new greenness over Chiangnan[1] is bedecked with flitting orioles, floating butterflies, and budding peaches and plums. About three hours after departing by car from Nanjing, the hub of ancient Chinese culture, the boundary of Yangchou is in sight.

From time immemorial Yangchou has been well known to people. It was one of nine provinces of the Hsia dynasty [*c.* 2205 - 1766 B.C.E.]. And, with the opening of the Grand Canal during the reign of emperor Yang of the Sui dynasty [589 - 618], it was

[1] The region south of the Yangtze.

where cultural and economic forces converged. Moreover, this city, situated at the estuary of the Yangtze, has been a favorite sojourn for the literati of all ages. Emperor Ch'ien-lung of the Ch'ing [1644 - 1911] dynasty was known to have traveled through Chiangnan six times while he was sovereign. T'ang [618 - 907] poet Li Po [701 - 762], in bidding his peer Mêng Hao-jan [689 - 740] farewell, once wrote:

> Heading west, my old friend
> departs from Huang-ho Lou
> (Chamber of the Golden Crane);
> Amidst the mists and blossoms
> of the third moon,
> he sails for Yangchou.
> Into the azure yonder recedes
> the distant image of
> that lonely sail,
> Leaving behind the sight of
> the Yangtze flowing toward
> the sky above.

Few other verses convey so simply the beauty beyond description of Yangchou which, in a country now overtaken with change and reform, is fast emerging as a dynamic metropolis.

Blessed hometown of Chiangtu

Accessible by a forty-minute drive from Yangchou is the county of Chiangtu which, in its pureness and tranquility, has never been a tourist hot spot or a strategic transport location. But, there is a certain character about the place, a certain wondrousness about it because it is in Chiangtu where one of this century's most illustrious religious leaders was reared.

There in a gray-brick courtyard west of Hsien-nü (Goddess) Temple was the homestead of Venerable Master Hsing Yun of Fo Kuang Shan (The Mountain of Buddha's Light).

On the twenty-second day of the seventh moon on the lunar calendar, 1927, an infant's cry rang from the abode of the Li family who ran a humble incense business. It was their second son. An elder brother and sister had come before him.

Unlike those of his siblings, the birth of the boy, then named Kuo-shên, was anything but ordinary.

The matriarch Madam Li [Nee Liu Yü-ying][2], now a spirited and healthy old lady, still recalls every vivid detail:

"In labor with your master, I had a dream of a little golden figure. He was rummaging through the odds and ends by my bed, not uttering a sound.

'Hey, what are you looking for?' I asked.

'He's looking for stalks of rice [grain],' said a graying elder nearby.

'My bed happens to be stuffed with hay. How can there be any stalks of rice!' At that moment, the little golden figure did manage to pull a stalk of rice from under the bed.

The old man then told me: 'This *tao* (way)[3] shall be fruitful.'"

More unusual happenings ensued. The chubby newborn was rosy-cheeked on one side and quite pale on the other. Between his nose and upper lip a pair of fine reddish lines were in evidence. Neighbors were soon gossiping about the

[2] Master Hsing Yun's mother passed away in May 1996.

[3] *Tao*, rice, is a pun for *tao*, the way.

"little monster who was born into the home of Li Ch'êng-pao."[4] Not to cause further uproar among the villagers, his mother would have him leashed with a piece of string and kept indoors most of the time until, fortunately, these unusual birthmarks vanished by age two or three.

Plum of the Li family[5]

Of the mythical tales Hsing Yun himself has no recollection whatsoever. But each time his mother spoke at great lengths about the past, he would sit and listen smilingly as a son should. When others passed these stories on, he would neither object nor seem to care.

After a lapse of half a century or so, that old house in Chiangtu has been renovated. As good as new, the two-story single-family home with a spacious courtyard today houses the youngest brother Kuo-min and his family. A stroll up Li-min (Benefit People) Bridge close by

[4] Master Hsing Yun's father.

[5] Li, Master Hsing Yun's secular surname, is a pun for *li*, plum or a choice object. It is the same character in the Chinese language.

Goddess Temple brings into view the Grand Canal, now polluted and stagnant. Madam Li in her reminiscences, it seems, had known what awaited this son of hers:

"Daily necessities in those days had to be purchased on the opposite bank. With the nation engulfed in war, nobody would risk their lives ferrying others back and forth for a mere dime! Your master though, then only ten, would strip to his waist, tie his shirt round his forehead, and plunge right in. The rushing current of the canal daunted many, but he would always bring home the necessities. Everybody thought this second son of ours was special: of all the plums in the Li family, this would be the one to watch for."

Grandma, the most beloved

Childhood gallantries meant little to Hsing Yun himself compared to the memory of his maternal grandmother Madam Liu [Nee Wang]. Though illiterate, she could chant the *Diamond Sutra* by rote, and had been a vegetarian for over half a century.

Years later in a Buddhist seminar,

Master Hsing Yun fondly remembered his grandmother and how the three- or four-year-old tot that he was first came into contact with religion: "My grandmother became a vegetarian at the age of eighteen. Rising daily at dawn for her morning prayers, she would chant Buddhist texts like the *Amitabha Sutra* or the *Diamond Sutra* despite her illiteracy. My sister and I were raised under her wing, and the two of us would try to beat each other in our vegetarian feats. I was three or four then and quite unaware of the Buddhist teachings underlying vegetarianism, I was merely trying to please Grandma.

"My childhood was spent in her company. Everyday, sometime between midnight and daybreak, she would get up to meditate, fold her legs, rest her shoulders, assume the full lotus position, and control her breath. In the process, her tummy would roar like rushing rivers and swelling seas. The sleepyhead that I was, often roused from slumber, would ask: 'Grandma, why is your tummy crying so!' 'This is called mastership. Mastership from practice.' was her reply."

The devoutness of the grandmother gave this grandchild and his older sister ample opportunities to accompany her to nearby temples where they paid homage and prayed to the Buddha. Other times she would invariably return home with the altar offerings, which the children gladly consumed. That was how Hsing Yun first became connected with the Buddha.

On occasion, monastics were received into the household. Grandmother was naturally the factor behind these visits. In an era of war and turmoil, the monastics impressed him tremendously with the lightness of the cassock, the serenity of the demeanor, and the reverence from the common folk. "How nice it is to be a monk!" he began to think.

Hsing Yun held his grandmother up as a consummate role model due to the nobility of her character. She was industrious, frugal, and kind. He missed her most dearly. Some years after becoming a monk, he returned home to see her. He had turned twenty. They were sitting beneath a tree one day. She, sewing in hand, began relating to him what she would expect for her own funeral should the event take place. She hoped that things would be left in the hands of this grandchild, who was now a monk.

Two years later, the communist regime took over the country. That was the last time the two of them were together. When his grandmother passed away, Hsing Yun was already in Taiwan and had no way of tending to her funeral as promised. Close as he had been to her, he could not quite get over his remorse. For the last decade or so, he made a regular practice of supporting his three uncles at home, hoping to return – if only in the slightest manner – what he had received from his grandmother.

Buddha nature in the tot

Hsing Yun would eternally be gratified for the inheritance of character, not glorious lineage or bedazzling riches, from his parents. He took after his father in moderation and rectitude and his mother in gallantry and fairness. His grandmother's compassion added to the wealth of qualities from which he was to benefit for life.

Among the siblings, Hsing Yun has, since his youth, been especially affectionate toward Su-hua, the sister who is three years his senior, and they share an exceptional harmony. Separated for forty odd years and reunited not long ago, they have not managed to be together as much as they would like. Reflecting on their childhood, Su-hua brimmed over with the same tenderness: "He was so different from the rest of us." She could not remember her kid brother ever fighting with anyone. In fact, the family candy-can would be dragged all the way to the courtyard by the then three-year-old, its contents given to friends in the neighborhood and himself ending up the laughing stock – the foolhardy son of the Li family – for knowing little except how to give away everything to others.

Reliving the childhood life they shared, Su-hua realized how the Buddha nature had been apparent in her younger brother and that monkhood probably stemmed from causes and conditions of many, many past lives.

Another time, the five-year-old Hsing Yun spotted a bunch of little chicks huddling together in the rain. Back he carried them, one by one, and placed them before the wood-burning furnace to help them dry off. One made a dash into the fire in panic. When the child snatched it back, he found its lower beak had been burnt quite badly. To help it to eat, he dug a tiny hollow in the earth, put in some rice, and let it feed from there. The chick was nursed back to health and eventually grew big enough to lay eggs.

One other episode has never quite faded from Su-hua's memory. It happened on a deep, wintry night. During a family gathering for fireside stories, one of the elders began a narrative of human suffering in which the main character was a white-bearded, impoverished, ailing, and hunger-stricken old man living in the mountains ... Before the storyteller ended, the little brother was out of sight – only to be found underneath the table, weeping and feeling sorry for the poor old man! Even when told that it was but a tale he would not come out, and he rejected dinner altogether because he wanted to give his portion to the old man. Not until he was sent to his maternal grandfather, to whom he gave his dinner, was he finally appeased.

Last year, at the knowledge of her brother's homecoming, Su-hua, together with her daughter and two sons, came all the way from Liuchou, Kuanghsi, to Nanjing by way of a forty-eight-hour train ride.

In the courtyard of the brand-new lodging which her brother had built for their mother's retirement, a reposed Su-hua looked every bit as handsome and genteel as she must have been in her youth. Recent travels have brought her to both Hsi Lai Temple in America and Fo Kuang Shan in Taiwan. Of course Su-hua recognizes the potent public figure that Hsing Yun is today, but deep down, he will always be the same chubby, dimpled kid brother to her.

Mother, mentor of wisdom

That there were quite many homes where "the wind sweeps the floor and the moon lights the house" evidenced the stark reality of the northern Chiangsu province where the Li family resided. Manual labor was the main means of livelihood and schooling was only for the privileged few who could afford it. Hsing Yun's folks, though somewhat better off than others, were unable to send him to a private school. Before he turned eight, he found his first mentor in none other than his illiterate mother!

The young Madam Li was frequently ill and often bedridden. Her loving second son would read to her from the *ch'i-tzu-tuan* (seven-character passages),[6] then popular in Yangchou. She would correct his blunders as he read on and, in time, help him build a fine vocabulary, encourage his avidity for reading, and reinforce in him the principles of loyalty, filial piety, integrity, and righteousness. Years later, he still remembers the names of all one hundred and eight characters and their respective characteristics in the classic *Shui-hu Chuan* (Water Margin).[7]

[6] Folkloric literature primarily of mythological, historical, and chivalrous themes, written in a prose made up of structured seven-character (or word, as in the Chinese language) sentences.

[7] A masterful fiction set in thirteenth-century China about 108 characters compelled to flee social chaos under the decaying Sung dynasty. It is said to be authored by Shih Nai-an. Many English translations exist.

Private schooling during the two or three ensuing years was interrupted by raiding local bandits and flight from the Japanese invaders. Little would he have expected that the bits and pieces of Confucian texts picked up during this period should become his life's schooling in its entirety.

Strictly speaking, he never spent a single day in a regular school, or earned a graduation diploma, a multitude of which he has handed out in later years. He never attended a university but founded Hsi Lai and Fo Kuang universities and has been awarded an honorary doctorate. His devotees, among the most highly educated in the history of Chinese Buddhism, hail from Harvard, University of California, Berkeley, and similar institutions; countless intellectuals have taken refuge with him. To them, he is the Master.

His triumph over the illiteracy of northern Chiangsu tells one thing: Hsing Yun did it on his own, not on the wings of fortune.

Half a century separation

On the day he entered the monastery, Hsing Yun became a monk who had leapt out of the three realms.[8] The vast sentience of his greater self has since been offered to all living beings. Still, the innate attachment to loved ones is hard to sever and relinquish. For the longest time, when folks at home were held incommunicado and he had no way of knowing whether his mother was alive or otherwise, he would not celebrate a single birthday, which is really a day of suffering to those who have mothered a child. Each year he would rise early, go before the Buddha, quietly light incense, and chant in solitude. All merits he would transfer to the blessedness and longevity of his mother. Finally in 1986, Venerable Tzu Chuang, then abbess of Hsi Lai Temple, Los Angeles, tracked down Madam Li, who was indeed alive and well. So on his sixtieth birthday, Hsing Yun held

[8] Of desire, form, and formless, in which living beings are reborn time and again.

a grand Dharma function "to show gratitude and celebrate birthday." Invitations were extended to a thousand fellow sexagenarians in the sangha and lay community. For in no other way would the Buddhist spirit of filial piety be better manifested than treating all parents as one's own and all who share the same age as one's own siblings.

As family visitations from overseas resumed in China, his mother was able to join him on various trips to Japan, the U.S., and Taiwan. And, at long last, mother and son spent the lunar New Year together at Hsi Lai Temple – their first in fifty years and their first since the start of his monkhood. It is in the arms of a loving mother that a child shall find eternal paradise.

As much as he missed his mother all those years, she too suffered. She was condemned to hard labor, making a meager living. The family was considered outcasts for having a son who resided out of the country. Not even a photograph of him could she keep. When circumstances went from bad to worse, she was detained many times and interrogated thus: "Leniency if you confess the whereabouts of your son, and punishment if you don't."

The worst is behind them now. For a monk like Hsing Yun, who must travel widely to spread the Dharma for the benefit of all sentient beings, he nonetheless tries to fulfill the role of a dutiful son. Aside from entrusting some of those duties to his brothers, he has paid three of the old village folks to play mahjong with his mother who loves a daily game of it.

In the spring of 1994, Hsing Yun left Kaohsiung to go home. With a birthday cake, peach-shaped buns, longevity noodles, and flowers in hand, and disciples and devotees tagging along, he went to celebrate his mother's big day. "How I've cried for you! My eyes are failing!" the mother was heard to whisper as she held her son's hand in hers. The towering master proceeded to feed his mother a small mouthful of cake.

Her gift to all living beings

Madam Li, at ninety-four,[9] is a walking historical text. Having braved storms of epic proportions – the fall of the Ch'ing dynasty, the Hsin-hai Revolution,[10] the rise of modern China, the strife of the warlords, the Sino-Japanese war, the civil war between the nationalists and communists, the Cultural Revolution, and the recent reconnection between Taiwan and the mainland – she has come to philosophize in everything she says and does. Once while walking about the grounds of Hsi Lai Temple with her son in the moist, coolish morning air, they arrived on the slope, to the left of the entrance. Hsing Yun, turning the key to a side door, announced: "This door opens to a shortcut that leads to the temple." "Main door or side door," responded his mother, "in this world of ours, the best people take the main door, the mediocre wait for one another, and the worst get nowhere. There's no shortcut!" That was such a poignant statement about reality.

9 In 1994.

10 The revolution led by Dr. Sun Yat-sen which overthrew the Manchurian Ch'ing regime in 1911.

Her life's greatest decision, Madam Li feels, was to have offered her son to Buddhism by letting him take the tonsure. The clan seems to have been blessed with exceptional longevity: she and her three brothers together add up to over 350 years of age; her four children, over 280 years; and both generations, over 600 years.

Some years ago, Madam Li was visiting Fo Kuang Shan when, on the occasion of a meeting of the devotees, she was asked if she would like to say something. It turned out that, contrary to her son's concern over her possible stage-fright, she took the podium before an audience of twenty thousand and spoke with confidence: "Fo Kuang Shan *is* the pureland; heaven *is* among us. May the Master guide you; may you attain the Way at Fo Kuang Shan. You're all so kind. This old grandma has little to offer you: I can only make you a gift of my son."

Afterwards, when they were alone together, Hsing Yun teasingly asked his mother: "How could you give me away like that? Don't you want me any more?" "So many need you. How can I keep you all to myself? You're not mine; you belong to everyone," she replied.

It is true that from the instant the tearful Madam Li agreed to her son leaving home to become a monk fifty years ago, her beloved son has been offered to all sentient beings.

Chapter 2

Promise on Cloud-dwelling Mountain

The bloodiest chapter in contemporary Chinese history opened with the eruption of Japanese gunfire on Lu-kou (Rush Waterway) Bridge, Hopei, on July 7, 1937. Thereafter, Japanese militarists proceeded to impose havoc on millions of innocent lives across the land.

To destiny via the unknown

It was under those circumstances that Hsing Yun's father left home on business. Nothing was ever heard of him again. The next couple of years saw the family slipping into financial ruin. His mother decided to take him, then twelve, with her to look for her husband in Nanjing. The year was nearing its end and the northern winter was unrelenting as ever. As the delicate young woman and her little boy, who had never in his life crossed the county gate of Chiangtu, took the road, they had no inkling where it would lead.

The road, it turned out, led to the child's destiny - the fruition of many lives of karma with the Buddha.

Hsing Yun recounted what happened: "Midway to Nanjing, we bumped into the newly formed peace corps at drill. As I gazed intently at the scene, from behind me came a monk who was one of the receptionists at the temple on Ch'i-hsia Shan (Cloud-dwelling Mountain). Probably thinking I looked cute with my round cheeks, big ears and all, he asked, quite casually, whether I was willing to become a monk. As if out of instinct, I replied: 'I'm willing!' Before long this message came from the abbot Venerable Master Chih K'ai: 'I've heard that you want to leave home to become a monk. You may do so under me as your master!'"

But how could the mother have let go! Trying to find her husband, she was about to lose her son. How was she going to face those at home! Then again, the young Hsing Yun insisted that he had given his word and that in no way would he go back on it. In tears, she at last nodded to his plea.

Forlornly his mother headed home, and Hsing Yun stayed on at Ch'i-hsia Temple. His father continued to be missing. Villagers speculated that he was probably one of 300,000 innocents who perished in the Rape of Nanjing [1937]. Although Hsing Yun did not remember much about his father, on his first homecoming he had the ancestral shrine renovated, the memorial tablets of both his maternal grandmother and father positioned, and told family members to light incense and pray regularly.

Ch'i-hsia was both a mountain and temple of historic renown. Under Master Chih K'ai, Hsing Yun received the Dharma name Wu Ch'ê (Thorough Realization), and the alias Chin Chüeh (Instantaneous Awakening), and became a disciple of the forty-eighth generation of the Lin-chi division of the Ch'an school. He became the youngest student at Ch'i-hsia Vinaya College, which was open to monastic students from all over. The fact that Hsing Yun was tonsured there did not make Ch'i-hsia his ancestral monastery. In accordance with the monasterial propriety of the time, Ta-chüeh (Great Awakening) Temple of Yihsing where his master was tonsured became his ancestral monastery instead.

So many monks in northern Chiangsu

As one looks at the circumstances of Hsing Yun's renunciation, one may ponder over the phenomenal number of Buddhist monastics in contemporary China who hailed from the northern Chiangsu province. Other well-known monastics from this area include Venerable Masters Chih Kuang, T'ai Ts'ang, Nan T'ing, Tung Ch'u, Yen P'ei, Chu Yün, and others. Was there something special about this region?

First, there was the harsh environment. The lowland of northern Chiangsu is where the hopelessly silted river Huai is redirected by way of the constricted Grand Canal, which floods every year between summer and fall when the Huai swells. Moreover, its formation being a result of the continual rise of the sea level, the soil simply contains too much salt to be suitable for agriculture. Residents, lamenting over life's impermanence, are often compelled to turn to religion for relief.

Second, driven by the region's poverty, there came a flux of the rural population to urban cities like Shanghai. Most were engaged in manual labor, that is, [professions employing] the razor, scissors, and cleaver. On the other hand, with their robed sobriety and dignified bearing, the generally better educated monastics had little problem keeping villagers in awe.

Third, the belief that "one son in monkhood will elevate nine clans to the heavens" was so prevalent at the time. When monkhood for fathers and brothers brought along a better living for those at home, they, in all probability, returned to lead sons and nephews onto the same path.

The supreme monastery from the Six Dynasties

How the Chênchiang, Chinshan, Chiaoshan, and Yihsing counties in Chiangsu abound in historic temples! One of them is Ch'i-hsia Temple, built during the Six Dynasties. There in the shade of the luxuriantly forested Cloud-dwelling Mountain, where maples spread like evening clouds, the gathering literati used to stand and stare.

Passing through the mountain gate, the steps leading to the temple are seen to be lined with old trees and new blossoms. A halfmoon lake beyond shimmers in the light. First a two-yuan admission is collected in the garden, and then again at the temple. Even Ch'i-hsia Temple is turning into a lucrative attraction.

In the cool April air stands the majestic P'i-lu[1] Shrine. On the lawn surrounding the five-story Sarira Stupa[2] young Hsing Yun

[1] Vairocana, originally the sun, meaning the pervasive Buddha's light upon all living beings or the ultimate enlightenment attained from endless kalpas of practice.

[2] The stupa or pagoda storing the sarira, relics left after the cremation of a Buddha or saint.

whiled away many hours after school. Parts of the hexagonal stupa have crumbled away. Inside the 1,500-year-old stone cave of a thousand Buddhas, figures of the Bodhisattvas and arhats[3] still maintain the full lotus position, but not their heads – evidence of violence against them by the unknowing Red Guards. The authority's cementing efforts hardly help salvage much of the beauty that once was.

Its cloud-dwelling remoteness was probably what kept Ch'i-hsia Temple from total ruin during the siege of the Cultural Revolution. The main shrine and side halls are intact. But the waft of incense is thin and the presence of devotees, rare. At times an old monk, frail and alone, emerges. The sramaneras (novice monks), in groups of three or five, look too languid to do anything. All in all, the temple, though structurally sound, has little left of its heyday spirit.

Even the Buddha, in the face of half a century of desolation, is speechless. And one can't help but wonder about the dawns

[3] Saints of the Hinayana (Smaller Vehicle) Buddhism.

and dusks Hsing Yun spent among those many-splendored maples and within those long, motley walls.

Poor as a temple mouse

Not unnaturally, the scantiness of wartime livelihood – as depicted in the analogy of common folks "who, in raising their hand to touch their collar, bare their forearm" – meant there was a shortage of devotee visitations and donations to the temples. Most simply could not afford any offerings even though they wanted so much to accumulate more merits. In those early days at Ch'i-hsia Temple, indeed, Hsing Yun was as poor as a temple mouse.

Each letter he wrote his mother he had to keep for a year because he could not spare the postage. A torn robe he would mend with paper; a worn sole he would fix with some cardboard; a lost sock he would replace with a reject from another. He cannot quite recall having ever worn socks of the same shade because they seemed so hard to find. He remembers too well the one bucket of water shared by all for the morning toilette. The act was restricted to the so-called *two times and a half* – soaking the towel being the first, wiping the face and soaking it again the second, and wringing the towel the last half. In the end, the water turned to mud. Still, it was carried off to flush the latrine. Needless to say, the face-towel was always filthy.

Food was in short supply: there was literally too little gruel for too many monks. Hsing Yun remembers that Ch'i-hsia Temple had housed a sangha of over four hundred monastics from all over China. Rice, often mixed with other grains, was served twice a month. Otherwise the daily gruel, more watery than anything, was accompanied with either beancurd dregs or salted turnips. Leftovers of the dregs, when sun-dried again, were added to droppings of birds who came to feast on them, and the turnips were often infested with maggots. The vegetable soup, quite free from grease, would probably be clean enough for laundry. Sometimes, with little snails and earthworms lining its bottom and afloat with bugs, it started to smell quite badly even at the chanting of the offering mantra.

He would only close his eyes, hold his breath, and gulp it down.

We are but human and prone to sickness and pain. But in those circumstances, even sickness was a luxury. One time, he came down with a case of skin ulceration so horrendous that each time he removed his garb, his skin was torn again and again. He did not even get to see a doctor.

Another time, he had malaria. Monasterial discipline disallowed sick leave and he was compelled to go about the daily routine like the others despite bouts of chills and fever. It was not until weeks later that his master, who headed the Buddhist college, got word of his condition and sent someone over with half a bowl of salted vegetables. In tears, Hsing Yun ate them and was quite beside himself with gratitude.

To anyone living in the affluent modern life, a half-bowl of salted vegetables would be trivial, but to the stricken Hsing Yun, it was comparable to the most palatable delicacy. Reception of it gave rise to his determination to spread the Buddhist faith in order to reciprocate his master's graciousness, and it reinforced his view on hunger - no one should go hungry. Today, kitchens in all the branch temples are ready, around the clock, to provide for whoever might drop by.

Nonsentient vs. sentient, unreasonable vs. reasonable

There is no ending to the suffering of the body; nor do the trials of the spirit seem any easier.

The new kid at Ch'i-hsia Temple often attended lectures for seven or eight hours at a time, palms joined and kneeling on the gravel until his arms were so numb that they no longer felt like his own and the gravel had sunk into his little knees. He was only twelve.

When, at fifteen, he received the complete precepts of monkhood,[4] he began to realize what it means to take on the

[4] Referring to the Triple Platform Ordination: the first in which the novices receive 10 precepts; the second in which the bhiksus and bhiksunis (monks and nuns) receive 250 and 500 (actually 348) respectively; and the third in which the preceptees aspire to be Bodhisattvas.

sentient with the nonsentient, to take on the reasonable with the unreasonable.

"I remember answering in the negative when the preceptor asked if I had ever killed. The next instant a whole bundle of willow twigs came down on my head: 'Not even mosquitoes and ants?' I quickly changed to the affirmative. But down came the willows once again because, regardless whatever it is, killing is a sin. Then the preceptor asked: 'Did your master send you?' 'I've come on my own,' I replied as I was whacked the third time. 'So your master didn't send you. In deciding to come yourself, you deserve to be beaten,' the preceptor said. 'Yes, the master sent me,' humbly I corrected myself once more. 'What if you weren't sent? Would you have come just the same?' And I was hit the fourth time."

The willow twigs smashed arrogance and obstinacy; the beatings transformed adherence to the ego to the absence of it. As Hsing Yun's religious sentiments and integrity took form, so evolved a personality that "is content with every encounter, lives according to circumstances, is carefree as the mind, and commits for the sake of others."

To the keenly inquisitive youth, that was only the beginning of the preceptoral period. It got harder in the next fifty-three days. Each time he raised his head, wondering where sounds of the mountain or streams came from, the leading master in the preceptoral hall would catch him and the bamboo cane would strike: "What is there to listen to? Close your ears now! Young as you are, what sound can you claim to be yours?" At that, he would hasten to gather mind and spirit and block out the leaves that rustled like waves and rain that beat on the eaves. But again the master's cane caught up with him: "Open your ears to hear! What sound can you say is not yours?" At other times, he would be hit for peeping at the happenings at the preceptoral shrine: "Your eyes are drifting! What is there that is yours?" Then, on exiting the hall, he became aware of the grass that swayed with the breeze and the geese that soared with the clouds and, in panic, shut his eyes to them. "Open your eyes to see! What is there that isn't yours?"

He was hit once more.

This form of training – one of "damned if you do, damned if you don't" – laid the groundwork of his practice and preaching, as well as a personality that is equally at peace with having and not having, hunger and fullness, day and night, more and less, advancing and retreating, largeness and smallness.

Master Chih K'ai, disciplinarian and reprimander

Venerable Master Chih K'ai treated his disciple with austerity, not lovingness. At most lunar New Years, everybody else would take time off to go home. Not Hsing Yun. He yearned to be reunited with his family but not once had the master given his consent. In ten years, in fact, he had given his disciple only two sets of clothing. During the occasional tutorial, he treated Hsing Yun the way a traditional master treats his disciple, disciplining and reprimanding him rather than guiding and encouraging him.

Once Hsing Yun was chided in class

by another teacher. Master Chih K'ai, thinking he might be wronged, sent for him. After the master asked about his circumstances, he raised the tea-cup before him and said: "You thought telling me your needs would get you something from me, didn't you! Listen, even the tea money that I could have spared would be more than you could spend. But you're not going to have any of it! Why, you may not understand now. You will appreciate my intentions someday."

As he grew in years and wisdom, he did come to appreciate the profundity of those intentions.

The reason for barring him from going home was his immaturity. Despite the possession of good roots and a good nature, it was feared that exposure to outside elements might be distracting, and that he might retract and lose the desire for the Truth. Rigorous training was purposed to teach him to prevail with mental fortitude. That entailed the endurance of pain and poverty. In the end, he learned to let go of material life and ceased to ask for more.

After four decades, Hsing Yun

returned to Ch'i-hsia Temple to sweep the stupa of his master for the first time. He, who rarely sheds a tear, prostrated before the memorial tablet of Master Chih K'ai, told of his own struggles in fulfillment of his master's wishes, prayed, and wept.

Media producer Chou Chih-min who toured with him records what she witnessed:

"The parade was overwhelming; so was the sound of the bell and drum. But the master's gait was weighty and his eyes were aglimmer with tears. Speechless, he prostrated before the Buddha time after time, again and again. When finally he was invited to speak, he broke down before he could begin. Some ten minutes passed, and the abbot posed the request once more. So the master began again: 'I was tonsured at Ch'i-hsia Temple. Forty-six years I have been away and today I am home to my ancestral monastery. How well everything is kept around here! With their lives the venerables must have guarded this place, I know! How you must have been there for him when Master Chih K'ai suffered, consoled him when he would rather die! I cannot honestly begin to thank you! ... I thought I would be strong but, here I am in my ancestral monastery, I know not what to feel any more ...' At that, he wept again."

Master Chih K'ai died defending the Buddhist faith in the turmoil of the Cultural Revolution. He was buried in his hometown Haian, Chiangsu. Hsing Yun has since taken upon himself the support his master's family and, during every homecoming, chants the sutras and prays in gratitude at his master's graveside.

The fact that Hsing Yun never complained to his own family did not stop them from missing him badly. His mother visited as often as she could. To be near him, brothers Kuo-hua and Kuo-min also lived and worked at the temple for a few years. Sister Su-hua, worried sick about her brother's badly worn shoes, resorted to learning the special skill of making monastic footwear from a nun who lived miles away. Unsure of his exact size, she made two pairs – one larger and the other smaller – which she asked someone to deliver. It was years later that Su-hua realized that Hsing Yun gave them away to a couple of sramaneras worse off than himself, and he continued to make do with the pair that he had.

The young and valiant monastic

The six years on Cloud-dwelling Mountain laid the cornerstone for Hsing Yun's lifelong commitment in Buddhism. By the time he was admitted to Chiao-shan Buddhist College, Chênchiang, in 1945, he had matured into a valiant young monk.

Chiao-shan Buddhist College, among the most heralded higher institutions, was home to an outstanding faculty and student population. Its chancellor Venerable Master Hsüeh Fan is now the abbot of Ch'i-hsia Temple. There Hsing Yun studied *Abhidharmakośa* (*Compendium of Abhidharma*) under Master Yüan Chan and early Buddhism under Master Chih Fêng. Master Ming Shan, the vigilant octogenarian abbot of Chiao-shan and Pao-hua temples, coached him on the doctrine of Yogacara[5] for half a year and remembers the young

[5] The Mind-only philosophy that nothing exists apart from the mind.

man in his late adolescence as "very focused on his studies, very reticent then, but quite eloquent now." They have taken time to get together a few times these past years and, whenever credited for having been the renowned mentor to a distinguished student, Master Ming Shan smiles and says: "Hsing Yun has done much to revitalize Buddhism. Really he is my master now!"

Shih Ming, a classmate from Chiaoshan, takes pride in Hsing Yun and recounts those days they shared: "You were so supportive of my two feature columns, *New Voice* and *Kalavinka*,[6] in the local Chênchiang newspaper! Each time I asked for a piece of your writing, you would always shake your hands first. This was to tell me that you would have it when you gestured to me that you wouldn't. Then you would lower your head in silence, and the exchange and laughter of the mountain stroll would come to a halt. I knew you were organizing your thoughts and beginning to compose on your own. Then at self-study that evening, you would place

[6] Wondrous sounds.

in my hands the completed work.

"I became a reporter for Nanjing's *Buddhism Monthly*. Once I was packing for another trip when you slipped a bundle of cash into my pocket, saying: 'Work aside, you need to feed yourself, too.' When we met again on my return, I lifted my garb and jokingly asked you: 'Lost any weight?' And you roared."

Books, the causes and conditions

China in the 1930s was witness to the unprecedented scenario of Western culture impinging upon its own. While not a newspaper was to be found within the typically reclusive orthodox Buddhist monastery where Hsing Yun was, the young minds among the sangha, eager to keep abreast of the times, were far from content. Fortunately for them, however, an evacuated country school left behind a library. The older monastics could not have cared less, but Hsing Yun would spend hours in this newly-found retreat away from the monotony of the monasterial life. He lost no time but flung himself into the sea of Chinese classics and, to this day, admits to savoring history and biographies the most. And in perusing translations of Western works, for the first time he came in touch with contemporary Western thought. This opened a window within his heart to the world without.

Today Fo Kuang Shan provides some twenty libraries for its international department, the lay community, students, and children. These facilities can be traced to the causes and conditions which first bonded Hsing Yun to a library five decades back.

Once into the joy of books, Hsing Yun, not schooled in the conventional way, never looked back. Every cent he had would be expended in the acquisition of new titles; he would miss a meal rather than a book. These days, a delightful volume becomes the gift of choice between the master and his disciples.

More important, Hsing Yun reads to comprehend and seeks to draw his own conclusions. He pens commentaries and annotations, makes generous notes, jots down the unforgettable lines, and always indicates the sources. Thumbing through personal notes each time is the equivalent to another read. Such a practice enables him to tutor the most erudite scholars among his disciples and to become a best-selling author and a most sought-after public speaker.

By the time he left Chiao-shan Buddhist College in 1947, Hsing Yun had studied in the monastery for close to ten years. The journey from Ch'i-hsia Vinaya School to the preceptoral hall of Pao-hua Shan, and from Chiao-shan Buddhist College to the meditation hall of T'ien-ning Temple, Chinshan, completed Hsing Yun's training in the Buddhist discipline, teaching, and doctrine, as well as allowing him an immersion in the Mahayana[7] spirit of the duality of practice and understanding. Afterwards, with youthful ardor, he stepped into a gravely afflicted society and found himself embroiled in the survival of both the nation and his faith.

[7] Greater Vehicle. Salvation for all as all are the Buddha and will attain Buddhahood.

Chapter 3

Facing the turbulent times

The Chiao-shan Buddhist College graduate first became director of Ta-chüeh Temple and then principal of Pai-t'a (White Pagoda) Primary School. Stepping beyond his monasdic Buddhist background and into society, Hsing Yun came to take, first-hand, the pulse of a great epoch.

It was a madding time. The belligerence of the warlords, the aggression of the Japanese, the strife between the nationalists and communists, and the suffering of the common folk outraged him like they did thousands of young patriots. Further, because of his Buddhist compassion the circumstances saddened him. Most of all, the Buddhist religion in China was heading to a dead end. Hsing Yun realized this and could not stop thinking about reform, about breaking through: "Don't ask what Buddhism can give me. Ask what I can give Buddhism!" That was the beginning of the formation of a body of thought which would continue to evolve in the years to come.

Buddhism in China, its ups and downs

Indian Buddhism was introduced into China during the reign of emperor Ming [58 - 75] of the Eastern Han dynasty and, through the next 400 years, flourished particularly in the Sui and T'ang dynasties. Mainstream Buddhism during the period was society-oriented. Many eminent monks were active in both political and literary circles. Some were highly regarded in the imperial court, like T'ien-t'ai (Heavenly Terrace) school's Master Chih I [538 - 597] in the court of emperor Yang of the Sui dynasty, Fa-hsiang (Dharma Mark) school's Master Hsüan Tsang [602? - 664] in the court of emperor T'ai-tzung of the T'ang dynasty, and Hua-yen (Garland) school's Master Fa Tsang [643 - 713] and Ch'an school's Master Shên Hsiu [605 - 706] in the court of empress Wu Tsê-t'ien of the T'ang dynasty; others were known to befriend such literary luminaries as Po Chü-i [772 - 846], Wang Wei [701 - 761], Li Ao [772 - 841], and others.

The Buddhist community sought to receive the masses by way of literature, drama, and art, and in so doing became responsible for enriching the cultural contents of the era. Through other undertakings, especially financial and charitable, religion and livelihood were further interwoven. These include such the establishments of *the inexhaustible treasury;* which was a banking system offering interest-free and contract-free loans,[1] *clinics* which offered medical services for the sick, and *fields of pity* to help the needy. All were immense successes during the Sui and T'ang dynasties.

The tide turned drastically by the Sung [960 - 1279] and Yüan [1279 - 1368] dynasties,

[1] In the original text, established by San-chieh Chiao (Three Period Sect).

however. Political persecution and the rise of *li-hsüeh*[2] doomed the prosperity Buddhism had previously enjoyed. The intellectuals drifted away from the monastics, and the monastics themselves, from secularity altogether. The founding emperor, Chu yüan-chang [1328 - 1398], of the Ming dynasty had been a sramanera in his youth. He fully recognized this all-embracing faith,[3] its popular appeal, and its non-negligible potency. Concerned that religion might brew trouble, he took action to control it. To do this, he allocated vast mountain properties to the monasteries and the monastic population was relocated therein. From that point on, Buddhism made a distinct departure from society, and its contact with the masses was cut off. Behind the closed mountain gate, Buddhism

2. A school of learning in Sung which employs the rational approach in the study of the classics.

3. In the hereditary caste system of ancient India some 3,000 years ago, social distinction was drawn in accordance with the four castes: brahmins (priests), rulers and the military, farmers and traders, and serfs. But Sakyamuni Buddha preaches compassion for and equality among all living beings who, he maintains, all possess the characteristics of wisdom and virtue, and will all attain Buddhahood. Such an advocacy invariably illuminated the despairing lower class at the time, who rallied around in zealous support.

assumed the format of a conservative, reclusive, and unsecular religion. Clearly, it was on the wane.

Venerable Master Lien Ch'ih [1532 - 1612] of the Ming dynasty wrote in the *Leisurely Writings by the Bamboo Window* about corruption in the sangha which so anguished him: "Some act like geomancers, like prognosticators, like physiognomists, like alchemists. ... Some hold their book of donations like earth gods. ... Some carry around a mere copper piece, beating it with a bamboo stick like child's play. ..." The former behaved virtually like roving practitioners of the occult and the latter like paupers. "This is the absolute worst of *mo-fa*!"[4] lamented Master Lien Ch'ih.

Turning into a faith of doom, Buddhist monastics seemed to have little more to do than perform funeral services to deliver the dead from hell. The religion totally dissociated itself from the masses and the literati dissociated themselves from a

[4] The last of the three formal periods of the Buddhist teachings in which its deterioration will lead to its eventual extinction. The first period was *chêng-fa* (period of correct doctrine) and the second was *hsiang-fa* (semblance period).

now degraded sangha. Ironically, the occasional monastic expressing a concern for worldly affairs or having a reputation on a par with the literati was criticized as overly secular. Venerable Master T'ai Hsü who lived at the turn of the century was among those who fell victim to this common misconception of Buddhism, which is, unfortunately, still alive and well to this day.

With the founding of the Republic came the movement against Confucianism engineered by young intellectuals who had but skimmed Western thought. Buddhism also took a public beating at this time. In the eyes of these intellectuals, the clay buddhas and country monks were feudalistic, backward, and superstitious hybrids, and they avoided monastic ceremonies like the plague. Many upheld the belief of "down with the temples and up with public education" as a form of national salvation. In 1927, warlord Fêng Yü-hsiang, nicknamed *the Christian General*, ordered the annihilation of Buddhism in Honan province, where monastics were either murdered or exiled. Likewise, the provincial authorities of

Chêchiang wanted to oust the sangha, and the central government's minister of internal affairs Hsüeh Tu-pi proposed that monasteries be converted into schools. The entire nation was inflamed by an anti-Buddhist sentiment. This was one of the lowest points in the history of Buddhism in China.

Master T'ai Hsü, the legend

Finally, the young sangha saw a light. It relit their hope in their religion and showed the way for their patriotism. This was Venerable Master T'ai Hsü [1889 - 1947].

Many of Hsing Yun's teachers at Chiao-shan had studied under Master T'ai Hsü. Hsing Yun read his works extensively. The young sangha at the time was particularly impassioned by his call: "Every national is accountable for the rise and fall of a nation; the sangha is accountable for the rise and fall of Buddhism." Master T'ai Hsü taught a redirection of Buddhism from the passivity of reclusion onto the positivity of humanity. In spearheading massive reforms in the Buddhist hierarchy, monasterial assets, and doctrinal teachings, he urged that "worldly matters be tackled with unworldly spirits."

In restructuring the Buddhist hierarchy, Master T'ai Hsü urged that the slack sangha be trained anew with the purpose of making every monk a competent preacher and every nun a qualified teacher and nurse. In reforming doctrinal teachings, he urged that the fatalistic belief that "life is suffering" and other obsolete conceptions be substituted with the affirmation of a valuable life, a correct view of it, and a positive attitude to live it. In revolutionizing monasterial assets, he urged that private ownership be returned to the entire monastery, reliance on the monastery be replaced by self-sufficiency, and self-sufficiency be attained through individual efforts and cultivation.

Master T'ai Hsü was also the designer of the contemporary format in Buddhist education. In 1918 the ground-breaking of Min-nan Buddhist College caused a stir across the nation. Unfortunately, the relationship between the school and the monastery where it was housed was a quarrelsome one. The operation broke down after a decade or so. Similar endeavors followed at its heels but none possessed nearly the same consistency.

Master T'ai Hsü was an intellectual who knew that Buddhism could not exist without a United China. Hence he called for active monastic participation in anti-Japanese activities in the then-beleaguered country. For, he pleaded, "the nation, society, and all living beings are one."

As much as the senior sangha repudiated Master T'ai Hsü and condemned him as a traitor, the younger monastics rallied to his support and hailed him as the savior of Buddhism in modern China. At the end of the war, Hsing Yun found himself in the master's Personnel Training Class in Chinese Buddhist Affairs. A classmate was heard to say: "Should Master T'ai Hsü ask me to tread boiling water and prance on fire, I would not ask why."

Language, the tool of reform

While stationed at White Pagoda Primary School as principal, Hsing Yun groomed the young and pondered long and hard on how to carry out Master T'ai Hsü's ideal of a new Buddhist faith. Like Hu Shih-chih [1891 - 1962][5] who maintained that "China's doom was poverty and ignorance," he realized language was the tool of reform and bridge to the masses. A series of literary undertakings ensued: *Raging Billows*, a monthly he founded with classmate Master Chih Yung ran for more than twenty issues; *Hsia-kuang* (Splendid Light) *fu-k'an*, a supplementary he edited for the newspaper *Hsü pao*; and extensive essay contributions to local papers in Chiangsu. His writings commanded a considerable readership among the young. Barely twenty himself, Hsing Yun was ready to bring Buddhism to a new height by urging that service conventions be revised and monasterial management be devised. In the meantime, he absorbed information like a sponge and read with gusto the literature of the 1930s.

At the surrender of Japan, China was hardly back on its feet when the country became embroiled in civil war again. Hsing Yun was compelled to halt before he could

[5] Educator and philosopher.

take another step. With Master T'ai Hsü's passing away in 1947, his call for reform was silenced. Little would he have guessed that, years later, his ideal would be launched from Taiwan by the renewed efforts of a young monk whom he had met but a few times.

Nanjing fell into the hands of the communists in 1949, and the nationalists were about to lose Chiangnan. Daily the wounded multiplied and the country agonized. Members of the sangha, under Venerable Master Lê Kuan, took to organizing medical relief groups. They would provide services for all living beings as they had vowed.

The Dharma lineage is preserved

Hsing Yun's close friend Master Chih Yung had worked about two months trying to bring a 600-member medical relief force to Taiwan. On the tacit agreement not to perish together, Chih Yung decided to stay behind and defend their religion, while Hsing Yun headed the relief group to Taiwan.

Hsing Yun, heavy at heart, returned to Ch'i-hsia Temple where Master Chih K'ai was and bade farewell. His plan to spread the Dharma in Taiwan delighted Master Chih K'ai, who gave his immediate approval. The night before Hsing Yun's departure, the master prepared a sumptuous meal in the refectory to honor his beloved disciple. But when dinner time came, neither had the heart to raise his chopsticks. Speechless, their eyes were riveted on each other. Then, tears welled.

Back in Nanjing, Hsing Yun learned that a Taiwan-bound vessel was soon to set off from Shanghai. He lost no time and took the night train to Ch'angchou. In the pitch-darkness of the Buddhist college, schoolmates he knew and some he didn't were roused and invited to join him in the brave new world of Taiwan.

Over a hundred had pledged to follow Hsing Yun but only seventy – including Masters Yin Hai and Hao Lin who now reside in U.S.A. – actually boarded in Shanghai. With the vow to preserve the lineage of the Dharma, he and the others took the sea. The voyage would chart a new course in Hsing Yun's life; it would also draft the next chapter in the history of Buddhism in China.

Part II

Crossing the nighted sea, light in hand

In his thirties

The way he was in Ilan

屆畢業紀念
五十二年七月

With the class of '63 at Tz'ŭ-ai Kindergarten, the first Buddhist Kindergarten, Ilan

Lecturing at Lei-yin Temple,
Ilan, 1953

Promoting the reprint of the Buddhist Canon in Changhua, 1955

With a young audience, Ilan, 1959

At a charity sale of Buddhist memorabilia in support of the Tibetan Buddhist movement in the late 1950s.

Departing from Sungshan Airport, Taipei, in the 1960s

Chapter 4

The T'ang monk[1] sets sail

Immigrants from Fuchien and Kuangtung provinces[2] brought their Buddhist faith as they set sail for Taiwan, then under Dutch rule, near the end of the Ming dynasty. Duly rooted, Buddhism began to prosper when Chêng Ch'êng-kung[3] [1624 - 1662] took over. The Mi-t'o (Amitabha) Temple was erected by his son Chêng Ching, a

[1] Referring to Hsing Yun here. *T'ang Shan sêng* in the original text, indicating that the monk hailed from China, referred to as T'ang Shan (Mountain of T'ang). The Chinese people are commonly known as *T'ang jên* (people of T'ang) after the mighty T'ang dynasty. Hence this coinage.

[2] In southern China.

[3] Leader of resistance against the Manchu invaders at the fall of Ming. He later regained Taiwan from the Dutch.

devout Buddhist, and K'ai-yüan Temple by his mother, who invited the sangha to care for the place.

By the Ch'ing dynasty, more of the sangha followed the same route as the early immigrants from Fuchien and Kuangtung. Taiwan became the site of not a few Buddhist temples. Chu-hsi, Fa-hua, Ch'ao-fêng, Ling-yün, Ling-ch'üan – all centenarian in age – are still standing.

The occupying Japanese brought along a version of Buddhism that was light on precepts and discipline. This subsequently produced a glut of monastics who went to the extent of abandoning celibacy and vegetarianism. Worse, some would wear their cassocks within the temple but not otherwise. Together with practitioners from such minor sects as Lung-hua and Hsien-t'ien who were not required to take the tonsure, they formed a picture so blurred that there was no telling who were the monastics and who were not. The common folk did not get a correct understanding of Buddhism.

Just a shirt on his back

The civil war ended in 1949. Thereafter a million more Chinese followed in their forefathers' footsteps and crossed over to the enchanting isle of Taiwan. The youthful Hsing Yun was among them. Some months before, the notion of spreading the Dharma in Taiwan never crossed his mind. He had heard little of the land, which remained as outlandish to him as depicted in archaic texts. He was also told tales of the rich and powerful who fled the country and ended up paying prodigiously for a place to sleep – on the streets.

Like the other passengers from T'ang Shan scurrying east, Hsing Yun landed in Taiwan with no more than straw sandals on his feet and a shirt on his back. The only baggage he had was misplaced, and he made a gift of his robe to his fellow monastic Venerable Chu Yün. Locals saw his sandaled feet and gaped. It embarrassed him. So he went barefoot like everyone else.

His group was disbanded. Like the others, Hsing Yun, then twenty-three, was on his own. He was in Taipei two days when he was told that the monasteries there were either "full" or not prepared to accommodate travelers from out of the province. At one point, a venerable monk spoke with uncharacteristic coldness: "How are you qualified to be here?" The night was cold, a storm was raging, and he was hungry. He stumbled into the knee-deep rain water and was soaked through. Finally under the big bell at Shan-tao (Good Guidance) Temple he curled up for the night.

The stranger in the strange land did not even speak a word of the dialect. However, he decided the next day to look up an old classmate at a monastery in Keelung. By the time he arrived, it was past one in the afternoon. Asked if he had eaten, a visibly embarrassed Hsing Yun replied: "No, I haven't eaten or drunk anything. Not since noon yesterday!" Just when his classmate was about to show him into the kitchen, a portentous voice thundered: "We can barely feed ourselves. Please let him seek help elsewhere!" That was understandable. In those days, everybody had difficulty just surviving, not to mention lending others a hand. Hsing Yun looked around and realized he must hit the road again. He turned to go but was halted by his friend. A pot of congee was cooked for him. His friend had paid for the rice from his own pocket. As Hsing Yun held the bowl that day, his hands could not stop trembling from hunger.

At the finish of the meal, he thanked his host and bade him good-by. Next he thought of going up Ch'êng-tz'u Liao in Kuan-yin Mountain. But rain flooded the road, leaving him stranded at the station, famished and shivering. How the lone monk must have felt, no one would ever know.

At long last, Yüan-kuang Temple

Ultimately, it was the compassionate Venerable Master Miao Kuo of Yüan-kuang (Perfect Light) Temple in Chungli who put him up. Hsing Yun, with utmost gratitude, toiled hard to reciprocate the kindness. He would pull 600 pails of water out of the bottomless well for the daily consumption of the 80 or so inhabitants of the monastery. Before daybreak, he would tread the shadows on the moonlit dirt road, pushing the handcart, and traveling 15 *li*[4] to the market. Amidst breezes through the boughs, the idyllic peace over the land, the barking dogs from afar, and the clatter of his own wooden clogs, he would silently recite the name of Avalokitesvara Bodhisattva. When he reached the market, the venders were still asleep. He would then knock on their doors, make his daily purchases, and take the same dirt road back.

Few were young and robust as Hsing Yun in the monastery. It was he who must also clean the latrines and, when somebody passed away, help wrap and bury the body.

All those chores aside, Hsing Yun never in those two years deserted his reading and writing. Once he earned a small sum helping out in a chanting service. With the money he hastened to buy himself new stationery. The elation was ineffable. Many a time fellow monastics and devotees

[4] One *li* is about one third of a mile.

caught him writing and thought he had nothing better to do. He still recalls the cordial exhortation of an elderly devotee and regular helper: "Master, you must go and work. Else you'll starve!" During the same period, he took three months off to tend the woods around Fa-yün (Dharma Cloud) Temple in Miaoli. There on the grass he churned out *Singing in Silence,* edited a monthly magazine, *Life,* and penned radio scripts.

Hard to tell the Buddhas and deities apart

Life was a grind, to say the least. Most people dared not venture beyond dreams of domestic well-being and a livelihood free from care. For Hsing Yun, however, there was more, much more. Not for a moment did he relax the will to carry on with Master T'ai Hsü's humanistic Buddhism in Taiwan so that more would be taught the correct knowledge and correct view of the Dharma. Inside he was as driven as ever. But then again, Taiwan forty years ago was not exactly the best stage for this!

Scholars of Taiwan's religious evolution have long maintained that polytheism was the natural answer to a life at the mercy of the elements: typhoons, earthquakes, and threats of like magnitude. There was simply nowhere to hide. Except, maybe, in the asylum of the Taoist temples that went up one after another. Many of these temples had their eaves bedecked with ornate figures from mythology, deities like Matsu,[5] Lü Tung-pin,[6] the earth gods, rock gods, and tree gods, and borrowed portions of the Buddhist etiquette and monasterial structure. In the end, it was hard to tell one from the other.

On another front, Buddhist monasteries in Taiwan were unlike the land-owning, self-sufficient establishments of China. Donations from devotees and contributions to the monastics were their main sources of sustenance. Taiwan was in an economic plight and purse strings were, more often than not, tight. Hence, for the longest time,

5. Goddess of the sea.

6. Taoist immortal.

the Buddhist community was busy enough trying to stay afloat. Progress had to wait.

In addition, the monastics in those days were not well educated. Most were competent in chanting the sutras and delivering the dead from hell, but the preaching of the Dharma was a seldom touched subject. Buddhism was for funerals. That was about its only social impact. Needless to say, the intellectuals were apathetic.

Worst of all, an overbearing American presence in postwar Taiwan and incredible economic prowess propelled Catholic and Protestant influences to the cities and villages. President Chiang Kai-shek and his wife became converts; so did social leaders and luminaries. Christianity was in; Buddhism was out.

Some would have no difficulty remembering how events were sent spiraling into disaster, how the sanctitude of the temples were violated, how Taipei's Shan-tao Temple was once transformed into recruiting offices for the military, how the main shrine of Yüan Shan's Lin-chi

(Gracious Regard) Temple was turned into Chung-shan T'ang,[7] and how the centenarian Tung Pên-yüan (East Original Vow) Temple in Taipei almost became a mosque when the authorities were intending to make their imperial friends from the Middle East feel at home (but was saved from ruin when a sizable mosque was put up elsewhere, with the government footing the bill).

Incarcerated three times

The [nationalist] government barely got a foothold in Taiwan. Uncertainty was in the air. Newcomers from the mainland were viewed with suspicion. Intelligence gathering and security were of high priority. Of all people, the monastics suffered the most.

Hsing Yun has been incarcerated three times during his lifetime. The first happened when he was running White Pagoda Primary School. Hot on each other's trail, the nationalist military would hunt for the communist guerrillas in the day, and the

[7] Memorial hall for Dr. Sun Yat-sen, founder of modern China.

communists would assault the nationalists after dark. He was nabbed by both and subsequently pressed for *enemy* intelligence.

One time in 1949, rumors were rife that 300 monastics were sent to infiltrate Taiwan. Hsing Yun, along with Venerable Master Tz'u Hang – who later founded Maitreya[8] Inner Court in Hsichih – and other monastics from the mainland, were jailed for alleged espionage. For twenty-three days they were bound and shackled and shoved around. There was not even room in the cell to lie down. Eventually the group was bailed out by devotees Sun-Chang Ch'ing-yang, Wu Ching-hsiung, and others.

Sometime afterwards, the police acted on anonymous reports alleging that he was receiving radio broadcasts from the mainland in the day and, incognito, disseminating procommunist literature at night. He was tailed around the clock. A year passed. The reports ceased. Those sent to follow him became his followers.

[8] Friendly, benevolent. The next Buddha, now in the Tusita heaven, who is to come after Sakyamuni Buddha.

Amidst the white terror[9], Hsing Yun accepted a teaching appointment offered to him by Venerable Master Ta Hsing at Ch'ing-ts'ao (Green Grass) Lake Buddhist College in Hsinchu. He found himself having to apply for leave with the local sheriff whenever he took time off. Years later in Kaohsiung, Fo Kuang Shan was again faced with the allegation of storing some 200 rifles. By then, Hsing Yun had wised up to the affairs of the times and fared well in communicating with those in power.

A rising star

Taiwan continued to benefit from the eminent presence of Buddhist monastics arriving from China. The true splendor of the Buddhist doctrine was unveiling before society. Indeed Buddhism was to come back. While all this was happening, Hsing Yun emerged from his ordeals quite unscathed. Not only that, he could no longer contain the burning thought that

[9] Terror happened in the daytime.

"Buddhism depends on me." The young monk drilled in orthodoxy would soon soar like a rising star.

He reaped a tremendous amount of affinities during his two-year stint at Yüan-kuang Temple. He was Master Miao Kuo's true protégé. His earnestness and diligence endeared him to many. Grass-roots support was mounting. He still talks about a gracious old lady who used to sneak him a bowl of noodles: "Each time I saw her deeply wrinkled hands reaching through my window with the steamy bowl, soup spilling on the sill, I was touched beyond words!"

So, a little later Master Miao Kuo lent his guiding hand to those next steps. A little further on, Hsing Yun stepped into society and began to walk with the masses. He had come to know the place and its people, and figured out what he must do for them.

Chapter 5

Ilan, the cradle

The Buddhist scene in Taiwan resembled an arid plain, where the prerequisites for the spread of the Dharma and cultivation of living beings would have to be no less than the right circumstances, courage, wisdom, and perseverance. Taking his position in Ilan, northeastern Taiwan, he had all four attributes at hand.

Going to the mountain city

It all began one day in 1952. He bumped into layman Li Chüeh-ho during an executive election of the Chinese Buddhist Association. Li was anxious to find a monastic willing to teach the Buddhist doctrine in his hometown Ilan. But Ilan was poor and simply out of the way. The Taipei-Ilan highway was winding, with perils at every turn. The train ride from Taipei took about five hours – complete with sooty tunnels. A few teachers of the Dharma would come once but not again.

Taking note of Li's problem, Hsing Yun eagerly volunteered his service. At year's end, he set foot in Ilan and never spoke of leaving. The folks of Ilan, too, went from appreciation and reverence to become wholehearted followers.

In those days, going to a place like Ilan took courage. Plenty, in fact. Hsing Yun's courage was born from a fiery determination to spread the Dharma, laced with a certain come-as-it-may placidity.

Geographically, Ilan is situated on a delta. Overlooking the Pacific at one end, the city is blockaded from the vast plain in the northwest by mountains at the other. Life was insulated and the people were introverted. Hsing Yun's destination was Lei-yin (Sound of Thunder) Temple in Peimên (North Gate). Built during the reign of Tao-kuang [1821 - 1850] of the Ch'ing dynasty, the former residential structure with the traditional courtyard was wrecked by a typhoon in 1963. Locals, headed by Hsing Yun, sought to rebuild it. Construction completed in 1978. That was also where Hsing Yun's career took off.

Treading the premises of Lei-yin Temple for the first time, Hsing Yun discerned why the place failed to keep other teachers of the Dharma.

He remembers leaving Taipei early that day and reaching Ilan past noon. Across the temple threshold came the sight of three military families squatting inside. The shrine was there; the cushions for worship were not – they had been turned into pillows. Clothes and footwear were scattered all over. A stove blocking the latrine was still smoking; it had to be removed to gain entrance into the latter.

Hsing Yun let his eyes roam awhile until they alighted on an elderly bhiksuni – Venerable Abbess Miao Chuan – who was chanting the sutras for devotees to relieve suffering. When done, she emerged with the query: "Are you the monk coming to lecture?" "Yes," he responded. Another halfhour passed before she returned with a cup half filled with tea – cold.

Finding a niche in the shrine

He commuted a few times. Devotees took to his teachings. He stayed. He found a niche in the main shrine. It was windowless and the ceiling was low. Once inside, he could not stand up straight. But it would do fine.

People who were there in those days might still remember that they had to pay for the installation of every light bulb in the household. To pinch expenses, he hung the bulb before the Buddha in the day and dragged it to his quarters to read at night. The cord was short, so he read and wrote at the threshold – the buzz of the mosquitoes kept him company until daybreak. The soupspoon was of scrap lead so light that it would go with the wind at any time, and he would be up chasing it. The first six months he slept on the floor. Finally the devotees chipped in for a prison-manufactured bamboo bed and chair. The bed squeaked with every toss and turn. But this resting spot would do just fine.

Hsing Yun knew hardship and everybody was poor then. Somehow, life's limitations never bothered him nearly as much as the circumstantial shortfalls surrounding the development of Buddhism as a whole.

Time was not exactly ripe for the spread of the Dharma. Taiwan was still reeling from half a century of Japanese rule. For its socially suppressed and educationally deprived people, religious orientation would be a difficult leap. On top of that, the prim little Ilan was paranoid about anyone and anything from outside. Needless to say, the coming of this young monk turned more than a few heads. Some would seek to put his wit and endurance to a few rude tests.

Master of North Gate

Buddhist lectures at Lei-yin Temple were often disturbed by clamor outside. Quick-witted, Hsing Yun turned the light off and left the spark of the lit incense before the Buddha. The blusterers, shocked by the sudden darkness, saw the magnificent sitting posture of Hsing Yun, and heard the lectures clearly. By means of "silence," many hostile people were transformed from having attitude of arrogance to that of friendliness.

Another time, Hsing Yun was practically stoned before a huge congregation. He was in the middle of an evening lecture in downtown Ilan where seven avenues converged. It turned out to be the doing of a bunch of Christian zealots. Within his own circle, things got a little explosive, too. Like the founding of his youth choir, which rubbed many the wrong way. The radicals even threatened to remove him altogether.

He rode the gales. The people of Ilan were eyewitnesses to his energy and bearing, his maturity and wit, his knowledge and charm. They did not know his name, but to them he was the master of North Gate. The older devotees certainly remember how he used to look. A-yao Ku, eighty-something, is among Hsing Yun's earliest followers. "He was so cute!" she grins, showing her gold teeth.

Not unnaturally the young monk with the commanding air was an item of enormous interest to the girls. *Shih-ku*[1] Hsiao Pi-hsia, who has followed the master for almost four decades, recounts the time he went over to the office where she worked to make a call. The next thing she knew was that Ilan was literally incommunicado because all twenty or so operators – their supervisor included – were out to size him up! Today, most employees in the office are Hsing Yun's followers.

First site for humanistic Buddhism

Tough might be the way of the folks of Ilan. But once converted, Hsing Yun realized, they would be the eternal buttress of Buddhism. He was ready to let Ilan be the first site in which to practice humanistic Buddhism.

To combat the prevalence of illiteracy in the 1940s, he decided the method of convenience would be to call on the name

1. An unmarried female devotee serving for life in a monastery.

of the Buddha and to chant the sutras. *Nien-Fo hui* (sutra-chanting sessions) were formed in which devotees would learn to recite the Buddhist texts. These sessions, in fact, were a legitimate form of public education. A formal lecture hall was added to Lei-yin Temple to accommodate the needs of the increasing attendees in 1956. At its inauguration, many highly-cultivated masters, including master Lcan-skya, came to offer their congratulations.

The chanting sessions were his first triumphant venture into the genre of regular lectures. To announce a forth-coming lecture, a devotee would carry a board with the inscription *Please heed the sutras* through the streets, and another would be the crier tapping a hand-drum. The site of the chanting sessions was virtually the birth-place of Buddhism in Ilan. North Gate's bus-stop still reads *nien-Fo hui.*

Sower of Bodhi seeds

Flexing the muscles of the youthful Buddhists would be next. Although not a singer, Hsing Yun formed a pool of gregarious song-birds – the first-ever Buddhist choir. His lyrics were set to music by Yang Yung-p'u. The kids flocked in. They brought their own chairs and poured tea for one another. Then came a creative writing workshop. He treated every submission with the utmost attention. The young intellectuals were enthralled. Venerable Tzu Hui, a first-generation disciple much touted for her literary talents, was frank about her initial intention: "I went to the master to learn writing, not Buddhism!"

In her article, Venerable Tzu Hui reflects on the mood shared among her peers at the time: "The chanting sessions in Ilan included a range of projects to expressly receive and guide the young. ... I have no words for the grace in his demeanor, the profundity of his thought, the extent of his knowledge. I was simply touched. ... We used to place our writings into a drawer beneath the altar in Lei-yin Temple. We would retrieve them the next morning when we turned in another batch. Our papers were always meticulously critiqued. We could not wait to exchange them. Everybody was excited. After a while, the master would round us up for an overall critique, and we would be taught the mechanics of composing."

Bodhi seeds were sown among the little ones, too. Groups were formed for those attending junior and senior high schools; subject tutorials for the under-privileged were provided by teachers among the followers. To some of their unbelieving parents, these young people became living proofs that "children of the Dharma never go astray."

Chêng Shih-yen, educator and a best-selling author on Ch'an studies, was in one of those tutorials. He recalls how the master went to great lengths in devising the most attractive projects for the kids, how well he understood them, how he would pat them on the shoulder and sit them down to chat, and how the bunch of them would fly to his side after school. Members of the student body, too, Chêng muses, used to walk extra tall. Years later at Fo Kuang Shan's first international Ch'an conference, Hsing Yun ran into the kid from the tutorial and he said, fondly: "O the willow carelessly planted is turning into a shade tree now! I'm so glad to see you again!"

Roots of compassion

Viewed from the standpoint of modern marketing, he practiced his understanding of grouping and was apt in the cultivation of *consumer habits*. Early training in Buddhism brings out innate good and compassion, he believed. Preschool and primary level classes soon expanded into Sunday schools complete with all kinds of contests in the arts. Bodhi seeds, indeed, must be sown in the spring.

Venerable Yi Kung, who holds a master's degree in Indian philosophy from Tokyo University, attended one such class for children. She took the tonsure two years after university graduation and has followed the master for two decades. She tells of frequenting Lei-yin Temple with her two sisters at four or five, and being drawn solely to the snacks – Buddha or no Buddha! For the promise of a gift of affinity, like a steamed bun, a peach-shaped longevity bun, candied crispies, or a

Buddha's Hand made of flour, the bouncy little girl would settle down to chant the sutras for the length of a burning incense (– also a common practice in Christianity). "Wanting to lead one onto the path of the Buddha, one must be satisfied with one's want." The master knows best! In time she began to resonate with the Dharma. "A lot of us probably were delivered while munching a little Buddha's Hand!" Venerable Yi Kung laughs heartily.

He moved the average devotees with his sincerity and diligent service. He conducted the seven-day chanting, set up the lecture hall, cooked the vegetarian meals, and waited on tables. Of course he played all the Dharma instruments during chanting. And, whenever the pet monkey in a nearby kindergarten ran off, somebody would invariably yell: "Master! The monkey's gone! Go after it!" He would lay down whatever he had in hand to go after the creature.

Ilan, this is forever

There was simply no stopping him. He would buy several hundred issues of the *Life* magazine he edited and give them away. For *Awakening the World* he actually went out soliciting subscribers. Income from his writings was channeled into the purchase of silver chains and sauvastika[2] pendants which he hoped young devotees would wear with pride, and notebooks and pencils for the students and children's classes.

The first sign of a harvest was a lantern parade in 1958. It was the Buddha's birthday. Tibetan Buddhists under the Dalai Lama were rising against communist oppression. Hsing Yun decided to echo their cry. Every district in Ilan was represented by a float. The parade of lights ran forty-eight kilometers. Three fifths of

[2] 卍 a sign on the Buddha's chest. A symbol of the sun or lightning; a sign of omnipotence over evil and all favor to the good.

the populace took part. All in all, it was an eye-opener. And the Buddhists had their first taste of solidarity.

During the course of twelve years, the alien monk and the city among the hills had become inseparable. "Coming, no one is there to greet me; going, no need to bid good-by. That's the feel of home," he says. No matter how far he roams, home is where the heart is. Always, his heart is in Ilan.

Truly Hsing Yun loves Ilan like no other. At Yüan-ming (Perfect Light) Temple by Chiao Hsi (Rocky Brook) he finished *Biography of Sakyamuni Buddha's Ten Great Disciples* at the speed of 10,000 characters per day. How he still misses the restful walk along the brook at the end of each day!

Ilan is all for Hsing Yun. It reared almost all his first-generation disciples: Hsin Ping, Tzu Chuang, Tzu Chia, Tzu Hui, Tzu Jung, and others that form the nucleus of Fo Kuang Shan.

The most *diehard* devotees of Fo Kuang Shan, too, come from Ilan. Wêng Sungshan, founder of China Buddhist Art Center, is one. The former painting apprentice reciprocated Hsing Yun's support in learning to carve Buddha statues thirty years ago by a huge donation to the Fo Kuang University foundation. He also thanked the master for the chance to do so.

Lei-yin Temple, the beginning

Without Lei-yin Temple, there would not have been Fo Kuang Shan; without Fo Kuang Shan, there would not have been the some hundred branch temples around the globe, the thousand disciples, and million devotees. Enshrined in the temple is Vairocana Buddha. Lei-yin Temple was where it all began.

The source of one of the century's supreme masters and the springboard to Fo Kuang Shan's full flourish – that is Ilan. To call Ilan the cradle for the modernization of Buddhism in Taiwan would not be an overstatement.

Chapter 6

Master of innovation

Sakyamuni attained Buddhahood at age thirty-five.[1] Venerable Master Hsüan Tsang journeyed to India to acquire the Buddhist classics at age twenty-six. Hsing Yun, at thirty, was at the threshold of his mission to modernize the spread of the Dharma. Moreover, he had positioned himself to take some creative risks.

Buddhism in China, for all its characteristic oriental subtlety, had been passive when it came to the spread of the Dharma. In other words, devotees were

[1] Different versions exist, some of which record age thirty-one.

welcome but not courted, and a generally low profile was kept. But, the times were changing and the age-old religious experience must change too. Technology, politics, the economy, the society as a whole, even the makeup of the congregation, how could these be incorporated? How could orthodox Buddhist doctrine and this brand new state of life connect? And, who should help Buddhists awaken to the causes and conditions of this new age? The difficulty with Buddhism is not in abstract semantics, Hsing Yun realized, but is in adapting the spread of the Dharma to the times and in following causes and conditions to explain them. Still, he was set to go.

No stranger to the dynamics of the modern media, Hsing Yun employed them on a massive, systematic scale to further the spread of the Dharma in Taiwan.

Language, his beloved medium

Throughout his career, Hsing Yun has never ceased to resort to the prajna[2] of

[2] Wisdom.

language as a vehicle for the joy of the Dharma. Language is his beloved medium.

Early in the days of Chiao-shan Buddhist College, he collaborated with classmate Master Chih Yung in founding *Raging Billows*, a monthly; and edited *Splendid Light*, a supplement to the newspaper *Hsü pao*. He also wrote for local papers in Chiangsu. In Taiwan, he lost no time taking up publishing commitments to the magazines *Awakening to Life* and *Life*. During 1957 - 58, he took over one journal and started another, *Awakening the World* and *Buddhism Today*, respectively. In 1979 he founded *Universal Gate* magazine. The original 58-page black-and-white production has evolved into a 200 page, stellar publishing venture in terms of content, design, production, and distribution. The glossy magazine is read both by Buddhists and non-Buddhists.

As an author, too, Hsing Yun has fared well indeed. He was never schooled in writing as such, but he harbors an unbridled passion for the printed word. The pen is to him the duster with which to clear away the mind's defilements and obstructions.

His first work, *Discourse on Avalokitesvara's Universal Gate Chapter*, took form at Yüan-kuang Temple. Then came *Singing in Silence*, composed in the woods at Fa-yün Temple. Special mention must be made of *National Master Yü Lin*, a bestseller that turned into a big-screen feature and TV series.

Once, traveling across Taiwan on speaking commitments, Hsing Yun and friend Venerable Master Chu Yün spent the night at a farm in Yuchih, Nantou. The pair found the raw presence of the commode bucket beside them insufferable. Sleep was out of the question.

"Hey, Chu Yün, tell a story! I can't sleep."

Master Chu Yün was the consummate story-teller.

"Let me tell you about Master Yü Lin then!"

By the time he finished, morning had broken.

"I won't let your efforts go to waste, Chu Yün!"

Returning to Lei-yin Temple, he

laboriously wrote the story down.

He used to write under the pen-name Mo-chia[3] and was regarded as an up and coming author. Once a friend even suggested that he should consider becoming a professional writer: "With that pen of yours, why don't you just go and be a journalist!"

Hsing Yun's brain-child, Fo Kuang Publishing House, has been very energetic in putting out Buddhism-related publications. Genres range from biographies, articles on doctrine, literature, to etiquette. And in recent years, cassettes and videos. But most important of all are the *Fo Kuang Tripitaka*, the award-winning *Fo Kuang Encyclopedia*, and English translation of sutras. His monthly journals, which appeared in *Universal Gate* magazine over a four year period, have been published in a set of twenty volumes. They are deemed an excellent way to connect with his disciples and followers worldwide, and are a most effective way to spread the Dharma. Currently, Fo Kuang

[3] An abbreviation in Chinese for Mahakasyapa, one of Sakyamuni Buddha's early disciples known for his asceticism.

Shan is collaborating with UC Berkeley to computerize the Buddhist Canon.

In his own words: "Via the prajna of language, not only those of us here and now are able to connect with the thoughts of the Buddha, but also all beings living millenniums from now and light-years from here shall be helped to the wondrous wisdom of absolute reality!"

Going the electronic way

In keeping with modern advancement, new electronic technology has become a tool of Dharma propagation. As early as the days in Ilan, there was the Buddhist choir. Then came the radio programs, *Voice of Buddhism, Sound of Awakening the World, Gate of Faith, The Wondrous Use of Ch'an*, and *Wisdom of Life*. The latest addition to the list is home visit for Chinese-speaking audiences in Los Angeles, California. These have also been made into television broadcasts: *Sakyamuni Buddha*, 1972; *Sweet Dew*, 1979; *Gate of Faith*, 1980; the award-winning *Venerable Master Hsing Yun's Buddhist Lectures*, 1983; *The Sixth Patriarch's Platform Sutra*, 1985; *Hsing*

Yun's Ch'an Talk, 1987; *A Verse Per Day*, 1989; the award-winning *Hsing Yun's Dharma Words*, 1991; *Hsing Yun Speaks a Verse*, 1991; and *Hsing Yun Says*, 1994. These programs are on all three channels in Taiwan – often simultaneously.

Music from the heavens

The original Buddhist music was *fan-pei*: *fan* being the music of Mahabrahma,[4] and *pei* being clearness and pureness. *Fan-pei* is truly music from the heavens. In quietness, the heavenly music can expand and elevate people's mind. Instrumental in early preaching, *fan-pei* was later employed in the praise of the Buddha. Musical instruments that the Buddhist devas are depicted with include the *p'i-p'a* (Chinese lute), *chêng* and *ch'in*,[5] all of which Chinese music has adopted.

Hsing Yun cut the first-ever 10-inch Buddhist records in 1957. The six of them,

4. The third heaven of the first dhyana (literally meditation), the self-existing origin of all living beings. Its ruler is infinitely protective of the Buddhist doctrine.

5. Both string instruments.

totaled some twenty numbers. Wu Chü-ch'ê, who was teaching at the polytechnic college in Taipei, was offered a key role despite the fact that they had not even met before the project. The two had no dispute whatsoever about popularizing and humanizing this time-honored faith. Wu applauded Hsing Yun's originality and offered his help without reservation. The half-dozen records which resulted struck a chord with wide audiences in Taiwan and all over Southeast Asia.

Three decades later, a 200-member choir from Fo Kuang Shan Buddhist College gave a historic Buddhist chanting performance at the national music hall in Taipei. The event helped lift Buddhist music to an unprecedented status.

The growing popularity of karaoke and KTV has sparked notions of putting the various Buddhist praises in like format. Hsing Yun wants Buddhist chanting to fill every household.

From radio, TV programs, records to Karaoke, Hsing Yun has shown himself a modern master of Dharma propagation.

Alongside the simple folk

In 1954 Hsing Yun began to systematically lecture on the Tripitaka (Buddhist Canon) in Taiwan.

Tzu En, then a teacher at the polytechnic college in Ilan, narrates his experience in following the master into the country: "We'd bike when the distance was manageable. ..." So the youthful monk crisscrossed the countryside, his thirty or so equally youthful followers tagging along. In the evening breeze they'd race against the setting sun. ..."The master would either lead or follow behind everyone. At times bikes broke down, or there was an uphill ride. Then we'd all dismount to walk our bikes up. When a typhoon struck, we'd just *bask in the Dharma rain*! On our return we'd sing aloud the master's *Song of the Dharma Preacher* and make our way back to Lei-yin Temple."

"We'd take the train when the destination was far off. We had to scramble somewhat for the train, which ran infrequently in those days. Later on, however, the people manning the various stations along the Ilan route became so touched by us that they made sure all of us were on board before the whistle blew."

As the day of a Dharma function approached, locals would sound the gong and announce: "The Dharma is coming!" When the day finally came, there would be parades of the deities and the divine personages leading the way. One such event drew a crowd of 5,000 in the tiny town of Yuli, Hualien. Whether it was out in the open, inside the minute town theater, or on the grain-drying ground, Hsing Yun and his young friends busied themselves setting up the microphone, extending wires, screwing in light bulbs, putting up posters, arranging the seats, and ushering in the audience. The young preachers then took the podium and, simultaneously in both Mandarin and the Taiwanese dialect and aided by a slide show, read from the scripts their master had perfected for them. By the end, the crowd was overjoyed.

The next thirty years saw Hsing Yun lecturing in towns and villages, schools and factories, national museums and memorial halls, art centers and sports stadiums. They also witnessed how the compassion and wisdom of the Buddha reached far and wide.

Across the oceans

Hsing Yun began moving his stage across the oceans about a decade ago. Especially in Hong Kong, he was visibly stepping up his teaching. Late in the summer of 1993, he made his way into the jam-packed Hunghom Coliseum, which seats 20,000. For three consecutive days, he spoke on topics *from the Diamond Sutra to the Research on the Prajna of the Nature of the Immaterial*. Media coverage was overwhelming. Each evening the coliseum was full well before the lecture was to start. On hearing that some people couldn't get into the coliseum, Hsing Yun arranged with Venerable Tzu Jung and the stadium officials to have a mega screen set up for those unable to gain entrance. For two hours [the minds of] those who attended – seated or otherwise – took a refreshing shower in the ambrosial rain.[6]

6. *Kan-lu fa-yü* in the original text. The Buddha Truth.

Like Catholic and Protestant preachers, Hsing Yun has for years been speaking in prisons. His lectures in Taiwan prisons are by formal appointment from the legal department. A few disciples and followers do the same on a regular basis.

When he was last in Hong Kong he spoke in the Stanley prison for the third time. With compassion, he talked to murderers, robbers, and drug dealers who were serving time in isolation. "These walls are nothing. Real incarceration is within the mind," he told them. That day the Buddha must have seen the thirty or so incarcerated men as the living beings that they were, not the deadly menace perceived by the eyes of others. Quietly the group listened to Hsing Yun's counsel to seek the Dharma for an end to their ferocity. Many were brought to tears when, during the refuge ceremony, the master sprinkled their heads with sweet dew to dispel calamities and to bring about repentance.

There is no end to Hsing Yun's innovativeness and unwavering dedication to the revival of Buddhism. He has an insightful grasp of the societal pulse. The construction of Taipei's P'u-men Temple in 1978 launched another series of Dharma functions, namely, the gathering of bright lanterns, the gathering to reciprocate parents' kindness, Dharma meetings for women, and Ch'an and Pureland practice. The "cross-island alms-round" function, a contemporary version of a time-honored monastic tradition, and home visits, titled "lighting up the homes," are regarded by some as a form of direct marketing in the spread of the Dharma.

Others at his heels

Hsing Yun's projects have received their fair share of support and pressure. Not unexpectedly, he has been condemned as garish and revolting, and feared for his charisma and popularity. As time went by, his strategies not only stood firmly but were also eagerly borrowed by monastics of other monasteries. No one can write him off as not being a significant modern Buddhist leader any more.

Once a student questioned Hsing Yun's eloquence: "Master, how come you always have so much to say?" During his early years in the monastery he had never crossed paths with a stranger and, if he had, would not know how to talk with one. Ten years of his life had revolved wholly around teachers and peers, and the first public lecture at Lei-yin Temple was petrifying. The whole time he had to hold the edge of the table before him to hide his quivering. Off-stage, he found himself drenched with sweat. As appearances increased, though, so did his confidence and carriage.

In the beginning, his lectures were not all *sellouts*. To disciples he confesses his life's most embarrassing moment – when , forty years ago in Ilan, he went on-stage to find not a single soul below. "The time and date were correct, I mumbled to myself. I waited and waited. Finally a handful of latecomers sauntered in. I began somehow. By the end of the lecture, the crowd hadn't gotten any bigger."

Now, he speaks eloquently. Unexpected quests at Fo Kuang Shan, wanting to hear him speak, need only allow him the benefit of the five-minute walk from Hsi Ling (West Range) to Pao Ch'iao (Treasure Bridge) to come up with a peerless script. For over ten years he has needed only to look over television scripts thirty minutes before shooting. The record of 100 episodes shot in a single day without a retake still has many people amazed.

Giving society what it needs

Too often people leave a lecture saying how wonderful it was. "What was it about?" others may ask. "Not a clue!" might be the answer. How true it is that speaking on the Dharma in ways no one can understand is so much easier than otherwise!

To explain a popularity that seems uniquely Hsing Yun's, Academia Sinica social researcher Sung Kuang-yü gave this analysis: "As convention goes, all that a Dharma lecture needs is a building spacious enough to house a few rows of seats. Hsing Yun overrides this convention. He is capable of discerning society's needs and seeks to design a preaching format accordingly."

People who have been to one of his

lectures rave about how sound effects and stage design are wedded with religious fervor: "The curtain goes up to reveal five images of the Buddhas resting on a crimson carpet with an azure backdrop. Flower-, candle-, fruit-, and tea-bearing lay attendants in four groups solemnly walk through misty effects, generated by dry ice. Their guide is the drum. The lighting turns magical. Fifty cassock-clad monastics take the stage with Dharma instruments in hand. It's all so arresting."

With the atmosphere established, Hsing Yun ascends to deliver a speech drawn and timed to perfection. Legend has it that once a total of 72 applauses broke up a 30-minute lecture.

Monastics usually make a practice of teaching one sutra at a time and expounding on each word and every phrase. This may take months. Venerable Master Chih I of the T'ien-t'ai school, teaching the *Sutra of the Wondrous Truth of the Lotus,* spent 90 days on the character *wondrous* in the title alone. Modern life is by far too crammed with work and social functions and more work for such a time commitment. Nor can bits and pieces of lectures here and there serve us any better as Buddhists.

Aware of society's pursuit for conclusiveness and analysis, and its emphasis on time management and efficiency, Hsing Yun is a master of innovation with his topical lectures. In terms of a singular topic, listeners course through the Dharma within hours. The topics always pertain to an aspect of everyday life and human psychology. His topics include emotions, well-being, the role of religion, and even a top-ten list about life.

Greatness of wisdom and completeness of harmony

Hsing Yun still speaks with a slight Yangchou accent. There is a charismatic ineffableness about his figure, countenance, and demeanor. Whatever he does – proving a theory with a case or discussing a case with a theory, stating or understating a point, borrowing from history or citing a handy instance – he does ever so neatly. Few around him go away untouched, or unconvinced.

Longtime follower Chang P'ei-kêng of the Chinese-Tibetan Cultural Association of the Republic of China looks at his master as a walking Buddhist lexicon and a human compendium of modern humanities and sciences: "The master's realm is the realm of prajnaparamita[7] – that of the greatness of wisdom and completeness of harmony. He juggles and employs information with seamless skillfulness; he trails cross-references without deserting the theme; he sets off from the Dharma, traverses the ocean of knowledge, and always returns home to the Dharma. With such ease he comes and goes in the maneuver of information and knowledge!"

Once, some years ago in Japan, after finishing a talk, *The Message of the Twenty-first Century*, a middle-aged lady came up to Hsing Yun and expressed utter amazement at her sudden comprehension of the Dharma. She told him that after attending more than 200 lectures and spending years

[7] Wisdom of salvation.

in a tireless quest through Buddhist literature, his speaking finally opened her mind. An astounded academic noticed the absence of the mention of the Buddha throughout. In spelling out ways to purify the mind, Hsing Yun shared his rounded interpretation of the Dharma. Much benefited, his audiences were ready to regard him as a living Buddha.

Adapting to conditions

Hsing Yun knows how to adapt the contents of his lectures to fit the audience. Like the time a dance troupe visited. He was brimming over with stories of devas scattering flowers, flying through the heavens, and making offerings to the Buddhas. Then he focused on Buddhist chanting and Buddhist songs of praise. To the musicians and dancers he represented song and dance as another vehicle of the Dharma. They were spellbound.

Still another time, Hsing Yun spoke on *Buddhism and Chinese Literature*. He steered the gathered literati through an entire course in the translation of Buddhist texts:

how Buddhism came to China, how Buddhist textual translation enhanced the Chinese literary vocabulary, how many literary works came to have the imprint of Buddhist thought ... He went on and on. His audience had no idea that the master had tread the same path as they.

He even discussed *Religion and Strategy* with strategist general Chiang Wei-kuo. Citing personal experience in the understanding of the Dharma and the living of life, he delved into the depths of diverse types of contingencies. His listeners were his *captives*.

With scientists he debates the scientific viewpoint of Buddhism; with economists, how material value is explained from a Buddhist conception; with engineers, monasterial architecture. His method of teaching and inspiring in accordance with objective timing is such that people from all walks of life are led to the Dharma. At times, like Master T'ai Hsü's blackboard, which was once feared as wizardry, Hsing Yun's innovations and reforms have been called monstrous.

Unfazed, he says: "Modernization is a form of exploration. It encompasses betterment, anticipation, adaptability, and promotion. As nations, societies, and religions evolve over time and through space, they must seek progress. That quest, and the will to be in agreement with the Buddhist doctrine, combined with the capacities of those attending, climax in timely, versatile representations of the Dharma allowing Buddhist teachings to be accepted easily. In fact, since the days of Sakyamuni Buddha, this is what Buddhist preaching has always sought. Like passing on the Dharma through speech during the Buddha's lifetime. There were pattra[8] sutras, engraved sutras, and printed sutras after his nirvana. Now, the computerized Tripitaka!"

The new generation of Buddhists are totally at home with markers and whiteboards, slides and projectors, and mega cinematic screens. Nobody has any qualms about the Buddhas enshrined in the halls of

[8] Palm leaves used as a writing material.

government, or the audible drum and bell in the metropolis or the country. Hsing Yun's innovation and foresight have made possible the modernization of Buddhism and the spread of Buddhist teachings to every corner of the world.

Part III

'Tis with him perpetual Buddha truth

With Venerables Tzu Hui (left) and Hsin Ping where the overgrowth of jute and bamboo were cleared for the construction of Fo Kuang Shan

Gauging distances

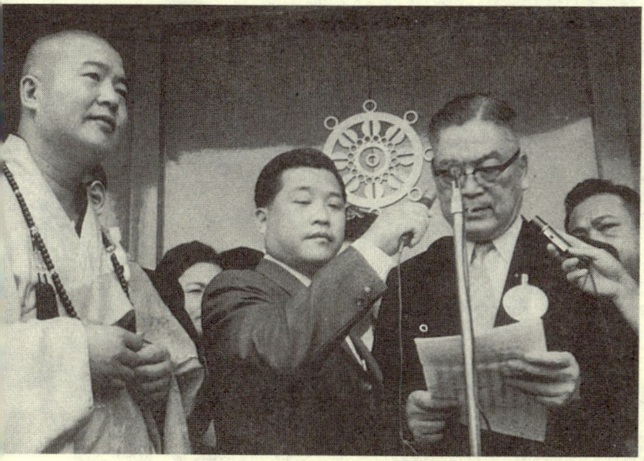

Listening to internal affairs minister Hsü Ch'ing-chung at the opening of the Great Compassion Shrine

With Hao Po-ts'un, R.O.C. presidential advisor, Hsi Lai Temple, 1993

With Chen Lian, head of the supervisory council, Fo Kuang Shan

With Chiang Ching-kuo, head of the executive council, Fo Kuang Shan, 1972

Receiving an honorary Ph.D. from
University of Oriental Studies, 1978

With friends in the literati (l-r),
publisher Kao Hsi-chün, editor Wang Li-hsing,
and media executive Wu Shih-sung

With U.S. vice-president Al Gore, then senator, at Fo Kuang Shan, 1988

Officiating at weddings

Chapter 7

Heading south

A good walker walks far; a good swimmer swims further. After the lovely and cherished Ilan, a spacious and resourceful expansion must be pursued. Kaohsiung was the place.

According to Buddhist doctrine, all things spring from causes and conditions. Hsing Yun was able to begin by exploring one aspect of Kaohsiung's potential and end up with a multifaceted endeavor hinged on conditions of all forms. But most important of all, the cause was the master spirit of Hsing Yun himself.

Actually, his relationship with Kaohsiung took root when he was excused from his commitments at Lei-yin Temple to make frequent excursions there to preach the Dharma. He soon generated adequate support for plans to construct a temple. He was twenty-six then. A place of worship and a cultural service center were followed by Shou-shan (Longevity Mountain) Temple right in the heart of Shou-shan Park. Eventually he had to commute between the north and south, Ilan and Kaohsiung.

Monastics are instructed

Deep down inside, Hsing Yun knew temples and monasteries alone could not revive Buddhism, purify minds, or rectify bad tendencies. Education could. It must always be a priority in nurturing new leaders in the Buddhist lineage. Then, one can start projecting into the future without end, he thought.

On that note, the class of '64, was the first to attend Shou-shan Buddhist College inside the temple. From the then small group of twenty or so, annual admissions quickly mounted until the temple became over crowded. To Venerable Tzu Chia, a graduate and director of Fo Kuang Shan cultural department, it was like yesterday when she and her peers studied in the evenings within the confines of the hall of relics. Meanwhile, to seek improvement in the learning environment while positioning the college for the anticipated enrollment boost, Hsing Yun made plans for a modern institution of multiple functions – educational, cultural, and religious. Just like the monasterial pattern and scale in which he matured.

Many people rallied around him at the revelation of this aspiration. As one thing led to another, Cheng Ching (Pure and Clear) Lake where the Grand Hotel now stands was the choice site. Purchase of the property was made possible by the sale of the building housing the Buddhist cultural service center.

Perhaps the sequences of events were meant to turn out differently. Or maybe it was Hsing Yun's sense of independence that was at stake. The funds were there. The contract was there – pen waiting. Then a disciple's words changed everything. In hindsight, of course, one realizes that Fo Kuang Shan would have been a different story if not for this particular episode. This was what disciple Venerable Yi Yen said: "The lake is a tourist hot spot. For sure our temple is going to share that trend. People are going to stream in, sightseeing while paying homage to the Buddha. President Chiang might even be an occasional guest."

Hsing Yun was perturbed by that view. He did not want the temple to become an addition to the lake. He hoped visitors from far and near would come with joined palms and a heart full of devotion to the Buddha. He dropped the plan. The decision was not nearly as appreciated then as it is now. Through the years, Fo Kuang Shan has attracted thousands of people from Taiwan and abroad to come and pay homage. Some people have even developed scenic spots in the vicinity. The President did not come. One of his sons came three times and at least once as president.

During the impasse, a debt-laden Chinese couple from Vietnam let Hsing Yun know that their vast, hilly property in

Machu Yuan (Jute Grove), Tashu Hsiang (Big Tree Village), Kaohsiung, was up for sale. They pleaded for his help without which, they said, suicide would be their only other solution.

No doubt Hsing Yun was moved, being the way he is. And he pondered. The most extolled Buddhist monasteries in China are deep in the mountains. "Of all the celebrated mountains under heaven, most are taken by the monks," so the saying goes. Like E-mei (Lofty), Wu-t'ai (Five-terrace), P'u-t'o (Potala), Chiu-hua (Nine-flower), all in China. It was time to carry the torch and found another monastery in the mountains of Taiwan.

Looking divine as he advances

Hsing Yun was adamant: he wanted to see the land firsthand. Thirty years has since passed but he remembers what he did that day. A bus was hired; a few devotees were invited. The road was rugged; the ride took more than an hour. Once there, the treacherous thicket covered land stretched as far as the eye could see. Everyone was stupefied; no one would leave the bus. Except Hsing Yun.

"Forget it, master! Who would care to come up here to pray? Except you, that is," mumbled the group.

"Fine, fine," he replied, not at all losing steam. "Let me go then."

He took his cane and vanished into the thorny grove.

Some disapproved of his determination; others were transfixed.

An hour elapsed. Then he emerged – weeds and red dirt on his collar, and a broad grin on his face.

"My apologies! I've made you wait too long!" he said as he wiped the sweat off his forehead.

He still teases some of the older devotees who went along that day: "You said that no one would care to climb this mountain. Haven't you been doing just that all these years?"

When asked about his intention, he says that the raw mountain offered opportunity. The monasteries then existing in Taiwan were run by monastics many years his senior. Hsing Yun, in his thirties, virtually had nowhere to go. Furthermore, when he finally settled down, he discovered he had more time for politics and socializing than for education and preaching. There was no strife up on the mountain. It would be right for starting from scratch.

The pioneering days

Those were pioneering days. Only a few devotees supported his decision. A follower who joined Hsing Yun at Shou-shan Temple and one of the key figures in the construction of Fo Kuang Shan, Hsiao Ting-shun says that no other experience would mean as much to him. Hsiao used to ride a motorcycle – with the master at his back – up the untraveled path, traverse three hills, and go on foot for another two hours before making it to the construction site (where the Buddhist college now perches).

"There's little we could do but stick to the geographical contours," recounts the shy former carpenter. "I'd snatch a piece of bamboo and sketch in the dirt. The two of us would think hard, and plan where to dig and where to build."

"We'd be drenched with sweat one moment and dry another. Discussion went nonstop. Often we didn't sleep until the wee hours and would rise to work again at the break of day."

"The land wasn't even flat. I've lost count of the thousands of truck-loads of dirt that it took to level it."

"Resources were limited. When they ran out, work would halt. Really, all we wanted was a small place. A few parking spots before the mountain gate. That'd do!"

Decades of southern sunshine has tanned Hsiao and seems to have energized him. Rapport between he and the master is like no other. With the latest project – Triple-gem Shrine – behind him, this character, who is short on oratory and long on substance, and who maintains an old fashioned demeanor, sums himself up: "I didn't make much money working with Fo Kuang Shan. Instead I have received a lot of joy. Each time somebody speaks well of Fo Kuang Shan, I feel this life of mine has been very worthwhile."

Consider the ways of the ant, and be wise

Abbot and Director-in-chief of the Committee of Religious Affairs[1] Venerable Hsin Ping was the first among the monks to join the construction. He was stationed in a shack in a bamboo grove with no electricity. To fetch water, he had to descend to a brook half an hour away. At night, he had to patrol the grounds in pitch-darkness. The bulldozer could not climb by itself; students in the second and third classes at the Buddhist college had to give it a shove. The hourly rate of the machine was exorbitant considering living costs at the time and their own financial circumstances. So Venerable Hsin Ping's most pressing charge was to ensure that the machine was put to full use. "Not a dollar from the devotees should go to waste," he used to say.

Venerable Tzu Jung had come to

[1] The highest policy-making body of Fo Kuang Shan.

Kaohsiung from Ilan with the master. She was there, too. "The roof of Dragon Pavilion on East Hill was being laid," she tells of the time when they were on hands and knees. "Midway through the process, the worker mixing the cement left for the day. We didn't want the pouring suspended for fear that the roof might crack and leak in the future. The master and the bunch of us expected the job to be completed, so we picked up where the man left off. Into the night we worked with the two motorcycles' headlights on us. Venerable Yi Yen was up on the roof to smooth the cement, which kept sliding back down the steep surface. She exerted herself so much pushing the cement back up again that her hands started to bleed ... "

The most frenzied time was when a typhoon caused a stupendous downpour washing away the upper dam of the Release Pool[2]. Hsing Yun plunged into the clay red rapids, and the others followed. First rocks and then their own quilts they passed along to block the opening and blanket earth. They banded together and struggled until

[2] Pool for the release of living creatures to save lives.

the storm gave way, and there was light behind the clouds.

Hsing Yun looks out from the balcony of Founder's Quarter and remembers: "Like ants moving T'ai Shan."[3]

From nonbeing, being springs

Chronologically, the first-phase construction of the Fo Kuang Shan complex included Tung-fang (Eastern) Buddhist College, Ta-pei Tien (Great Compassion Hall), Kuan-yin Release Pool, Dragon Pavilion, and the image of Maitreya Buddha.

The second phase: Ta-tz'ŭ (Great Compassion) Nursery, Ch'ao-shan Hui-kuan (Pilgrim's Lodge), Chieh-yin Ta-Fo (Great Welcoming Buddha), Fo Kuang Vihara, and Ta-chüeh Temple.

The third phase: Main Shrine, Ching-t'u Tung-k'u (Pureland Cave), P'u-mên High School, Wan-shou Yüan [Longevity

[3] The eastern sacred mountain in Shantung, China about which folklore abounds.

Park, a cemetery], and an exhibition hall.

The fourth phase: Machu Yüan [a guest house], Ksitigarbha[4] Hall, E-mei Chin-ting (Lofty Gold-roofed) Samantabhadra[5] Hall, Ta-tz'ŭ An [named Great Compassion, a living quarter for nuns], and a service center for devotees.

The latest additions have been T'an-hsin Lou [Devotee's Chamber, an activities center for devotees], Chin-yü Fo Lou (Chambers of Gold and Jade Buddhas), and Ju-lai Tien (Tathagata[6] Hall).

The Great Welcoming Buddha, standing a lofty 32-meter, beckons those on their way to Fo Kuang Shan. It ranks sixth on the global top-ten list of oversized images of the Buddha.

It was with bare hands that Hsing Yun created a Buddhist holy land of world renown. Verily, from nonbeing being springs.

Whether viewed from afar or up close,

[4] Earth Treasury. Deliverer from the hell.

[5] Universal Sagacity. Bodhisattva of the great practice.

[6] Absolute Come. One of the titles of the Buddha.

Fo Kuang Shan seems to have been sculpted out of its location. Each element has been rendered with sterling precision: the grandeur of the architecture and openness of the temples, artistry of the Buddha images and design of the courts and gardens, decor of the halls and chambers .... "There is a world in each bloom, and a Buddha on every leaf."[7] How well put!

Most inscrutable of all, Hsing Yun has been the one to irrigate the wilderness and rear a holy land, he with his papers and meter rule, and Hsiao with his random bamboo sticks. Architectural expertise or construction committees were never a factor. Just how did he do it? "I'm certainly unlearned in architecture," he says. "From the mainland to Taiwan to the rest of the world, I've walked many miles and seen many houses. Each and every case I observe and contemplate. I ask myself would I have executed a design for a property differently if I were in the architect's shoes. By the time conditions are ripe for a temple or a school, construction plans have long been in place.

[7] Buddhist truth can be manifested in our daily life.

That practically eliminates the prospect of complications." The answer to his success is a simple one: "Just pay attention."

Many-splendored land

Outwardly, Fo Kuang Shan is a palatial, aesthetically classical attempt to represent the abstractness of the Dharma. Its interior, however, is a quintessential, technologically sophisticated scheme of multifaceted functions. The complex has a state-of-the-art multimedia audio-visual center, a conference hall complete with simultaneous interpretation facilities at every seat, a brand-new lecture hall with a capacity for 2,200, and a top-notch internal and external communications network. Fo Kuang Shan is the first-ever computer-managed monastery.

At the same time, devotees and visitors sip Fo Kuang tea to quench their thirst, savor a restful interval in the shady pavilion, enjoy the amenities of the guest house, drop by the service center for a tour, or consult the monastics on various issues.

Monasteries used to be a picture of gloom and doom. The many-splendored Fo Kuang Shan has turned all that around. It is the expression of its leader's disposition and traits, and projection of his reason and concepts. Critics have called Fo Kuang Shan wealth-oriented. The business world, as well, yearns to know what – in terms of vision and planning – makes it tick. Meanwhile, thirty years of weekends continue to see an incessant traffic of devotees and visitors, some better known than others but all earnest. They come from the ten directions.

Fifty lasting *firsts*

The million or so devotees and hundred or so branch temples aside, Fo Kuang Shan has fifty lasting *firsts*.

Namely, the first Buddhist choir, Dharma radio programs, music recordings, television appearances, Dharma lectures in the halls of government, hard-bound texts, devotee's uniforms, monthly sutra-printing, monastic hierarchy, cross-country preaching, religious souvenirs, student body, public discussion sessions, children's class, Sunday class, ten-thousand Buddha hall, preschool education workshops, bright lanterns,[8] slide shows, weddings, Indian cultural research, postsecondary summer camps, city college, devotee study programs, mobile clinic, public library, home for the terminally ill and lodging for their families, devotee service center, thanksgiving Dharma functions, annual meetings for devotees, Sangha Day, temple housed in a high-rise, alms-round Dharma functions, global examinations, triple practice sessions in the Ch'an, Pureland, and esoteric schools, *Return to the Epoch of the Buddha* functions, museum and exhibition hall, Dharma-passing ceremonies, short-term monastic retreats, home visits and service, art gallery, the *Fo Kuang Tripitaka*, the *Fo Kuang Encyclopedia*, preaching to the militia and on the outer islands [of Taiwan], world organization (Buddha's Light International Association), 200-member pilgrimage to India .... The list continues.

To Hsing Yun himself, the creating of each and every one of those organizations

[8] Lit for a year's blessing at Fo Kuang Shan.

and functions climaxes decades of collaborative efforts. Fo Kuang Shan being what it is today, its creator wants the "glory to be the Buddha, achievement to be for all, benefits to the monastery, merits to the devotees."

Declining to bask in the reflections on the lake, Hsing Yun picked Kaohsiung county, which in turn has since been basking in Buddha's light. The value of real estate in the vicinity has soared; public utilities have been updated; highways added; employment has multiplied; schools built. Neighborhood and village get-togethers and festive revelries are now standard. Each year opens to an endless string of community activities which take advantage of the amenities of Fo Kuang Shan. To Kaohsiung, it is no longer only a momentous religious landmark; it is also the basic promoter of community spirit and a dynamic cultural institution.

The view of Fo Kuang Shan is nothing less than awe-inspiring: the five peaks undulating like the petals of an orchid, the tidal sea of lush green woods, the heaven-touching Buddha, the parade of halls, the overpowering heights of the structures, the juxtaposing eaves. This is where twentieth-century Buddhism exemplifies itself as a religion, a culture, education, charity, and a scenic attraction.

Chapter 8

Epoch of Buddha's Light

As one looks toward the Great Welcoming Buddha, the one sees the shimmering Kaohsiung-Pingtung Brook. Fo Kuang Shan, since its inception in 1967 has had to come a long, long way before becoming southern Taiwan's most unique landmark and Asia's foremost Buddhist holy land. Yet, based on the Buddhist concept of matter or becoming, dwelling, deteriorating, and nonexisting, Fo Kuang Shan must not be gauged by the dazzle of its shrines and halls, its form alone. For Fo Kuang Shan's essence of being lies in its principle and practice, theme and rationale.

Coming out of the mountain gate

Humanistic Buddhism[1] is what Hsing Yun and Fo Kuang Shan's principle and pratice are about. From Master T'ai Hsü, he learned that monastics must come out of the mountain gate. Fo Kuang Shan was to be the testing ground of the principle.

He defines this theme in one of his lectures: "To have the Dharma isolated from life is the worst failing of Buddhism today. The most seasoned believer can't seem to get rid of greed, anger, and ignorance, and the most learned in the doctrine are still bothered by gossiping about people's ideas of right and wrong.

"Once Buddhism breaks away from real life, the Dharma stops serving our needs and ceases to be our guide; once it fails to enrich the content of our lives, its existence becomes meaningless. The Buddha's teachings are for the improvement of life, purification of mind, and uplifting of character. It is a Buddhism which is pertinent to life and living that I want to spread."

[1] A form of Buddhism that one can pratice in life.

"A living Buddhism hinges on the correspondence to the Buddha's teachings while sleeping, talking, walking, or any form of activity. The Buddha spoke about resolve of the mind. To apply that teaching, we resolve our mind in the way we conduct our daily lives, in the way we give, and, overall, in the way we practice Buddhism. Sleep done with resolve becomes extra restful; food eaten with resolve becomes extra tasty; a road trodden with resolve becomes smooth before our eyes; a problem tackled with resolve turns into a delightful challenge."

"The resolve of the mind is an aspect of Dharma teaching useful in the harmonizing of all levels of human relationships. Not rhetoric, the Dharma is to be exercised and, with utmost thoroughness, to be fulfilled. There is no way that life and the Dharma should part company."

Carrying the Buddha's light

"Let others have faith; let others have joy; let others have convenience; let others have hope" – those of Fo Kuang Shan live their faith under this code of ethics. What today's business world upholds as its maxim, "create the future, form a unanimity," Hsing Yun has long put into practice. Many times he has lectured on what it means to be a Fo Kuang Buddhist in order to explain these concepts.

To begin, a Fo Kuang Buddhist is first worldly and then unworldly. Buddhism, dismissed as passive and world-weary, is on the decline because, in looking for deliverance from existence, it overlooks issues arising from existence. Truly, how can Buddhism be accepted by society, if it departs from the reality of life and becomes unpatriotic, unfilial, and unfriendly? Hence, it is for the Fo Kuang Buddhist to seek attainment within the world before delivering it without.

Second, a Fo Kuang Buddhist is to be a vehicle first for the living and then for the dead. The greatest misconception of Buddhism is that it is a religion in which to chant and to deliver the dead only. Without any misgiving whatsoever about Buddhist services for the purpose of gathering merits, the Fo Kuang Buddhist believes the living, much more than the dead, needs Buddhism, and hence will spread this faith within the home, in temples and in society.

Third, a Fo Kuang Buddhist first tackles life and then tackles death. True that to end [the cycle of] life and death, is the ultimate Buddhist practice. Yet to merely have on one's lips the yearning for a clear, clean life or cultivation in the mountains is unrealistic, even presumptuous. The virtuous and eminent masters of the past all began with the resolve to serve the masses. Some promised to shoulder people's burdens like an ox throughout many lives; others vowed to serve and suffer through endless winters. Ch'an master Huai Hai of Paichang [720 - 814] initiated the austere rule of toil and productivity – no food without work. Be adequately prepared; live well. Then talk about ridding oneself of the cycle of rebirth.

Fourth, a Fo Kuang Buddhist is small before becoming big. Unlike the rattling half-filled vessels in this vanity fair of ours, a Fo Kuang Buddhist weathers the vicissitudes of time like a thousand-year pine, and withstands the test of ice and snow like the winter-worn plum tree. Only the patient will know success; only the small shall be big.

Culture is the vehicle of the Dharma

Fo Kuang Shan is structured upon the four aspirations "to spread the Dharma via culture, to nurture talent via education, to benefit society via charity, and to purify minds via joint cultivation." Fo Kuang Shan is no longer just a reputable temple in Tashu, Kaohsiung. It represents three decades of dauntless efforts by a thousand-member sangha and million-devotee populace around the globe.

Alms-round donations commemorating its twentieth anniversary have funded Fo Kuang Shan Cultural and Educational Foundation in the financing of Buddhist scholarly conferences both national and international. This funding also sponsored the publication of Buddhist journals *Benevolent Teachers, Blessing,* and a weekly *Buddhist News,* and gifts of books to libraries, schools, and prisons. A decade was expended in researching, annotating, and indexing the *Fo Kuang Tripitaka*. In 1989, the *Fo Kuang Encyclopedia* was awarded publishing's golden cauldron award in Taiwan. The *Buddhist Historical Chronology* was named the most distinguished textual tool. The three monumental works of the Tripitaka Editorial Committee are collectively heralded as the triple gems of Buddhist scholarly research.

Awakening the World[2] is provided free to a readership of 100,000 in 42 regions and nations. Published three times monthly since 1957, the publication continues to function as an information carrier for Buddhists worldwide. *Universal Gate*, a medley of popular articles, modern living, literary trends, and universal appeal, is running a global circulation of 30,000. Launched in 1979, this polished Buddhist magazine is the only advertising-based product of computerized management, distribution networking, and financial self-sufficiency.

[2] It was changed to a monthly publication in Aug. 1995.

Hsing Yun is an accomplished and dedicated author, editor, and speaker who has ensured that his disciples, like himself, are duly groomed. Venerables Tzu Hui, Tzu Chia, Yi Kung, Yi Yu, Yi Sheng, Yi Chun, Yung Chuang, Yung Yun, and Man Kuo represent three generations of published writers. And sales of Hsing Yun's four-volume lectures have never slumped; nor have the sales of other titles: *Biography of Sakyamuni Buddha, National Master Yü Lin, Hsing Yun's Ch'an Talk, Hsing Yun's Dharma Words,* and *Hsing Yun Speaks a Verse,* among others.

Fo Kuang Publishing House has, during four decades, put out hundreds of serial titles; namely, sutras and discourses, scholarly journals and literary anthologies, biographies and doctrinal commentaries. The latest ventures are children's books, comics, cassettes, and videos – all attempts at giving orthodox Buddhism a contemporary appeal. The publishing house, together with *Fo Kuang Scholarly Journal* and Fo Kuang bookstores, form an intricately diversified cultural body.

In addition, the Buddhist exhibition

hall, art gallery, and exhibits of Tunhuang[3] paintings and Buddhist art not only demonstrate an elevated social mentality, but also show multiple exemplifications of the Buddhist faith.

Education is the nursery of talent

From Shou-shan Buddhist College, established in 1964, to the current three-year sangha education program (see also chapter 9), application for admission has been on a continual upswing; so have the credentials of the candidates - about one third of whom possess a university education. Many of these can boast of ample work experience yet simply aspire to return to school to learn the Dharma.

Ilan's Compassionate and Nurturing Kindergarten was the first-ever Buddhist kindergarten,with graduates totaling over 30,000. Three others have followed, Tainan's Compassionate Vehicle, Shanhua's Wisdom

[3] City in Gansu, China, near which cave temples of a thousand Buddhas were unearthed in the early 1900s. Invaluable finds include 5th- to 10th-century manuscripts and other block prints and paintings.

and Compassion, and Fo Kuang Shan's P'u-mên. Chih-kuang (Wisdom Light) is a secondary-level school of commerce. Last but certainly not least, P'u-mên High School, located at Fo Kuang Shan, went from 91 students in 1972 to 1,600 today and has emerged as one of the most outstanding private institutions in Taiwan. Hsi Lai (Coming West) University in Los Angeles, California, is a small-scale institution of higher learning with a brilliant faculty and an international student population. It is also positioned as the hub for international Buddhist academic exchange. And, to top off Hsing Yun's passion and tenacity in education, the brand-new Fo Kuang University is scheduled to accept applications for its graduate school in 1995.

The establishment of a city college at P'u-hsien Temple, Kaohsiung, in 1983 sparked similar projects in continuing education at other branch temples. It offers three-month courses in Buddhist studies in answer to the need of the work force to exploit off hours for academic and professional advancement. Such a format is as in-depth as it is broad-based and takes the

Dharma further into society.

A range of specialty classes also have been arranged in response to increasing social diversity and devotees' demands. These include courses in vegetarian cooking, calligraphy, T'ai-chi, and others, as well as choirs and orchestras.

Charity is the vehicle of benefit

Few are familiar with the history of Fo Kuang Shan's charitable endeavors which, though long-standing and encompassing, are downplayed.

The Compassion Foundation, working to "benefit society through charity," conducts charitable and social welfare activities, which span the length of a human life through the Great Compassion Nursery for orphans, Fo Kuang retirement home, Ilan Graciousness Home for the needy, Fo Kuang walk-in clinic, mobile clinics, a foundation fund for the sangha, a home visit and service plan, a cemetery which has allotted 2,000 free cabinets for ashes to Kaohsiung's county social welfare department, regular functions to release live creatures, winter collections of food and clothing for the poor, and disaster relief.

A case in point was Wang Hsiao-min who remained in a vegetative state from a traffic accident three decades ago. Her treatment exhausted family resources, and her mother and sister have since then been under the care of Fo Kuang Shan.

Ilan Graciousness Home is an indisputable instance of the tenacity required of charitable ventures. It was a former Christian-owned charity which ran into financial strain. Hsing Yun took over the operation together with the fate of its occupants. The freshly graduated Venerables Shao Chueh and Yi Jung volunteered their services, and thereby consummated the Bodhisattva Way by devoting half of their lives to washing, feeding, nursing, and, eventually, laying to rest those frail, lonely folks. Both of them have received awards from the government for their exemplary deeds.

Be it the flooding of the Yangtze in the Mainland or catastrophic typhoons across Taiwan itself, Fo Kuang Shan has taken to fundraising and relief efforts of enormous proportions.

Behind its low profile in charity is a profound consideration for the self-esteem of the recipients. The hundred or so children in Great Compassion Nursery are sheltered as much as cared for in life. Hsing Yun calls them his princes and princesses, and insists they be fed and clothed like any other, and cherished like gems by those who attend them. He wants them to feel respected, and that they belong with him. To those who came without a surname he gives his own secular Li. The nursery is out of bounds to tourists; the children are raised away from the limelight. He will not have them hurt a second time. Amidst the sense of peace and security that prevails in the impeccable classrooms and dormitory, director Hsiao Pi-liang's tone is soft yet firm: "This is a home. You don't showcase it. The kids call me Mom. For that alone I must give them a safe, cozy place they can call home, too."

Some rough statistics indicate that over 30,000 low-income patients visit Fo

Kuang Shan's clinic annually; the mobile clinic's 23 ambulances travel through 28 cities, more than 50 towns, and over 100 villages to serve the sick in outlying areas; and 6 affiliated temporary lodgings in Longevity Park provide a form of consolation for the family of the terminally ill. Burials, provisions, and medical relief are standard.

Joint cultivation, a means to purify minds

Meticulously organized Dharma functions, joint cultivation, practice, chanting, and Ch'an meditation together form the mature religious composite into which Fo Kuang Shan has evolved. Devotees from all ten directions attend repentance services, solitary retreats, sangha-devotee joint practice, Eight Precepts and seven-day cultivation retreats, pilgrimages to the temple,[4] pilgrimages to India, tours through various branch temples, and annual

[4] Ritual in which the sangha and devotees call on the Buddha's name while following a three-step and one-bow routine toward the direction of the Buddha's shrine.

meetings for devotees. Led in the direction of the Buddha gate by causes and conditions of their own, those who aspire to let their good roots flourish discover there a dwelling for their minds and a core for their faith.

No doubt Fo Kuang Shan is a forerunner in terms of devotee popularity, social impact, and national repute. When a monastic – any monastic – is asked casually: "Aren't you from Fo Kuang Shan?" it more or less becomes an alternative title for Buddhism in Taiwan. And the finger on the button of this intricate, mammoth, and potent machinery, everyone realizes, belongs to Master Hsing Yun.

Prayer beads worn around the pulse of time[5]

He has no intention whatsoever of being pedestaled as the founder of yet another school in the history of Chinese Buddhism. Perhaps it could be titled Fo

[5] As in the original text. It refers to the tremendous sense of time Hsing Yun has maintained throughout his career.

Kuang, like supporters hope will happen someday. Hsing Yun, at best takes comfort in a good career, and plans that Fo Kuang Shan, a tour de force, will be

1. a contemporary religious body and system with
    a. gender equality in hierarchical advancement
    b. harmony between the sangha and devotees
    c. solidity in the foundation of religious undertakings
    d. notable cultural and educational achievements
2. an international Buddhist body and network which includes
    a. Buddha's Light International Association
    b. global branch temples
    c. international conferences
    d. non sectarian communication and exchange
3. a society founded on humanistic Buddhism, which is characterized by
    a. Dharma practice for everyday life
    b. the practice of Buddhism within the

family
   c. social application
   d. a multitude of activities
4. a bridge between the two banks[6] which encompasses
   a. cultural undertakings in the north
   b. educational undertakings in the south
   c. Buddhist Association as the foundation
   d. culture and education as the starting point

It began from nothingness; it will end in endlessness. Hsing Yun's prayer beads are worn around the pulse of time. He, with his unworldly spirit, will continue along the worldly path. Fo Kuang Shan will certainly leave its mark in the development of Buddhism in China.

[6] The mainland and Taiwan.

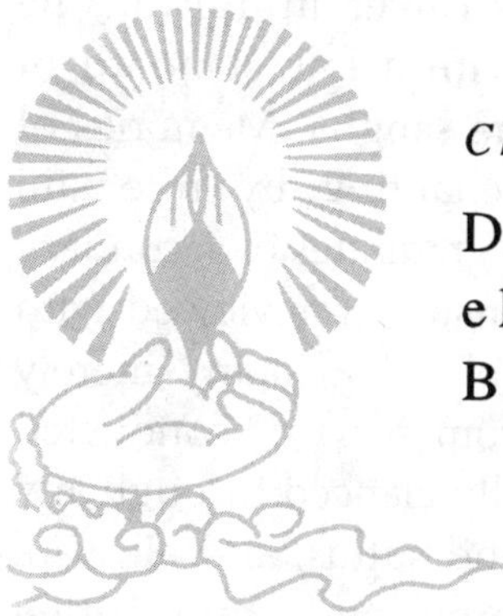

Chapter 9

Dragons and elephants of Buddha gate[1]

Ascend the realm of purity to seek the Truth; enter the mountain of treasure to learn the Dharma.

What propels the grand machinery that is Fo Kuang Shan is the energy of those whom Hsing Yun took four decades to raise.

His realization of how the growth of Buddhism is interwoven with cultivation of the young – and his conviction about handing down the light someday – must have stemmed from the integrity of his orthodox Buddhist background. Early

[1] Referring to the illustrious figures in the sangha.

during his teaching career in Taiwan, he came face to face with a low standard of education among the sangha. Memories of the semi-illiterate chanting by rote still haunt him. The rare graduates of secondary school taking the tonsure was viewed with disbelief by the public. Too many merely coveted earnings from services conducted for the dead, or hardly glanced through any pages in the texts and sutras, and all were damned as "withered buds and rotten seeds." The properly educated monastics were a rare breed, like "feathers of the phoenix and horns of the *lin*."[2]

Revival begins with the right people

As the revival of a nation begins with the right people, rejuvenation of Buddhism, Hsing Yun knew, would have to start from the beginning – the rearing of a pool of talent. In fact some of the young followers in Ilan had requested to be tonsured. He declined because he had no school for them. Not until the Buddhist college at Shou

[2] Mythical female creature resembling a deer.

Shan, Kaohsiung. Thereafter young talents were able to stay. Many were tonsured.

The class of '68 from Tung-fang (Eastern) Buddhist College (formerly Shou-shan Buddhist College) was to Hsing Yun an unprecedented yield from years of labor in Buddhist education. What was more, their graduation symbolized the crossing of Buddhism over the strait. The locally bred group would take leading roles in the future development of Buddhism.

Hsing Yun saw in Tung-fang Buddhist College a fertile field for the new buds in Buddhism. The amalgamation of traditional spirit and modern information was a scheme that would be the backbone of Fo Kuang Shan's educational body. Also, it was to be frequently referred to and widely adopted by other Buddhist colleges.

The credit system was employed in Tung-fang Buddhist College's three-year program. Members of its prominent faculty were Fang Lun who was a specialist in the Buddhist Canon, T'ang I-Hsüan, Venerable Hui Hsing, Master Chu Yün, and others. The array of courses offered included introduction to natural sciences, introduction to social sciences, introduction to philosophy, Chinese history, western history, Chinese literature, western philosophy, basic teaching in Chinese culture, foreign languages, business-writing, and sutra-chanting.

The first group of graduates – twenty in all – are now heading monasteries, assuming teaching positions in other Buddhist colleges, preaching the Dharma, or researching the Buddhist classics. The second and third classes totaled seventy graduates or more. By then Hsing Yun was concerned about the lack of usable space and was ready to look elsewhere. That, indeed, was the underlying cause for Fo Kuang Shan.

Young intellectuals are received and guided

As the saying goes: "Better to lead an army garrison than a sangha." The late Master Tz'u Hang also said: "Ask your enemy to run a school." Such is the formidable task of Buddhist education.

Hsing Yun worked feverishly to provide for everyone who attended the Buddhist college - free tuition and books, room and board, clothing and necessities. "You and your students are going to starve," others warned him with kind intentions. "Left with nothing, you'll end up losing your devotees altogether." He knew what he was doing. The first building that came up on the formerly thicketed land was the Buddhist college west of Treasure Bridge. That was the beginning of Fo Kuang Shan.

To keep the institution going, he, who has never favored specializing in services for the dead, would do so, sometimes through the night, to raise funds. At one point, the young woman in charge of academic affairs resolved to take the tonsure and joined him in those chanting sessions. That was Venerable Tzu Chuang. The teacher, who managed student affairs and worked part-time in a bakery to acquire extra sponsorships was Venerable Tzu Hui. The kindergarten teaching staff, Venerable Tzu Jung, Wu Pao-ch'in, Yang Tz'u-man, and others gave up their salaries. Devotee

Hsiao Pi-hsia sold her properties to finance the cultural and educational foundation. Venerable Tzu Jung would later direct the charities of Fo Kuang Shan and spearhead Buddha's Light International Association; Tzu Chuang would pioneer Hsi Lai Temple; and Tzu Hui would found two universities, Hsi Lai and Fo Kuang.

The inception of the postsecondary Buddhist summer camp in 1969 was designed to bring young intellectuals out of the ivory tower to tackle life's profundity. It sowed good seeds for the vibrant growth of Buddhism in academia years later. Harvests thereafter were bountiful. The cream of the crop included Fo Kuang Shan's own Venerables Yi Chun, Hui Kai, Yi Kung, and Yi Fa, together with the gallant Venerable Chao Hui – all pillars of the Buddhist circle now. The camp was their launching pad.

Strength of the mind, a very present constituent

Hsing Yun invested most heavily in rearing the young. Both in financial terms and, especially, in strength of mind. The odds were unspeakable. Just prior to launching the second postsecondary Buddhist summer camp for 600 participants, the water tower broke down. Overcome with anxiety, Hsing Yun supervised the emergency repairs during the day and stood guard, ear against the tower wall, all night, until the rumbling of the motor and water began at three in the morning.

Should the water not resume, he confided to disciples later, he vowed that his blood would turn into clear water for the consumption of the young people about to swarm in.

In fundraising for the research department of the Chinese Buddhist Research Institute, Hsing Yun and his students rolled up their sleeves and put on their aprons to cook for devotees, hoping they would be pleased with the rice and noodles and would be generous in their support.

His determination and sincerity touched a chord with many who did lend a hand. Venerable Tzu Chuang had an opportune experience, with a hint of the Buddha's apparition. She remembers that it was the eve of another summer camp. Funds were drained and delivery of provisions was still up in the air. Just when she was wringing her hands, she saw an elderly figure coming up the arched entrance. It was a peasant woman, straw hat on her head and shoeless, and she wanted specifically to see the abbot. Venerable Tzu Chuang received her and treated her to soup and rice noodles, which she ate with relish. Then, quite offbeat, she produced a paper-wrapped package and said: "Give this to the grand master. Do whatever you please with it." Then, she turned and was gone. Inside was a neat bunch of notes amounting to NT$50,000 in the then-new currency in Taiwan. The emergency was no more. Nobody to this day has the slightest inkling of who she was or where she was from.

The sangha takes on a new look

Hsing Yun believes that Buddhism is contemporary, progressive, and vibrant, not a hackneyed picture of frailty and boredom. "Buddhism needs the young, but the young need Buddhism more," he says. The Buddhist college at Fo Kuang Shan is now peopled by youthful, amicable, confident, and disciplined pursuers of the Dharma. Hsing Yun has bestowed the Chinese Buddhist monastics with a brand-new air.

If Shou-shan Buddhist College was a delicate, budding plant, Fo Kuang Shan's endeavors in Buddhist education are a luxuriant, fruit-bearing tree.

At the summit of Fo Kuang Shan's three-tier structure is the Chinese Buddhist Research Institute, which encompasses three-year research programs in the spread of the Dharma, sangha education, fundamental doctrine and systematic etiquette, and monasterial management. Research fellows with master's degrees and graduate students with bachelor's degrees produce, on completion, a thesis in Buddhist studies no shorter than 60,000 words in length. Acceptance of the thesis by the examination panel leads to the conferring of a master's degree in Buddhist studies.

Next comes Fo Kuang Shan Ts'ung-lin College which is divided into divisions of international and postsecondary studies respectively. The former is a center of global scholarly exchange, and it produces a constellation of international preachers of the Dharma. The latter runs a four-year program in each of these departments: sutra and doctrinal studies, management of ceremonial services, social application, and cultural preaching.

Last but not least, Tung-fang Buddhist College, which runs a two-year program divided between the genders.

The curriculum is a blend of tradition and modernity, practice and comprehension. From fundamental Buddhism to higher research, it is a tight-knit, integral composite. And, in answer to demands raised in international preaching, recent attention is expressly paid to foreign languages and computer studies.

No doubt, with 11 departments, 28 classes, a faculty of 200, and a student population of close to 800, this Buddhist college system has made history. From this point on, Hsing Yun will be looking in the direction of Nalanda's[3] record population of 30,000.

Equaling the Confucian sages

To cite statistics from 1994, Fo Kuang Shan's sangha had surpassed 1,100. Of this number 225 are bhiksus, 937 are bhiksunis, and 30 are of the *shih-ku* status. Annual increase averages 100. The majority are age 21-40. A good 70 percent are graduates of postsecondary education. Also, 35 hold master's degrees and 3 have doctorates. Most are from Taiwan, and about 10 percent from overseas, namely, France, Hong Kong, Indonesia, Malaysia, Nepal, Singapore, Thailand, the United States, Vietnam, and other places.

The monastics of Fo Kuang Shan pride themselves on their *record* of having many members of the same family tonsured under the same master. Venerable Tzu

3. Unwearying Benefactor. Name of a historically renowned monastery and Buddhist institute of higher education in India.

Chuang, her father Hui Ho, and nephews Hui Lung and Hui Chuan all follow Ven. Master Hsing Yun in the monastic life. There are sisters, like Venerables Tzu Jung and Yi Lai, and other siblings, mothers and children, all of whom come to address one another as Dharma brother.

Hsing Yun was alone when he landed in Taiwan. Now, the sangha of Fo Kuang Shan boosts three generations, including himself. After the founder, the succeeding generations of bhiksus are named, in order of tonsure, Hsin (Mind) and Hui (Wisdom); the third generation, Cheng (Vehicle). The second generation of bhiksunis is named Tzu (Compassion), Yi (Accordance), Yung (Constancy), Man (Completion), Chueh (Awakening), and Miao (Wondrousness); the third generation, Tao (Way). Historian Orient Lee regards such a lineup equal to the seventy-two Confucian sages.

3,000 splendid rules, 80,000 minute details

Hsing Yun has created a unique system with excellent capability to minimize internal strife. The monastics of Fo Kuang Shan, according to the master's rule, do not take disciples or build temples of their own. All disciples follow the discipline of Fo Kuang Shan, no one has a personal following. Venerable Tzu Chuang is the master of tonsure to the third-generation bhiksunis, and Venerable Hsin Ping [now Venerable Hsin Ting], to the third-generation bhiksus. Hsing Yun is the master to the second-generation monastics, and grand-master to the third generation.

Observers think this system, with its protective measures against internal division and even possible corruption, and its family-oriented justice, is a worthwhile reference for similar institutions.

Producer Chou Chih-min of the television program *Ai-hsin* (Loving Heart) is among those of the media who have become great admirers of Hsing Yun's management methods. She relates an episode in her career which illustrates the strength of the sangha under the mighty master.

"Late 1979, I was on an episode titled *Buddha's Light Throughout the Universe,"*

Chou recalls. "It was the sixth day of the Chinese New Year holidays. Holiday revelries were still going strong. I, along with four colleagues, went to Fo Kuang Shan. ... What transpired within the first halfhour we were there was absolutely eye-opening. I showed Venerable Tzu Hui our outline. She didn't say much. Fifteen minutes passed. She handed me a schedule which outlined when and where to work, and with whom and how. Even the theme was there. We couldn't find a flaw even if we had tried. The next two days we adhered to the timetable. The shooting was nothing short of smooth sailing."

This only mirrored Hsing Yun's personal style. Planning, open discussion, delegation of responsibilities, monitoring of progress, reflection of the process, projection into the future – the whole bit. Not a step skipped or wasted.

Outsiders are inclined to share the observation that the branch temples of Fo Kuang Shan, or its monastics for that matter, "feel different, just different." They have about them a composure and propriety which are uniquely Fo Kuang

Shan's. Indeed, in every move or gesture they make reflects "the 3,000 splendid rules, 80,000 minute details." These bhiksus and bhiksunis are not only well versed in the multiple chores and skills of a conventional monastery, but are also aptly armed with the knowledge and capacities needed for writing and theorizing, monasterial management and accounting, social work and teaching, computers and mechanics. For the Buddha's way is the fundamental, and the worldly way is the functional; together the two consummate the method for the deliverance of all living beings.

Ingenuity regenerating itself

Hsing Yun thinks that ingenuity regenerates itself. Therefore Tzu Chuang, Tzu Hui, Tzu Jung, Tzu Chia, Tzu Yi, and others were sent to Japan, despite the shortage of funds. Many asked him to think twice: "What a brain-drain it would be if they didn't return! But if they do, how will you rein in those elitist minds!" It will be a breeze, he answered, even though things were going to be tough for the next little while.

"They're going to be back to do a lot for Buddhism," he added.

As their master anticipated, Venerable Tzu Hui, an education major, took over Fo Kuang Shan's educational body in its entirety; Venerables Tzu Chia and Tzu Yi headed the compilation of the *Fo Kuang Tripitaka* and the *Fo Kuang Encyclopedia;* Venerable Tzu Chuang, who specializes in construction, masterminded one branch temple after another; and Venerable Tzu Jung, a major in social work, specialized in organizing, implementing, and supervising mega-scale functions.

Hsing Yun could now rest assured that his torch was in the right hands. He was able to step down, and he did. He has since been roving among the clouds and across the four seas preaching the Dharma. In the meantime, Fo Kuang Shan continues to thrive.

So is the selection of disciples with the ability and promise for further study. Presently in Japan are Tzu Yi, a doctoral candidate, together with Yi Yu, Yi Hsin, Yung Chuan, Man Ting, and others. Hui Kai is pursuing his doctorate at Temple

University, and so is Yi Fa at Yale University in the United States. Man Guan, Chueh Mu, and quite a few others, too, are attending universities and colleges across California. Yung Hsien and Chueh Hang are in France; Yung Yu and Yi Yi at Oxford University, England; Chueh Cheng at Sao Paulo University, Brazil; Yi Hua at International University, India; Yi En in Korea ... About a hundred of them in all. They know well why they are there and what they must do.

These disciples of Hsing Yun's are probably the most qualified ever in the history of Chinese Buddhism. Many of them are accomplished in the foreign languages they are destined to use to spearhead the dissemination of the Buddhist faith around the globe.

Life's greatest blessing would be the opportunity to read thousands of books, travel thousands of miles, do thousands of tasks, and deliver thousands of living beings. In dispatching disciples to go abroad and preach, Hsing Yun wants them to realize that "Fo Kuang Shan is but a preparatory station, not a terminal, in the spread of the Dharma." Based on individual seniority, dedication, ability, and contribution, he maps out for them ways to further their studies and their lives. Practically everyone has at some point been out of Taiwan. These monastics are a far, far cry from those who used to have only the oil lamp and *Wooden fish*[4] for company and died keeping watch over a lonesome temple in the mountains.

Knowing a gem when seeing it

The sight of a youthful monastic in the old days would invariably invite a lament or two: "What a pity! To have renounced the world at such a young age!" There is nothing *piteous* about joining Fo Kuang Shan, where heavy stakes are placed on training and the trained are allowed plenty of space. For, "being good at discerning the nature of all living beings and not ever being discriminative," Hsing Yun steers his disciples in their development based on

[4] Wooden fish. Two kinds exist, one for keeping time in chanting and the other for announcing meals. One version of its origin is that it serves as a reminder of alertness to the monastics, the fish with its eyes open at all time.

their strengths and inclinations. In "accommodating them, changing them, and employing them," he ensures that they become the best they possibly can be.

Among many, many others, the eloquent Tzu Hui, Tzu Jung, Hsin Ting, Yi Kung, and Hui Chuan have been sent to preach the Dharma; the literary Yi Sheng, Yung Chuang, Yung Yun, and Man Kuang keep publishing; the academic Tzu Chia, Yi Chun, Hsin Ju, Yung Ming, Yung Chin, and Man Kuo compile the Canon; the compassionate Hui Lung, Yi Jen, Yi Pin, and Yi Lai champion charitable causes; the serene Yi Yen, Hui Jih, and Chien Kuan concentrate on their practice; the studious Tzu Yi and Chueh San further their studies; and drafting specialists Tzu Chuang, Yi Min, and Hui Li build temples and undertake managerial duties.

Hsing Yun is like a miner and sculptor in the discovery of talents. "He knows us better than we know ourselves," disciples say, brimming over with gratitude and admiration. Once he was discussing the issue of examination and certification with a jeweler. "He knows gems; I know people,"

Hsing Yun beamed.

The young monastics of Fo Kuang Shan did not take the tonsure out of despair in love or in life; they did so with perfect will. With compassion – the love for all, not for one – they have come to serve living beings. In so doing, they radiate joy, drive, wholesomeness, and grace. The rest of the world will learn to think differently about Buddhism.

Some years ago parents were still heard insisting that their tonsured sons and daughters go home with them. These days, however, students of the Buddhist college arrive with their folks' blessings and take the tonsure in their presence. The ancient way of "grieving, the son relinquished to the gate of void" finally gives way to modern parents, "cheerily, walking their child to the gate of the Buddha."

Author Hsiao Hung sees Hsing Yun in every one of his disciples. "They're so affable – like their master. Passing by, they close their palms in greeting; if the path is narrow, they wait aside to let the others pass. One has to possess devotion within to display it without. It is not a mere act. Simply the master's virtues finding expression through his disciples."

Born to be an educator

Learned educator Chêng Shih-yen finds in Hsing Yun a natural educator with many concepts and theories that should be widely adopted in the educational field. In the past, Hsing Yun witnessed classmates who acted out of line at Ch'i-hsia Temple being ordered to pay homage to the Buddha or kneel before the shrine for the length of a lit incense. Thinking to himself that paying homage to the Buddha is such a thing of beauty, he could not believe it should take the form of penalty. Today at Fo Kuang Shan, misbehavior is punishable by "being sent to bed and disallowed to pay homage to the Buddha." Cooped up in bed and guilt-ridden, students have little problem recognizing their own follies. Permitted in the presence of the Buddha again, many prostrate in tears and kneel for a long, long time.

He emphasizes education of the mind. He replaces condemnation with encouragement and chiding with caring. A personal favorite for teachers is the story of Ch'an master Hsien Yai. A novice monk was prone to diversions beyond the confines of the monastery. Nightly he would jump over the wall and be gone. One time Master Hsien Yai was on his rounds in the temple grounds when he came upon a stool by the corner of the wall – evidence of an attempt to sneak outside. He removed the stool and stood himself in its place, waiting. The night wore on. At last, the novice returned from his merriment. Not knowing about the absence of the stool, he alighted squarely on the master's head. When he finally landed, to his consternation, he found himself face to face with the master.

"The night is deep and the dew is heavy," the gracious Master Hsien Yai said, as if nothing had gone awry. "Take good care of your body. Don't let it catch cold. Run on home and get yourself more clothing."

Not another word was uttered about the incident. No one even knew it ever occurred. Thereafter, though, among the hundred or so novices there were no more nocturnal excursions.

Like the cultivation of orchids, disciples have to be strengthened by the accumulation of learning and nourished by the accumulation of virtue, stimulated by the resonance of the Way and reached by the passing on of the Dharma. Nothing consolidates sangha members more than such a connection between the master and his disciples.

Yi Kung feels that Hsing Yun is just like a parent, "with whom we can pour our hearts out." Aspiring after Sariputra[5], his unsurpassed intellect and erudition, she says: "The master is the Buddha. I wouldn't have become a monastic if not for him." For the most obstinate of living beings would have bowed to his compassion and attained sagehood; the most incorrigible mules would have stooped to his tender care and been transformed into fleet-footed steeds. Yi Kung recalls the time she was to relocate to other quarters. The master made sure she was given a larger room "because

[5] A principal disciple of Sakyamuni Buddha.

Yi Kung has tons of books," and a table light "because Yi Kung has a lot of reading to do."

Venerable Hsin Cheng, too, has her share of reflections: "That year in Changhua I was hospitalized from a car crash. The master dropped in to see me. The sweat on his forehead was unwiped. He was just rooted there and kept staring at my bandaged leg and toothless mouth. I was so ashamed to have him hurting for me like that!"

Inevitable are the occasional disagreements and discontentments, disciples have this thought to bank on: "The master treats me like no other. He'll understand!"

Like friend, like teacher, like parent

Disciples rush to reciprocate. The master is followed on his rounds within the temple grounds and as far as preaching commitments may take him. And, whenever worn or delayed at meals, he is promptly served a cup of hot tea, a hot meal, or a hot towel.

Hsing Yun has for years been under

treatment for diabetes. Disciples will not leave until he is seen to have taken his medication at the end of a meal. And, each time the statuesque master boards or exits a vehicle, one of them always lays a hand on the doorway lest he may bump his head.

To the older disciples, he is both master and companion in the Dharma. To the younger ones, he is a parent. "The master is as colossal as a mountain yet endearing," they say. "He is rather like the air we breathe, spontaneous and vital. We cannot be without it. But then again, the pressure is never there."

On filiality, however, Hsing Yun's sigh is clearly audible. "When parents are young and useful," he ponders, "their service is eagerly sought after - like a basketball. As their effectiveness dwindles with age, they are shoved around - like a volleyball. Finally, old and incapacitated, they are kicked around - like a soccer ball."

"I left home to become a monk at twelve. I have no children of my own. But my disciples are more filial to me than any children I would have had. One day I shall be old. They are going to hold me and not let me go - like an American football."

In his bid to create inexhaustible brain-power for the Buddhist circle, Hsing Yun has broken out of the limitations of Fo Kuang Shan. Projects such as the Chinese Buddhist Research Institute, regular international Buddhist conferences and seminars, the annual international Buddhist examination, Fo Kuang Shan Cultural and Educational Foundation, and diverse sponsorships for international Buddhist scholarly research, all serve the same end.

"When rearing the young, they should not fear growth and independence," he has said many a time. Trained and matured, he vows to make gifts of them to society, to the nation, and to all living beings.

Modern guard for the Buddhist faith

Yes, Hsing Yun is fully aware of the widening gap between Fo Kuang Shan's awesome growth and the training of its forces. But he has every reason to believe that experiences shall be updated and wrongs be righted. It is a path for the next hundred years. They will get there.

Such a self-assured openness has created a modern guard for Buddhism. On the shoulders of the thousand or so dragons and elephants at the Buddha gate shall rest the future of the Tathagata. While his contemporaries are piqued by imminent concerns over posterity, Hsing Yun knows that "twenty years from now, Fo Kuang Shan shall stand as the most powerful religious body in Taiwan."

Chapter 10

Traditional monastery, current version

If we count Fo Kuang Shan as an enterprise, it will be in the list of the top hundred. Realizing its system and functions, you'll find that Fo Kuang Shan is a well-organized entity full of life, manpower, and financial resources. It inherited the spirit of the traditional monastery of the T'ang dynasty, and combined this with the ideals of modern management. Overall, Fo Kuang Shan embodies the modern version of Chinese Buddhism and provides a model for secular business management.

Product of teamwork

Organizational empires are usually the brain-child of the founder. Fo Kuang Shan is no exception. The formation and operation of Fo Kuang Shan is Hsing Yun's brain-child.

Maintaining that Buddhism is the enterprise of all living beings, Hsing Yun sees Fo Kuang Shan as a team innovation. The Committee of Religious Affairs is vested with decision-making in developmental directions, and interdepartmental communication and coordination. Committee members number 7 - 11, each serving six-year terms, with one third being elected every two years. A director-in-chief is elected from the committee to also serve a term of six years. Presently holding the position is abbot Venerable Hsin Ping.[1]

The next level is the abbot's office followed by the executive director's office which oversees ten management departments governing monasterial affairs, devotees' affairs, charity, social welfare, construction and maintenance services,

[1] Venerable Hsin Ping passed away in April, 1995. The new abbot is Venerable Hsin Ting.

financial affairs, human resources, systematic affairs, etc. along with the departments of education, cultural affairs, and monastic elders, Light-passing Committee[2], Fo Kuang Shan Cultural and Educational Foundation, Fo Kuang Shan Pureland Foundation, Compassion Foundation, Fo Kuang University Fundraising Committee, Buddha's Light International Association, and others – totaling over 180 units.

Headquartered in Kaohsiung, Fo Kuang Shan has a vast network of over 100 branch establishments. A majority of these were put up by Hsing Yun himself. A handful were cases of various temples voluntarily seeking to merge with Fo Kuang Shan after hitting financial snags, due to unsolvable internal strife, or the absence of a successor.

Chi-lê (Utmost Joy) Temple, Keelung, newly renovated last year, was one of them. The causes and conditions that bound the temple and Hsing Yun together through four decades dated back to the instant he

[2] The committee takes charge in looking after all monastics at Fo Kuang Shan pertaining to education, welfare, reward & punishment, medication, etc., and even the welfare of the monastics' parents.

set foot in Keelung. After having left his ship, he was on his way past an old, weathered temple. When he glanced inside, a monastic returned the look. No word was ever exchanged. Thirty-two years later, the director of the Keelung Buddhist Association and abbot Hsiu Hui of Chi-lê Temple – whom Hsing Yun had met fleetingly – invited him to conduct a three-day seminar. Venerable Hsiu Hui had read his works and readily identified with the concept of humanistic Buddhism, Hsing Yun was told. Another three years were to pass before Venerable Hsiu Hui made a gift of Chi-lê Temple and its surrounding properties to Fo Kuang Shan.

Yüan-ming Temple in suburban Ilan, where Hsing Yun completed his *Biography of Sakyamuni Buddha's Ten Great Disciples* and the *Enlightenment Sutra*, was another. In 1982 abbot Chüeh Yi entrusted Fo Kuang Shan with the temple just prior to his passing away. Yüan-fu (Perfect Fortune) Temple, Chiayi, erected at the turn of the century, was the third.

Expansion, peripheral and nucleus-oriented

Certainly with the hundred or so branches stemming from the nucleus of Fo Kuang Shan there is the need for the most intricate organizational structure.

Right below headquarters is the first level of branch temples which include major temples such as Taipei's P'u-mên Temple, Kaohsiung's P'u-hsien Temple; Los Angeles' Hsi Lai Temple, and Tokyo's branch temple. Each is categorized by its location in a metropolis of a million or more population, its ability to hold Dharma functions for 1,000 or more, and its 8- or more resident sangha members.

At the second level are those which maintain the outward appearance of traditional temples; lecture halls and temples, which are mostly established in the setting of modern buildings. Again, each is categorized for its location in a city of half a million or more population, its ability to hold Dharma functions for 500 or more, and its 4- to 8-resident sangha members.

At the third level are the Ch'an and Pureland centers. Each is categorized for its suburban location, its ability to hold Dharma functions for 200 or more, and its 2- to 4-resident sangha members.

Lastly, the preaching centers in outlying areas are run in a more mobile way by visiting monastics.

Financial independence of all branch establishments is required. Financial assistance, however, is often sought from headquarters in cases of major constructions.

This global setup of Fo Kuang Shan is unprecedented in the history of Buddhism. Similar to the Vatican but not quite, it is especially unique in the centralized training and delegation of its forces. Thus, no matter how vast the peripheral expansion, resource assignment will always come from Fo Kuang Shan.

The hierarchy

Two subsystems exist under the hierarchy of Fo Kuang Shan: gradation of seniority and appointment in administration.

The gradation of seniority falls into 5 classes and 15 grades. At the bottom is the class of pure and clean practitioner in 6 grades, one per year. The next 3 classes are, learning practitioner in 6 grades, one in 3 - 5 years; cultivating practitioner in 3 grades, one in 4 years; and teaching practitioner in 3 grades, one in 5 years. At the top is the class of master.

The appointment in administration pertains to the delegation of duties in other headquarters as well as branch establishments.

Hsing Yun has in fact designed a management scheme of tremendous flexibility and versatility, in which manpower is maneuvered in accordance with academic credentials both outside and from the Buddhist college, and accomplished study of the Canon; character, conduct, and practice; and contribution and seniority. This system is capable of promoting junior but outstanding performers to vital positions as well as warranting recognition of senior and responsible members.

No doubt corporate executives are

well acquainted with such a credentials- and accountability-oriented dual system, which maintains a business order by preserving seasoned workers and keeps the organization on its toes by boosting promising newcomers.

Most transfers come once every three years, usually during the first and seventh month of the lunar calendar. Before the transfer, individual preferences are filed with, and evaluated by, the Committee of Religious Affairs. Implementation corresponds to the demand of the relevant departments and units. Objections are rescheduled for further discussion. In tackling the enormity of such a personnel structure as Fo Kuang Shan's, this evaluation system prioritizes the placement of "the right person in the right place."

From regulated transfers springs a managerial fluidity. Nobody hangs onto a position, or grows powerful enough to abuse it. Promotion and transfer are as clear-cut as awards and penalties. Supply from a pool of talent is always ready, always fresh. The division of labor is best illustrated in large-scale functions, Fo Kuang Shan style. Called humanizing management, these are spectacular maneuvers in manpower from the initial delegation of authority through the ultimate execution of a project.

Devotees learn to "abide by the Dharma, not the person." They protect and maintain the temples instead of relating and attaching to a certain monastic. Exposure to constantly renewed leadership means the substitution of personal sentiment by an open system.

Economics

Hsing Yun leads in the personal example of not ever maintaining his own temple, raising his own funds, or pocketing his own savings. Every penny in terms of income and donations are channeled to the individual temples for maintenance and other expenses. Financial and administrative authority are distinctly separate; in the hands of junior executives lies the former, and in those of senior executives lies the latter. Everyone collects a monthly stipend on the basis of seniority and position: teaching practitioner, NT$400; temple head , NT$300 - 350; director,

NT$300; clerk, NT$200; cook at the guest house, NT$150; and so on. Daily necessities, room and board, and transportation are paid by Fo Kuang Shan. Salaried lay workers receive a monthly average of NT$3,000.

Hsing Yun thinks the feasibility of this relative leanness is empowered by the principle of selflessness upheld at Fo Kuang Shan, where the spirit of agricultural Ch'an practice so advocated by Venerable Master Huai Hai of Paichang in the T'ang dynasty – no food without work – is alive and well.

Critics have cautioned young people against seeking academic furtherance at Fo Kuang Shan in what is deemed a labor-intensive program. "The monastics are made to do drudgery work instead of being allowed to cultivate," some say. To Hsing Yun, who was raised performing diverse chores, manual labor is natural. Once separated from fetching water and chopping wood, wearing clothes and eating food, the expression of the Dharma is lost. The essence of Ch'an, or meditation, is reflected in work. The eminent masters throughout the ages had, without exception, built their characters through labor. The sixth patriarch Hui Nêng carried rocks and pounded grain; Master Huai Hai of Paichang moved firewood and fetched water; and, wearing a cloak of straw, Master P'u Yüan of Nanch'üan drove cattle. As for Hsing Yun, he spent six out of ten years serving meals, two years fetching water, and a year and a half tending the shrine and working in the kitchen.

Even those attending the Buddhist colleges have obligations alongside their privileges. At Fo Kuang Shan, the traditional monasterial daily routine, complete with the punctuating bell, drum, and board, is still intact. Wake-up signal is at 4:20 a.m., followed by morning liturgy, and then breakfast. Classes are conducted for three hours each in the morning and afternoon, and self-study is for two hours in the evening. The day closes with the evening liturgy, meditation, and then rest. Chores such as cleaning and cooking are included. For the latter, grand old wood-burning stoves are still ablaze because they are deemed indispensable devices in the training of patience and concentration.

Finances

In supporting its community of monastics and lay people, and financing diverse projects in education, charity, and construction, Fo Kuang Shan's financial burder is understandably unwieldy. To maintain self-sufficiency, Fo Kuang Shan has established kindergartens and schools, published books and magazines, and produced memorabilia and souvenirs. Though assailed for "multifaceted commercialism," Hsing Yun is at peace with his own intentions.

"Buddhists are not social deserters," he says. "Nor is there any call to feed on society. It is for us to trade our labor for our livelihood. For in personal practice and spreading the Dharma, we have to be self-sufficient before we can serve the masses. Most of all, Buddhism, having received donations from society, must give in return. This basically explains the business ventures of Fo Kuang Shan."

Indeed, the monastery needs donations to run its undertakings. Of the donations from devotees, Hsing Yun also has an exceptional view. The two main sources of income in a traditional temple are the conducting of repentance ceremonies and services for the dead, and soliciting the support of generous protectors of the Dharma. Concerning the former, in particular, he harbors no misgivings – except that he believes them to be a mutual relationship rather than a trade-off. While devotees give to the temple, it is only right for the sangha to provide for their needs. Hence repentance ceremonies and services for the dead at Fo Kuang Shan and its branch temples are organized and discreet.

Hsing Yun does not favor the mundane practice of keeping a few protectors of the Dharma with hefty check-books. For chances are lavish givers may also pose oversized ego problems and end up doing more harm than good to the general harmony. That is why Hsing Yun prizes small sums from countless humble donors over a handful of generous patrons. This is what building good affinities from far and wide means.

"These days most people don't mind

small sums any more," he adds. "When they do give, they certainly have no intention of seeking control of temple affairs in return. Besides, more visitors at Fo Kuang Shan means the accumulation of more and more affinities."

Drops in the ocean

Just how are good affinities from far and wide accumulated? First of all, those who contribute to the temple receive gifts "from the Buddha." In a way, the mammoth Fo Kuang Shan has been built from its little souvenirs.

Then, weekly pilgrimage tours, though not exactly profitable, have become greatly attractive to devotees as well as nondevotees, who spend two days and a night at Fo Kuang Shan. The tours prove to be one of the most effective means of creating the causes and conditions of Buddhism. Among others, Venerables Yung Ping and Yung Wen came in touch with Buddhism and, ultimately, their own destiny in the sangha, when they joined the tours.

On the conviction that the ocean begins with small drops, Hsing Yun had the City of Thousands of Buddhas together with the Chambers of Gold and Jade Buddhas erected – all of them products of collaboration of donors. These, along with 480 golden Buddhas surrounding the Great Welcoming Buddha, 8,000 images of Avalokitesvara Bodhisattva in the Hall of Great Compassion, 14,800 images of Sakyamuni Buddha in their respective niches in the Main Shrine, other pillars, Chinese roofing tiles, and relief sculptures are there for devotees to pledge their donations. Each donor leaves Fo Kuang Shan with a share of affinity.

Other Dharma functions such as the regular lantern of light, Chinese New Year's lantern of peace, and thousands affinities functions bring in tens of thousands of devotees and their contributions.

In the red

The fact of the matter is that Fo Kuang Shan is far from an entity of great wealth. In the words of a temple spokesperson: "Fo Kuang

Shan is not wealthy, but it knows how to utilize wealth – even that of next year, and the year after next." Rather, it is a center where resources are diverted.

Hsing Yun himself does not touch on money matters unless compelled to do so, and often tells disciples to refrain from paying too much attention to them, saying: "You're going to lose sleep knowing too much!" A budgetary system is fast taking shape, and various units are commercially registered.

Backed neither by a country nor any financial consortium, Fo Kuang Shan is accomplished in controlling resources. However, it must be noted that, estimated at NT$150 billion in assets, Fo Kuang Shan is far behind the top-ten list of Taiwan's wealthiest religious corporations.

Both a giver and taker

Hsing Yun is a monk who is unafraid of wealth, unafraid to create wealth, and unafraid to utilize wealth. "I'm both a giver and taker of wealth," he says, candidly discussing the prevalent view in the Buddhist circle that poverty stands for cultivation and wealth is another word for vulgarity.

"Catholics and Protestants are lauded for their financial strength. Why should Buddhists alone shy away from money matters so!"

"Wealth is a requisite unless one doesn't want to achieve anything. How best to put to use the devotees' good wealth, clean wealth, and sacred wealth for the benefit of all living beings – that is the question."

For years the media lost no time in painting this picture of Fo Kuang Shan: bustling, not the least tranquil; retailing soft drinks and profiteering from souvenir sales; air-conditioned and carpeted guest houses; monastics riding in sedans and – making phone calls. Their conclusion: Fo Kuang Shan is far too worldly, and Hsing Yun is just an enterprising monk.

Somehow, many visitors have come away with something else. Apart from areas open to the public, where modern comforts are for the convenience of devotees and tourists, the restricted areas are where practice and cultivation are conducted. Wood-burning stoves are still in operation. Sleeping quarters, neither air-conditioned nor carpeted, are lined with boards as in the old days. Monastics rise at 4:30 a.m. and go to bed at 10 p.m. They know no weekends or holidays, are never paid overtime, and wear the same clothing and two pairs of shoes year-round. Indeed they live a simple life. They do take the odd ride or make the odd call. But then again, in an age of electronics and telecommunications, insisting that monastics should go on foot and keep to themselves at all times would be ludicrous!

Hsing Yun admits he can do nothing about all the distorted rumors flying around. He only feels deeply for his disciples and followers. He urges them to continue to receive devotees and visitors with their affability and compassion, their diligence and service, hoping that, with a meal and friendship, more resources shall be gathered for the care of the old and young, running of schools, and the preaching of the Dharma.

The system

Suffice it to say that Taiwan has kept lit the incense of Chinese Mahayana Buddhism. Moreover, under Hsing Yun orthodox discipline and etiquette, kept intact at Fo Kuang Shan, have been modernized and perfected to accord with the times. Writing about the hope of revival, Hsing Yun prioritizes what he feels is a healthy system:

"In the past, the Buddhist sangha had a healthy system. The precepts and rules, for instance, were instrumental in ensuring monasterial peace. As well, the six points of reverent unity,[3] warrants monastic harmony. There used to be a monasterial order in the mainland because there was a system. That is not true in Taiwan: we have no system; we go our own way."

Hsing Yun grew up in a traditional monastery and traveled to various places. He thus cultivated his temperament and insight. The Fo Kuang Shan that he created

[3] Bodily unity as in worship; verbal unity as in chanting; mental unity as in faith; moral unity as in observing precepts and rules; doctrinal unity as in views and interpretations; economic unity as in community of deeds, study, or charity.

is a current version of a traditional monastery. "A temple has to be like a temple; a monk has to be like a monk." The tonsure has to follow a system; so does the passing of the precepts. In 1991, Fo Kuang Shan conducted a three-month Ten-thousand Buddhas Triple Platform Ordination. The reception of the complete triple platform precepts – the sramanera or sramanerika precepts, bhiksu or bhiksuni precepts, and Bodhisattva precepts – qualifies a monastic of the Mahayana tradition. Five hundred recipients attended the most systematically and meticulously executed ordination to date. Every single detail went by the book: work and rest, morning and evening liturgies, explication of the precepts, meditation, rehearsal, and labor. Abbot K'ai Chêng of Hung-fa (Spreading the Dharma) Temple called the event the most correct and accomplished monastic ordination in Taiwan during four decades. And, retired abbot P'u Ch'êng of Song Kwang Sa (Vast Pines Temple), Korea, found the sights and sounds to be invaluable references.

From propriety to professionalism

Everyone, though burdened with chores and duties, must adhere to the morning and evening liturgies, and not stop learning. Light-passing College is the school of continuing education and in-service training which Hsing Yun established for that specific purpose. Attendees take four courses per year for four years. In addition, a monthly letter comes from the master himself inquiring after their progress, with topical notes attached. The latter may range from doctrinal themes, textual research, case studies, preaching methods, or learning experiences. Students are required to delve into these materials and submit reports on them. Examinations are held twice a year, and diplomas are awarded to those who pass them. Flunking an exam is not an unusual occurrence.

Fo Kuang Shan's welfare system is about the most thorough there is, tending to everything from medicare, vacations, further studies, traveling, family visits, loans, to burials for parents.

There even exists a dining system called *kuo-t'ang*. For each meal, everybody is required to line up, join palms and chant the Buddha's name, and wait for the sounding of the board before entering the dining hall. Seated, everybody begins with the five contemplations and ends with the offering mantra before starting to consume the two bowls (of soup and rice) and one plate (of vegetables) set in front. Eating in the manner of "a dragon swallowing a pearl and a phoenix nodding its head," no one is to glance around or talk. Everyone absolutely must finish his/her share – a sign of cherishing one's blessings. At the end of the meal, the entire group leaves in single file, while tables are quickly cleared.

Life on the mountain can be aptly described as flowing with conditions while being disciplined. No one will dispute the professionalism with which Fo Kuang Shan conducts itself. It is but Hsing Yun's influence at work.

Chapter 11

Dharma should not be separated from worldly awakening

He lives on the mountain but thinks of those below. Feet on the ground, he eyes the universe. From temples the good run over for the benefit of all living beings. Heavens are fine; this world is finer.

Hsing Yun's lectures, his writings, his person, his temples, his disciples, and his devotees are all manifestations of the concept of humanistic and living Buddhism.

Some researchers of Taiwanese Buddhism think that Hsing Yun has set up a "Fo Kuang School" in addition to the eight traditional Buddhist schools.

Though Hsing Yun doesn't intend to set up another Buddhist school, tracing what he has thought and done in the past five decades, we can discover a coherent system in it.

The Buddha was human

The founder of Buddhism, Sakyamuni Buddha, was not a fleeting, feathered deity. Nor was he any pedestaled savior. He was human; he really lived.

Sakyamuni Buddha, originally named Siddhartha, was born on the eighth day of the fourth month of the lunar calendar, 544 B.C.E.,[1] in Lumbini, Kapilavastu, India. His parents were Suddhodana, head of the Sakya clan, and his wife, the immaculate Maya. His mother died seven days after his birth, leaving him to be raised by her sister Prajapati. Amidst the adoration of his people Siddhartha grew up the peerless leader his father had groomed him to be. At seventeen, he wedded Yasodhara, who in the ensuing year bore him a son, Rahula.

[1] Different versions of date and ages exist. This is the Chinese Mahayana version. The Buddha's story here is based on the *Fo Kuang Encyclopedia* and the *Chronology of Buddhist History*, both published by Fo Kuang Publishing House.

Somehow, in neither his nobility nor the affection of loved ones could he find the answer to his question about the truth of life and the meaning of the universe. Eventually he left his palace and went on his quest. He became an ascetic and for years practiced austerities. Finally at age thirty-five, he seated himself on the diamond throne[2] beneath a Bodhi tree, gazed at the stars above, and became enlightened: "All living beings have the Tathagata's wisdom and virtue." Subsequently he began to turn the wheel of the Dharma[3] and founded his sangha.[4] After preaching for forty-five years, he entered nirvana in a grove of Sal trees[5] near Kusinagara.

Most extant Buddhist literature is a record of Sakyamuni Buddha's teachings, compiled by his disciples after he passed away.

[2] *Chin-kang tso* in the original text. The Buddha's seat on attaining enlightenment.

[3] *Fa-lun* in the original text. The Wheel of the Dharma which crushes all evil, and which rolls on from person to person, place to place, age to age.

[4] On the basis of poverty, chastity, and insight or meditation. That was the founding of Buddhism.

[5] Teak trees.

Sakyamuni Buddha, as evidenced in history, was born in this world, raised in this world, attained enlightenment in this world, and entered nirvana in this world. Life's joy, anger, misery, and happiness he tasted; human birth, aging, sickness, and death he lived. *Buddha* in Sanskrit stands for the enlightened one; Sakyamuni *is* the Enlightened One. We are humans yet to be enlightened.

The Dharma as the Buddha taught it in his time was primarily geared for traveling, living, sitting, resting, thinking, and behaving in life. The result is a human-oriented Buddhism. What Hsing Yun does is apply the Buddha's teachings of 2,500 years ago to modern life. And in the process, he furthers the development of humanistic Buddhism.

The Five Precepts, cornerstone of worldly peace

When once asked at a military academy about the tangible contributions Buddhism has for the nation and society, Hsing Yun replied: "The Tripitaka along with its twelve divisions of sacred sutras are all beneficial to the nation and society. But then, the simple Five Precepts alone will suffice to govern a country and rule the world."

Specifically, freedom in the contemporary sense is that which does not interfere with the freedom of others. That is exactly what the Five Precepts are about. The precept against killing prevents [us] from assailing the safety of others, and thus is a respect for life. The precept against stealing keeps [us] from plundering the property of others, and thus is a respect for rights. The precept against adultery stops [us] from corrupting the chastity of others, and thus is a respect for virtue. The precept against lying holds [us] from ruining the name of others, and thus is a respect for morals. The precept against intoxication prevents us from losing our sanity, and thus keeps us from becoming a danger to others. Should we abide by the Five Precepts, respect one another, and are able to fully enjoy freedom within legal bounds, the nation and society will, no doubt, be safe and harmonious, happy and beneficial.

Though six decades have passed since the day he started school, he will always cherish the very first character that he was taught – *jên*, people! All his life, his respect for people has never diminished. Fo Kuang Shan is for the practice of humanistic Buddhism. Those who join its sangha must share the consensus of awakening oneself and others, benefiting oneself and others. Journalist Wu Ling-chiao once wrote: "Whoever seeks liberation for oneself [6] only must not seek Fo Kuang Shan."

Worldly life is affirmed

In humanistic Buddhism, the idealistic and realistic Hsing Yun sees an absolute affirmation of the value of worldly life. What is more, he insists that asceticism give way to joy in practice.

He does not think it realistic to be obsessed with the idea of liberation from birth and death, to engage solely in practice,

[6] *Tzŭ-liao-han* in the original text. The proper title is arhat, or lohan, the enlightened saint in Hinayana Buddhism, who seeks destruction of body and mind and extinction in nirvana.

to turn one's back on worldly affairs, and to live on others' support. That, he says, would be a parasitic existence. "Practice, practice! *Practice* is becoming another word for indolence," once lamented Master Yin Shun. For indeed practice is neither a slogan nor a ritual. Practice is the real-life application of the Dharma in the form of service and offering, diligence and patience.

"To tackle life is more important than to tackle death," Master T'ai Hsü once said. Living must be solved before seeking liberation from birth and death. Buddhism is to be applied to daily life because it is a living religion.

Venerable Master Hui Nêng of the Ch'an school spoke this verse in *The Sixth Patriarch's Platform Sutra*:

> The worldly existence of the Dharma
> Departs not from the worldly
>   awakening.
> Leaving the world to seek the Bodhi[7]
> Is like seeking the horn of the hare.

In a nutshell, "the Dharma is but the

[7] Perfect wisdom; enlightenment.

innate good of human nature." There in every aspect of daily life is the possibility of wisdom, waiting to be realized. The following verse gives a metaphorical depiction of such a state:

> Exhausting the days in quest of spring,
> nowhere is it to be found;
> Treading the clouds along the mountain
> range with [my] sandals of straw.
> Returning, in [my] hands [I] chance
> to hold the plum blossoms
> to [my] nose,
> Only to be told that, already,
> spring is on each and every bough.

The practice of the Ch'an masters is such that those in business follow the rules, not swindle, and not evade taxes; those in the military are valiant and guard their land; those in office are loyal and accountable, and serve their hometown; and those in academia focus in their study and teaching. In other words, when all shall play their roles the best they can, the Dharma will be in the air.

Religion of blessings

To Hsing Yun, the humanistic Buddhism of our times is one of sounds, colors, actions, and humor. "What I mean by humanistic Buddhism is a life of joy and interest, of gratification and affluence, of compassion and virtue. Such is the deliverance for all as taught by the Mahayana and the way as learned from the Pureland."

The *Amitabha Sutra* speaks about a world of utmost happiness in the West where the ground is covered with gold, chambers and attics are adorned with the seven gems, water is of the eight virtues, hued birds speak the Dharma, and gorgeous flowers never wither. It is an indication that the Buddhist practice does not necessarily mean eating badly, clothing oneself in rags, or being forever deprived of daily necessities. Quite the contrary, if joy after death should be sought after, why shouldn't the fortune of living be treasured first? Buddhism is not a religion of suffering but one of blessing. Hsing Yun wants the beautiful and good side of this world to be cherished with positivity, and defines the Pureland on earth as

> Courteous and respectful,
>   let kind words be uttered,
> Hopeful and content,
>   let happiness spring;
> Civil and harmonious,
>   let freedom come to hand,
> Compassionate and accepting,
>   let peace and wholeness
>   be celebrated.

He is probably one of the most listened-to storytellers around. His elucidation of the wondrousness and profundity of humanistic Buddhism by way of social concerns and familiar circumstances is deemed magnetic.

On wealth

Since everybody else is looking in the direction of wealth, Hsing Yun, too, speaks often on the Buddhist view of wealth.

"Buddhism does not deny wealth," he says. Many Buddhists absolutely refuse to discuss the subject, stigmatizing "gold as a viper," and certainly do not recognize *gold* as a sustenance of practice and necessary in the spread of the Dharma for the benefit of all living beings. The truth is, however, that the wise cherish wealth and know the correct way to acquire it. For when wealth comes in a proper way, the more the better. No Buddhist should have any cause for resistance against wealth.

Once a man took pains to stock gold bullion in his cellar. Thirty-odd years passed. It was not even touched. Then one day the gold bullion was gone. He thought that he would die. "Have you ever spent any of the gold?" someone asked. "Absolutely not!" "So you've never touched it all these years. No matter, let me get a brick, wrap it up, and put it back there. Wouldn't that be just fine? Why bother to mourn like that!"

Hsing Yun's story is about an understanding that "wealth is a blessing; knowing how to expend wealth is wisdom." Neither one who devalues wealth nor a miser is called wise. *Possessing* wealth is a pleasure, but to be able to utilize wealth for the benefit of others is truly *enjoying* wealth. Most of all, wealth appears in various forms in our life: stamina and health, thankfulness and content, a meaningful existence, peace and security for loved ones, a wholesome spirit .... All are worth cherishing and cultivating.

On fate

These are such evanescent times. Some seem to take a person to the constellations while others plummet one into the fathoms of disgrace and destitution. Hence predictions based on physiognomy, fortune-telling, and geomancy have been sought after by the public. A favorable prediction will send some walking on air; an unfavorable one will shroud others with fear. Humanistic Buddhism has none of this. Fatalism is not the view to adopt. Destiny is in our own hands, and fate, far from written, can be altered.

Here is Hsing Yun's illustration of how providence is depicted in humanistic Buddhism.

A master who had attained arhatship realized in meditation that his favorite disciple was left with but seven days to live.

"Why does this lovely child have to have seven days left of his life?" thought he. "What a misfortune! I can't honestly tell him the truth. So young, how is he going to take such a blow!"

At daybreak, the master laid aside his heartbreak and summoned the little sramanera, to whom he said: "My good boy, you haven't seen your folks for so long. Why don't you pack up and go home for a visit!"

Innocently, the sramanera took leave of his master and went home. A day went by. Then another. A total of seven days passed but nothing was heard or seen of him. Just when the master was mourning the loss of his disciple, the little one showed up in his presence, quite safe and sound.

The incredulous master took his hand, looked him up and down, and asked: "What brings you back? What happened in the last seven days?"

"Nothing!" responded the sramanera, shaking his head and quite perplexed.

"Try to remember! Did you see

anything? Or, did you do anything?"

"Oh, I came upon a pond on my way home and saw a group of ants caught in the water. So I picked a leaf and helped them back ashore."

The child's compassion at that moment – the master was relieved to learn – had sown such bountiful causes of good, that, in saving the ants' lives, he amended his own fate.

Though merely another parable, it once again shows how exhaustible fortune really is. Like a mountain of wealth stacked away, if abused, all the blessings in life may go down the drain. On the contrary, regular contributions to a savings account will in time amount to a substantial balance. That is also how a life of misfortune may turn around. In humanistic Buddhism, it is hoped that we rejoice in life, know our futures, clear our minds, change our ways, and create our destinies.

On politics

Politics is an ultra-sensitive topic especially in politically sensitive Taiwan. But Hsing

Yun, with unmistakable integrity in what he does and does not do, has long been speaking publicly on Buddhist political views. When cautioned by followers against the taboo – which most others would rather avoid, not to mention the monastics – he tells them that politics is a public issue. As gregarious as humans are, no one is an island, and therefore cannot live above and beyond politics. The Buddhists of modern society vote, pay taxes, serve when drafted, and live a life closely connected with the implications of politics. We may just as well view politics properly.

"I leave home but not the country," he often says, meaning that to accord with the concept of humanistic Buddhism, the monastics, too, are not unconcerned about the affairs of the state. Chanted monthly on the first and fifteenth days in *Praise of the Precious Cauldron*: "In deep respect, longevity is wished for the republic, as long as heaven and earth shall last ...." Ch'an master Ch'ang Lu once prayed for "all countries to be at peace and all frontiers stilled; all arms dismantled and forces dismissed; all winds gentle and rains kind; all men safe and women joyous." Records of politically influential monastics are ample. Venerable Master Hsüan Wan of T'ang, an imperial tutor, coached the heir to the throne in the ways to rule his country and love his people: practice charity, eliminate killing, follow nature, observe vegetarianism. In yet another case, Master T'ai Hsü countered Japan's accusation that China was corrupting Buddhism during the Sino-Japanese war by visiting with the Buddhist countries of Burma, Ceylon,[8] and others, and winning support in the process. Master Lê Kuan, too, called for a rally of the monastics in resistance.

Hsing Yun believes that Master T'ai Hsü's moderate and objective standpoint of "questioning politics without intervening" is the attitude for modern Buddhists. That is, caring about the well-being of the country, but not pursuing the glory and fortune of public office. Politicians may be advised to borrow from the Buddha's wisdom as recorded in *Ekottara-agama*: no corruption, no anger, no evasion, no isolation, no trespassing, no selfishness ....

[8] Sri Lanka.

On relationships

Relationships must top the list of modern defilements. Too many lives are seen spiraling into tragedy because an ego is inflated, a battle must be fought, or cheating and bullying seem like the things to do. Hsing Yun has seen enough of life to recognize the finest of causes and effects. He views one's existence as the result of causes and conditions binding one to another. How the affairs of the world are so plagued with pain and sorrow and anxiety stems from the common incapability to treat *them* with kindness and to cultivate *ourselves* with dedication. Indeed the strife between *them* and *us* is rife even between loved ones.

In the *Hundred-parable Sutra*, there is a story about a couple squabbling over a piece of cake.

A man locking horns with his wife over a fried cake thought to himself: "Women just can't hold their tongues. I can beat her in that one!" He proceeded to suggest that the two of them should battle in silence and that the winner would get the treat. His wife acquiesced. So in a mute impasse the pair sat, with the cake placed between them.

Then came a burglar upon the scene. Naturally he had no way of making head nor tail of the two rigid householders. So he stuck around. A few hours passed but nothing happened. This so emboldened the intruder that he, while combing the place for valuables, began edging toward the lady of the house. The next instant, he was laying his hands on her. Somehow, the husband was utterly unmoved by what transpired before his own eyes. Unable to contain herself any longer, the wife rose to her feet, screaming: "Are you blind or something? Can't you see I'm being molested?"

Incredible as it might sound, her man sprang from his seat, snatched the fried cake, and started munching it. "Ha, you've lost," said he, laughing. "The treat is finally all mine!"

To be as coldly calculating as that – bearing a grudge when there is triumph and disdain when there is loss, allowing boundless ignorance and hence triggering ceaseless defilements – is the source of strife and hostility in every form.

To resolve the multitude of issues in relationships, be they marital, friendly, sibling, or collaborative, humanistic Buddhism offers an axiomatic and feasible solution "You be big and I'll be small; you have much and I'll have little; you be good and I'll be bad; you rejoice and I'll suffer." To illustrate this, Hsing Yun has another story.

There were two neighboring families: the Changs, who were incessantly quarrelsome, and the Lis, who appeared to be forever basking in peacefulness. In time, the Changs felt compelled to take counsel from their neighbors.

"Why are we bickering from day to day while you seem so at peace with one another?" queried the Changs.

"You fight because you're all superb folks," replied the Lis. "And we're not even good enough to start a fight."

"Nonsense, but how so?"

"Now, take the breakage of a vase as an example. You each think yourself the last to be blamed and that somebody else has to be held accountable. The finger-pointing becomes perpetually vicious because you all insist you're in the right and everybody else is in the wrong.

"As for us, we would rather concede guilt than have others' feelings hurt. Thus, the apology of the one guilty of the blunder is met with apologies from others, who say: 'Surely it's not your fault, no, not at all. I was careless to have left the vase in that spot.' We always start by thinking we're in the wrong and holding ourselves responsible. No issue do we evade. Harmony, therefore, is a matter of course."

On responding to the times

"An effective writer is one capable of responding wholly to the times," once said humorist Lin Yü-t'ang. Likewise, humanistic Buddhism, not only a concept but a practice, is sociologically consequential. Hsing Yun *is* a religious master "capable of responding wholly to the times." Not only that, he acts in the moment, with incomparable aptitude, and charts his own course.

To assuage the agony Taiwan suffered from the severance of diplomatic ties with the U.S. in 1979, Hsing Yun conducted a grand chanting recital to raise funds for a patriotic foundation. To right wrongs in terms of social values and trends, he organized a series of campaigns in 1992, which were designed to purify minds by means of the seven precepts which, alongside the basic Five Precepts, are the seven means of self-discipline in modern society: no smoking and no drugs, no violence, no stealing, no gambling, no drinking, no indecency, and no quarreling.

And, to respond to the organ donation drive at Longevity Memorial Hospital some years back, the gracious monk led many others to follow suit by pledging to give his own. To play a role in preserving the environment, he rallied much public support by speaking up for the reforesting of Kaohsiung, to save the county's water resources, the recycling of used paper, and the protection of wildlife.

Perfecting a person, becoming a Buddha

Unlike some reclusive, puristic monastics, Hsing Yun adheres to the conviction that "the Dharma is for solving all issues in life," and that a Buddhist should exercise, without fail, every awareness and concern for social changes of all forms. Whatever new phenomenon, tendency, or problem arises, he counters with these questions: "What instructions exist in the principles of the Dharma? How is the contemporary Buddhist to respond?"

Take the controversy over abortion, which the Catholics have persisted in outlawing to this day. Where, then, do the Buddhists stand? Terminating a pregnancy is a violation of the precept against killing, Hsing Yun asserts, and retribution is an inevitability. However, he points to circumstances such as medically confirmed fetal abnormality or pregnancy caused by sexual assault, under which childbirth will in all likelihood encumber the society enormously and sink the mother irredeemably in a life of torment. Then, he maintains, as long as the mother is ready to shoulder the retribution for killing, the ultimate decision to end the pregnancy is hers and hers alone. By the same token, he makes it clear that he believes the crucial decision-making which pertains to euthanasia lies with those closest to the patient and must only be rendered with love.

Neither does he shun such touchy social issues as divorce and family violence, on which he says: "The Dharma has it all. I'm merely applying it to our times." A Buddhism failing to keep abreast of modernity and provide viable solutions to its problems resembles "a grown person stuck in children's wear." He cannot see how that can last.

Hsing Yun braved insufferable misunderstanding and mortification through four decades of his advocacy of humanistic Buddhism. Time has honored his vision. Master T'ai Hsü prepared an outline for humanistic Buddhism at the turn of the century, and Hsing Yun has succeeded in picking up where he left off. For contemporary Buddhism, he has paved the smoothest and broadest way with his lifelong rectitude to the "perfection of Buddhahood via perfecting the human."

Chapter 12

Good affinities around the world

The morning and evening liturgies always open with a passage in praise of incense-offering:

> Incense in the burner is lit just now
> To permeate the dharma realms;
> From afar, the assembly of
> Buddhas have heard.
> Auspicious are clouds forming above
> And intense is the piety about;
> The Buddhas appear wholly
> before all.
> Let us take refuge with the Bodhisattvas,
> [Let us take refuge with the Bodhisattvas,
> Let us take refuge with the Bodhisattvas.]

It tells of how the Buddhas, moved by pervading devotion, are glad to protect and guide the chanting and praying, and to ensure that merits are shared with all living beings in the ten directions.

Surrounded with good affinities

People-oriented, Hsing Yun has acquired countless affinities with friends and devotees. As visible as the auspicious clouds [depicted in the praise for incense-offering], these have come to be significant conditions in the career of both himself and Fo Kuang Shan.

Statistics from the department of civil affairs indicate, on average, the existence of one temple or church per 2.47 sq. km. in Taiwan today, with Buddhist temples totaling 1,560, right behind are Taoism and Christianity. In addition, the department of internal affairs estimates 4.85 million Buddhists, 3.63 million Taoists, 0.91 million devotees of I-kuan Tao, 0.42 million Protestants, 0.29 million Catholics, along with others.

Statistics from Fo Kuang Shan show that over 1 million have formally taken refuge there. This represents that 1 out of 5

Buddhists in Taiwan is a Fo Kuang Buddhist. More specifically, in the first half of 1994 there were more than 10,000 devotees who took refuge at Fo Kuang Shan in Kaohsiung, the temples in Taipei, and Hsi Lai Temple in Los Angeles. Moreover, some 200,000 donors have contributed to the newly erected Chambers of Gold and Jade Buddhas and Triple-gem Shrine; over 200,000 free subscriptions of *Awakening the World* are regularly distributed; and overseas Fo Kuang Buddhists number around 200,000.

Small wonder that, with such grass-roots support and subsequent impact, Hsing Yun and Fo Kuang Shan have become an apple in the eyes of political enthusiasts. Once he was appointed consultant of party affairs by the nationalists, and another time, honored with the title of member of the central committee, on which he remarked: "As committee member, I honestly don't know what I can do for the party and, in that regard, I certainly don't know what the party will want me to do!" The laurels are for the Buddhist circle as a whole, he insisted, not for himself only. In fact, all that the politicians have given him have been gifts of tea for mid-autumn festival or the lunar New Year.

Some seem more pragmatic than others though. Most of the time, they display little affinity with the Buddha. Come election time, they start streaming through the mountain gate. Invariably this is going to be headlined in the media: *Hsing Yun Pledges Support for....* As if it would happen. On occasion, political luminaries are seen at the head tables at Fo Kuang Shan's functions. "No headaches in getting the needed locations for sure," Hsing Yun quips. "Just ask a mayor or county supervisor to come and say something."

Political Monk no more

Being dubbed *Political Monk* was certainly not a pleasure. Hsing Yun probes his soul and still answers in the negative when it comes to officialdom or partisanship. Quite the reverse, the government had no part whatsoever in the growth of Fo Kuang Shan. Not even a single tree or a blade of grass. Except, maybe, for ten years of delay in matters of official registration.

He was a great sport about that, saying: "Mayors serve terms of three or five years; this monk serves for life. The permit will come someday."

Actually, it was the dissidents who opted for name-calling to vent their wrath over his friendliness with the nationalists.

Those who have walked the path of [contemporary Chinese] history with Hsing Yun will never forget how the nationalists fled the mainland, only to exercise another thirty years of despotism in Taiwan. Under those circumstances, no one would dare to befriend the dissidents. Lacking any backing, Buddhist groups were vulnerable back then. Like the rest of the population, the Buddhists, together with other religious bodies, had but the Chiang government to hail and the nationalist party to vote for. That was the political environment and psychological milieu then, and this is now. Why should Hsing Yun be singled out and left with the yoke?

Conditions are new; so are values. When the nationalist-backed Venerable Ming Kuang ran for a seat in the national assembly several years ago, no one ever called him anything.

About the appellation, Hsing Yun only comments about his dilemma with the circumstances. "The media, not I," he says, "especially rave over politics and hot topics like the future of the strait and the dissidents on the mainland. If I don't come up with a response, I'll be deemed unaware, unconcerned; if I do, overly political."

Friends in public office

Political monk or not, the rest of the world has come to know better. Nor does he care any more. "Defamation in itself is incapable of spoiling a character," he says, "unless the character is an unwholesome and hollow one. The way to confront slander is not to outright try clarifying oneself but to quietly reject the conflict." To some political figures, Hsing Yun doesn't try to shun them, but treats them without discrimination. Perhaps, some come to him with certain intentions at first. However, after getting along with them for a period of time, he has made a number of bosom friends.

Vice-chairperson Wang Chin-ping of the legislative council and legislators P'an Wei-kang and Shên Chih-hui are frequent visitors. P'an, the sole Buddhist in a family of Catholics, is so motivated by Fo Kuang Shan's creed of "Joy unto others; faith unto others; convenience unto others; hope unto others," that she has adopted this creed for her place of work.

Also, secretary-general Wu Po-hsiung of the president's office, judge Lin Fu-ts'un of the high court, mayor Lin Shui-mu of Keelung, and chairperson Chung Jung-chi of the provincial committee of the Kuomintang, stay in touch often. To commemorate the passing away of presidential political advisor Ch'iu Ch'uang-huan's parents, Hsing Yun took it upon himself to conduct the services for both. Former mayor of Kaohsiung Yü-Chên Yüeh-ying used to regard him as her personal consultant in municipal affairs.

His friendship with Chen Lian, head of the supervisory council, is next to legendary. Chen did not learn about Buddhism until age 50 but has since become a remarkably diligent and avowed protector of the Dharma. His family now shares the same devotion, and his eldest son Chên Yü-t'ing has entered the monkhood at Ling-ch'üan Temple. Moreover, with the unanimous endorsement of his siblings, Chen moved the remains of his parents, former vice-president Chen Ch'êng and his wife, from T'ai Shan to Fo Kuang Shan three years ago. Hsing Yun gave the occasion the most dignified arrangements. In last year's fundraising for Fo Kuang University, the executive representative of the entire body of Fo Kuang devotees literally packed two trucks of Chen's family antiques, paintings, and calligraphic pieces off to Fo Kuang Shan for auction.

Friends in business

Hsing Yun has more than a few business friends. Wu Hsiu-ch'i of President Corp. has been a great friend for over three decades and a strong supporter of Fo Kuang Shan. Chang-Yao Hung-ying, whose semi-conductor business Hsing Yun named Light of the Sun and Moon, played a key role in the founding of Hsi Lai Temple, Los Angeles. P'an Hsiao-jui, owner of the Grand Formosa Regent, Taipei, was there for the master from the very beginning of Fo Kuang Shan. "Donations are the most delightful of all wealth." Years of charitable endeavors with his wife show in his face a benevolence that resembles that of Maitreya Buddha.

Ts'êng Liang-yüan and Huang Li-ming, a couple in the construction business, fondly address Hsing Yun as "old pa" instead of master. Having striven hard to initiate the fundraising of Taipei's new temple, they gave a hearty gift to the master who is more of a parent to them. They call themselves the gleeful, ultimate beneficiaries.

Friends in cultural circle

Some of Hsing Yun's best friends are from the cultural circle. "Few in the early years had the impetus to lend a hand in Buddhist cultural affairs," he says. "Those who did shall forever be my guests of honor." Academics Chên Ku-ying, Yang Kuo-shu, Wei Chêng-t'ung, Hu Fo, and others share warm memories of the days they used to teach at the Buddhist college and, in particular, the amount of civility lavished upon them – a rarity today.

A driven writer himself, Hsing Yun knows well how to appreciate like minds when he runs into them. Painter Li Ch'i-mao's wedding he conducted. Script-writer Sun Ch'un-hua's daughter, now Venerable Miao Jung, is a disciple. Through various fundraising art auctions for Fo Kuang Shan in these last two years, he has been able to build unprecedented affinities within the cultural circle.

Thriller writer Szu-ma Chung-yüan, a friend of twenty years, describes Hsing Yun as "insightful and visionary; positive and pragmatic; modern and unconventional; historically innovative in the spread of the Dharma and the expansion of Buddhism; classically gallant in spirit and demeanor, like the legendary monk Lu Chih-shên who is said to have pulled out a weeping willow in one somersault. Other literary figures include Chao Ning, who took refuge under him and was given the Dharma name P'u Kuang, and veteran author Liu Fang who, though Hsing Yun's senior in age, calls him master with unquestionable readiness.

Essayist Ying Wei-ch'ih once dined with Hsing Yun at P'u-mên Temple. "Monastics receive their sustenance from all ten directions, as the saying goes," joked an apparently most satiated Ying afterwards, "this pen-wagging bunch received ours from eleven today!" Members of the media, Li Yü-hsi of *Min Sheng Daily*, Lu Chên-t'ing of *Central Daily News*, and Su Chêng-kuo of *China Times* came thinking they were just poking their noses around but could not leave without bowing their heads in awe.

The entertainment industry has certainly not been short of Hsing Yun's followers, like Kuo Hsiao-chuang, Chên Li-li, Chêng P'ei-p'ei, T'ien Wên-chung, Wang Hai-po, Kou Fêng who produced *National Master Yü Lin* for television, Yang Ch'ing-huang and K'uang Ming-chieh who played the leading roles, and many, many more.

Friends needing a friend

Those around him marvel at what a good

friend he is. Li Zijian, a painter from the mainland who found himself in a tight corner in the United States, was given his own residence. Li was assured that his creative endeavors must not be interrupted and that his wife and child would be with him. A year later, Li reciprocated his patron's kindness with close to a hundred works collectively titled *This World Needs Love*. Further aided by Hsing Yun, Li went on to exhibit at Hsi Lai Temple, Fo Kuang Shan, and Taipei's city art gallery, and is currently taking his works across Europe, North America, and Japan.

Hsing Yun came to the rescue of Gao Ertai and Pu Xiaoyu, both on the faculty of Nanjing University at the time of the June 4 massacre in Tiananmen Square, [1989], who were forced into exile in the United States. The couple's apropos encounter with him led to the finding of solace both physical and spiritual for themselves. Like another starting point to which the master had directed them, it was to them "the sighting of an image of light, by which images from ten thousand *li* would come to light."

Qian Jiaju, an economist of international renown from the mainland who had expended a lifetime delving into materialism and Marxism, left for the same reason as Gao and Pu, and was also Hsing Yun's guest in the United States. After attending the master's lectures three times on the sutra according to the sixth patriarch of the Ch'an school, he became a Buddhist at the ripe old age of 80. As much mentor and pupil as good friends, the two are often heard addressing each other as "Elder Qian" and "Great Master".

Friends are forever

Wealth is not forever; friends are. All along, he has been surrounded by undemanding friends. Chên Chien-ch'êng, a civil servant from Kaohsiung's department of financial affairs, was in the audience on every occasion when the master spoke, nodding in agreement as he listened. From the days of Shou-shan Temple to those of P'u-hsien Temple, he must have done that for twenty odd years now. The second- and third-generation followers, too, are catching up fast. Not a few of them the master has actually named. Lin Ch'i-sung, a devotee from an opulent background, is often spotted with an apron and a broad grin, working in Hsi Lai Temple's kitchen and serving in the dining hall during Dharma functions. Back in Fo Kuang Shan, wherever there is a singular painting job, it is under the auspices of a couple running a paint business, Chang T'ien-yung and Chang-Yün Wang-ch'üeh. The pair hardly ever get to greet the master in person, but year after year, they have made their offerings, never faltering, never saying much. One of the most unresolved identities was that of an elderly devotee who, at the close of offerings made to the sangha, shoved a red packet into Hsing Yun's hand. Inside were bundles of jewelry. It all happened so fast that Hsing Yun could not even get a good look at her face.

Just what transpired to make the lone monk from those lean years into the magnetic personage commanding so much amicable affinity? To put it plainly, devotees feel close to Fo Kuang Shan. They get help in weddings and funerals if only they ask; they get filled in monthly by an ample supply of journals and newsletters; they get to be reassured, both physically and spiritually, attending lectures, Dharma functions, chanting sessions, and workshops; they even get visits from the monastics, sometimes when they are sick and more often when they are not; they get to pray for added fortune and to be rid of misfortune. Some of the older devotees get birthday cards promptly a week prior to the day. What better binds people together than such a display of affection and drive toward harmony?

Lin Ch'ing-chih, a follower of four decades, recalls how caring the master was to him: "I was in the army back in 1962 when the master visited the Chinmen front. He brought along a pack of Buddhist texts which were intended for me. But his schedule was far too tight and I was stationed out in the islands. We didn't even get to see each other. So he had to take the books all the way home and mail them back to me again. I honestly had no words for how I felt when at long last the package reached me.

"After the draft, I was readying myself

for further schooling. The master was all for it. I used to take advantage of the lecture hall when it was free from chanting sessions and work into the wee hours. And he would keep me company either doing his own reading or writing something or other. At times he would pass onto me snacks given him by devotees. 'I don't snack at night,' he would say, trying to ease my mind. I didn't fare that well but got accepted eventually. The master was thrilled just the same and gave me a copy of the *Far East English-Chinese Dictionary*."

On graduating from National Taiwan Normal University, Lin returned to Hsing Yun's side and spent the next decade helping him found Chih-kuang, a school of commerce. Even the shade trees on campus he had helped transplant. For a while he had a horrendous stomach ulcer but never was he out. "I didn't bring shame on the master," Lin voices his gratitude from deep down. He and his wife, both teachers, have been faithfully sending in their monthly support for the last ten years – a commitment no longer upheld even between children and their own parents today.

Receiving with wisdom

Director Kou Fêng remembers how the master once received him with the most profound wisdom which, alongside a vast compassion, would be instrumental in drawing countless followers. "There seems to be this fully packed bookcase inside me," he told the master about his vexation. "In trying to reclassify my books, I knocked the bookcase over!"

"I'm vexed, too!" the master replied with a dash of humor. "Except that you're vexed a lot and I'm vexed somewhat; you can't let go but I can!"

And he added: "I've a bookcase inside, too. Neither is it in good order. If it were, I would be sitting there instead of here!" In so saying, Hsing Yun gestured in the direction of the shrine where the Bodhisattva was seated. What he meant to tell Kou was that one who is free from worldly cares is no longer human but a Bodhisattva.

Such is the way of Hsing Yun:

Awaken in the instant or
cultivate at length;

Never depart from the
worldly ways.
Flow with the masses or
go with all living beings;
Always help them bond
with the Buddha.

"I won't desert anyone," he pledges. To him, nobility and commonalty are the same; everyone is one of many. Bestselling author Lin Ch'ing-hsüan still relates in detail the hospitality which Hsing Yun extended him long before his success. The master literally went out of his way to greet Lin on the latter's first visit to Fo Kuang Shan. Last year, Lin went on a lecture tour in the United States on behalf of Buddha's Light International Association. The master, who had just returned to Los Angeles from Russia, made it a point to thank him in person. Lin ended up a quarter of an hour late for the appointment due to traffic congestion. But the moment his car drove through Hsi Lai Temple's main gate, he could see up the road a tall figure, cane in hand, and waiting in the hot sun of July. The sight was quite unforgetable.

The delicacy of his considerateness

makes working for him sheer pleasure. In fact, he always takes the initiative to have people comfortably settled before all else. "To direct volunteers," he says, "one must, first and foremost, be the volunteer to the volunteers. Have stationary and seats in place before asking volunteers to write; have buckets and hoses at hand before asking volunteers to water the plants. ... Tell them where the tap is, too."

Those gifted in the arts were exceptionally hard to come by during the early years in Ilan. When Yang Hsi-ming resolved to do the murals for the kindergarten, Hsing Yun was so thankful that he simply waited around day in and day out, preparing brushes, paint, easels, rulers, tea, and snacks like an apprentice. When Chu Ch'iao took up the editing of *Buddhism Today*, he often had to work into the night. Hsing Yun, too, would be there for him, cooking noodles or bringing him a glass of milk to keep him going.

To this day, during those tedious drives on the freeway, he is the one to keep the driver entertained – and awake – while the others nap.

All affinities are attributed to Buddhism

Though many have become devotees and supporters of Fo Kuang Shan out of admiration and respect for Hsing Yun, all affinities he attributes to the institution. "These are Buddhist devotees," the master expounds on the principle of selflessness, "not personal. Don't ask them for favors or donations unless absolutely necessary. Don't ever conduct monetary dealings with them. Don't lose your temper with them so that they lose their faith in you."

He keeps reiterating to disciples and staff what good affinities mean to him: "Coldness toward devotees is coldness toward me; leaving guests unattended is leaving me hurt."

On one occasion, the moaning of a young monastic in charge of a branch temple that devotees were becoming less compliant and that many were unwilling to do manual chores angered him visibly. "If my disciples should think such absurd thoughts," he said in shame, "I would have them mop the floor and scrub windows for ten years! Sure it's wonderful for devotees to resolve to serve, but it's just as well that they don't help at all. For they've come to pay homage to the Buddha, not to work!"

Preaching amidst the red dust[1]

Many a time the master teaches his disciples that, according to the Ch'an school, the gate of the Buddha is compared to the plants in a grove. A single plant cannot make a grove; nothing works unless in unanimity. Practice cannot be isolated; it has to be carried out such that "the blood flows with that of the masses and the pulse throbs with that of the masses." Hsing Yun's recognition of the potency of the people is really the backbone of his acute sense of popularization, contingency, and public relations in the spread of Buddhism in modern society.

The traditional Buddhist temple was either deep in the forested mountains or at the end of a blind alley and always a picture of somberness. Devotees either could not find it or would not dare get near. The

[1] The secular world.

monastics hardly ever stepped outside and were stern and uncaring. Fo Kuang Shan and its branch temples have reset standards and created a distinctive, pleasant, and upbeat image. As well as being places of worship, they function fully as premises for socializing and study. Some visitors even come away with a sense that everywhere can be a ground for preaching. A few of the lecture halls are even upstairs from so-called beauty parlors and the like. About those, Hsing Yun says with a laugh: "It's hell below and heaven above. Let's hope people will in time get promoted."

The newly opened branch temple in Taipei is right by Sungshan train station. Parking space is plentiful. The five stories from the 14th floor down house the shrine, conference room, meditation hall, dining hall, reception room, audio-visual room, gift shop, and art gallery. Directions outside the elevators are precise and clear, and the volunteer guides are very helpful. Plenty is always going on, and visitors are more than welcome to participate. In just about a year, this has gained the notable favor of devotees in northern Taiwan.

Wherever red dusts roll,
  the Bodhi is taught.
Wherever the heart is pure,
  meditation is complete.

Hsing Yun looks to the day when every city shall no longer be short of temples to visit so that Buddhism shall truly take root in the lives and minds of all.

Affinity before Buddhahood

Hsing Yun's affinity with millions of devotees and friends from all walks of life was not cultivated in a day. In the minds of these people, the master's deep yellow robe and towering figure are "awe-inspiring to view and heart-warming to be near." And, every move he makes, to them, reflects a childlike purity.

"Affinity with fellow humans comes before the attainment of Buddhahood." Fo Kuang Shan today is best summed up in the couplets which Hsing Yun composed for its main shrine:

Coming from ten directions,
Going in ten directions,
For all ten directions,
    undertakings shall complete.
Thousands of practicing,
Thousands of letting go,
For all thousands,
    affinities shall complete.

Part IV

Spreading the Dharma to deliver all beings

Handing down the abbotship to
Venerable Hsin Ping (right), 1985

Dharma propagation in Egypt

A visit to Dhammakaya Temple, Thailand.

St. Petersburg, Russia

Ensuring that all living beings are content

Reaching out to refugees in northern Thailand, 1988

Meeting Zhao Puchu (second from left) on his homecoming, 1989

Stating the case for Xu Jiatun with journalist Lu K'êng (second from right), 1990

Chapter 13

The baton, its passing and receiving

As the months and years have passed from the pioneering through the cultivation period, Fo Kuang Shan has grown from infancy to assume the vigor of young adulthood. Hsing Yun, parent-like, thought the time was ripe for it to move forward on its own. He was determined to pass the abbotship onto Venerable Hsin Ping, his first disciple among the bhiksus, on the 18th year of Fo Kuang Shan's founding.

A historical moment

September 22, 1985 was to be a moment of historical succession at Fo Kuang Shan.

As day was breaking in southern Taiwan, in front of the main shrine there were already a sea of devotees. Plainly clothed seniors, casually dressed youths, primely attired men and women waited quietly – all kneeling with palms joined. In reverence they heeded the sounding of the bell and drum and the chanting of a dozen young monastics before the Buddha. They eagerly awaited what would be the grandest succession ceremony in the history of Buddhism in Taiwan.

At ten o'clock sharp, with the August sun shining brightly, accompanied by senior Venerables Yüeh Chi and Wu I as witnesses, and with thousands of devotees watching, Hsing Yun unrolled the Dharma scroll and started to read aloud the names of all the ancestral patriarchs of the Lin-Chi school. Then, he handed down the abbot's cassock and alms-bowl, the constitution and rules, the jade scepter, the Dharma pole and the duster – all emblems of the abbotship. On receiving these, Venerable Hsin Ping pledged before the masses thus:

> The master's heart shall be my heart;
> the master's resolve shall be

my resolve.
[I shall] abide by the monasterial rules
and ancestral directions; spread the
Dharma to benefit all sentient beings,
Receive the masses from all
ten directions; preach the Fo Kuang
way to the ends of the world.

At that, music rose and thousands of doves flew skyward. Those on the ground felt both an enthusiastic welcome for the replacement and an unwillingness to part with the master.

Hsing Yun, accompanied by the new abbot, executive director Venerable Tzu Hui, and over a hundred abbots and abbesses of the branch temples, first bade farewell to the Buddha in the main shrine and then took the path down the hill. As he walked on, he looked at the familiar objects and scenes one more time.

Meanwhile, along the one kilometer path between the main shrine and the gate of non-duality emotional devotees lined up, many quite affected and pleading:

"Master, please take care!"

"Master, come back soon!"

"Master, remember us!"

Waving good-by, Hsing Yun kept his smile on to the end. Hard as it was to let go, one must let go; hard as it was to walk on, one must walk on. Thus he vanished beyond the mountain gate.

Handing over

Hsing Yun only gave the public a month's notice prior to the actual succession. But for those at Fo Kuang Shan, it was an expected move, not a surprise. The new abbotship meant a transfer of duties, not a change of an established system.

Hsing Yun has not only been the dreamer of such a system but also its doer.

Clause 22 in chapter 4 of Fo Kuang Shan's constitution states it clearly: "The abbot of Fo Kuang Shan is the director-in-chief, serving a term of six years, with one reappointment by popular vote and, under exceptional circumstances, a second reappointment by two thirds of the popular vote." Hence, toward the end of his second term, Hsing Yun was already searching for a successor both from within and from outside the community. By the time he completed his third term, his resolve to step down was unmovable. Venerable Hsin Ping was the unanimous choice to be the next abbot. Further, monasterial supervisory laws require the presence of an executive director, a position which Hsing Yun had also assumed while holding the abbotship. Venerable Tzu Hui was appointed in his place.

Venerable Hsin Ping, 58, had been a follower of the master through three decades since the master's time in Ilan. He was tonsured in 1961, received the precepts under Master Tao Yüan of Hai-hui (Assembly of Buddhas) Temple, Keelung, in 1963, and went on to attend Shou-shan Buddhist College and the Chinese Buddhist Research Institute. For lengths of time during the earliest days of Fo Kuang Shan, Hsin Ping was stationed in the construction quarters. In 1973, he was named the head of the bhiksus. Admired for his melodious voice in chanting and his kind and easy-going character, Hsin Ping was the best-loved of the leading monastics.

Venerable Tzu Hui, 60, also from Ilan,

hails from a prominent family. Acclaimed in the Buddhist circle for the excellence of her abilities, she would play her role as executive director like no other could. She began following Hsing Yun when he first set foot in Ilan forty years ago and has since been his personal interpreter in the Taiwanese dialect. She has indeed bridged the gap between Buddhism and the people of Taiwan. Venerable Tzu Hui graduated from Ilan's Lan-yang Secondary School for girls with high grades and from Japan's Ohtani University with a Master of Arts degree in Buddhist Studies, and has also studied at Kyoto University in Japan. For many years she has been on the faculty of the Chinese Culture University.

Rule of law, not of people

To clarify his intentions, Hsing Yun wrote this verse just before he, at age 58, handed over Fo Kuang Shan:

> Those of Fo Kuang Shan are
> heading west
> While Mahakasyapa[1] heads east;

[1] Referring to Hsing Yun himself.

Coming and going in like manner,
[I,] in this world, [shall] always
be the restful, busy yet free one.

The attachment of his disciples and devotees Hsing Yun takes lightly. He firmly believes that only a well developed system can ensure the continuous existence of a religious organization. At the succession ceremony, he stated unreservedly the four reasons for his stepping down:

· Rule should be of law, not of people
· No one is deemed indispensable
· Stepping down is not to be considered as retiring
· It is all a matter of quickening the pace to further the renewal of Buddhism

"I'm merely shedding the load of official commitments," he added. "A monk will always be a monk. I've no way of resigning as the master!"

Probably the only thing that troubled him was, along with the passing on of the baton and renewal of the system, the astronomical debts were now laid upon his disciple's shoulders. Hsin Ping, though, never spoke of these to others. Nor did he say much about the burden. If many mouths had to be fed, he would do whatever he could to ensure that each was sated. That was the stoicism for which he was most celebrated.

For Fo Kuang Shan, the succession enhanced its metabolism from within and helped make a modern Buddhist institution. For the rest of the Buddhist circle in Taiwan, however, it was like a gigantic rock hurled into an otherwise calm lake. The rippling effect left a long lasting impact.

First-ever term set for abbotship

Transference of the abbotship is a matter of course in the Chinese Buddhist tradition. The succession can go by lineage; it is deemed the handing down of the law. When succession is done by inviting an eminent master from outside to take over the abbotship, it is called monastery of the ten directions or passing onto the sages. For the time being, Fo Kuang Shan has followed the lineage tradition. But then, who can tell what may occur in the future? Still, why did its first succession cause such a stir?

In a rhetorical article published in *United Monthly*, Buddhist scholar Yang Huinan lauds the master's decision and hints that others should follow suit. He further points out that the term system might not exist in the traditional Chinese Buddhist monastery, but the abdication of the abbot was not unusual, especially in an established monastery where succession was an integral part of the operation.

Buddhist monasteries during the prenationalist era were at best dubious in identity. Properties were never defined; the rich and powerful would take over the place and run the sangha; or the abbot would simply refuse to let go. As philosopher Li Ao once put it, the elders in China would not only refuse to hand over the baton but also have the younger generation batoned. And, the current monasterial supervisory laws, though tough, have ironically been the factor behind many a conflict between the laity and sangha. More often than not, an old abbot's death within his term sparks triple-party contention over monasterial properties among his disciples, secular family, and the director of the temple. Litigation, fist fights, and other less honorable incidents, make glaring headlines. In the end, monasterial serenity is no more.

Yang believes that Hsing Yun's abdication set the first-ever term for monasterial abbotship and pointed to a brand-new direction in monasterial management. "Those abbots who harbor the intent of being there for thousands of years," Yang writes, "will have a lot to fidget about from now on. Should they follow what is right willingly? Or should they hold on to their titles until they die? Hsing Yun! O Hsing Yun, what an awful example you have set!"

As it turned out, Hsing Yun succeeded in setting the tone for the ensuing abdication of a number of elderly monastics, like Sung-shan (Pine Mountain) Temple's Master Ling Kên, Hua-yen Lien-shê's (Avatamsaka Lotus Society) Master Nan T'ing, and Hui-jih Chiang-t'ang's (Wisdom Sun Lecture Hall) Master Yin Shun.

Living the spirit of baton-passing

As Fo Kuang Shan continues to flourish, his

disciples – like him – uphold the conviction of "success not having to be of the individual" and take pleasure in their supporting roles. The senior monastics, in particular, are seen to manifest their master's baton-passing spirit and to be more than willing to take a back-seat to their up and coming juniors.

Venerable Tzu Chuang, known for her industriousness in the founding of branch temples, turned P'u-mên Temple over to the younger generation of monastics ten days after its opening and proceeded to another construction project. Venerable Yi Kung's study at Tokyo University was arranged by Venerable Tzu Chuang, who also accompanied her there. When asked why Yi Kung was sent to such a prestigious institution while she herself had attended the lesser Bukkyo (Buddhist) University, Venerable Tzu Chuang simply replied: "That's the spirit of Fo Kuang Shan."

One year by coincidence, to join Hsing Yun on a lecture tour in Hong Kong, all the abbots and abbesses left their posts at the branch temples in Southeast Asia and Japan.

"Wouldn't the notion of your abbotship being overthrown on your return faze you?" Hsing Yun asked Hsin Ping, smiling. "It's one of the worst military maneuvers, you know, for the entire leadership to be away like that."

"In that case," Hsin Ping replied, also smiling, "let's build a second Fo Kuang Shan!"

Everyone who heard the exchange smiled. It evidenced the absolute desire of the master to let go and the readiness of his successor to delegate. No matter who is at the helm, everything shall proceed according to the system.

Truly letting go

The first half-year after stepping down he spent in isolation in the United States to enable a smooth transition in his absence. These past ten years, Hsing Yun has really and truly *let go*. Now he leaves the entertaining of guests at Fo Kuang Shan to the abbot and all the construction and functions at the branch temples to their respective abbots or abbesses. Whenever he is asked for his opinion, he always asks:

"Have you consulted the abbot first? What does he think?" Neither is he prepared to intervene nor is he keen on giving advice any more – a definite show of confidence in the system and its operation and the support for the new leadership. "I can't stand people putting down the bowl but not the chopsticks," he notes. "Stepping down, one must absolutely let go."

He recently read about president Li Teng-hui's dream of peaceful transition of power within his own lifetime. "Mine has come true!" he says in earnest.

Titles mean little to Hsing Yun. Now cleared of all of them, he works just as hard. "Editing journals, helping in the kitchen, and everything in-between," he says, "I promise to give all my efforts." One lunar New Year, devotees were again expected to swarm the place. A plot at the foot of the hill was allocated for parking so that devotees would no longer have to pay for parking nearby. It was New Year's Eve, and everybody's plate was full. He got a job from the abbot – painting the lines in the parking lot. By six in the evening, dinner was ready but not he. He hastened to lay down his work and went over to greet everyone. Afterwards, he sneaked back to the parking lot and picked up where he had left off. Not until four o'clock the next morning did he, together with a couple by the name of Tsai, finish 80 new spots for trucks and 800 for cars. As devotees started to take up those spots one by one, it was time for Hsing Yun to go to sleep.

Another time, the exhibition hall was vacated following the first auction of pieces of calligraphy and paintings to raise funds for Fo Kuang University. In the middle of the night, he and a handful of disciples rushed to the scene and set up another display so that visitors would have something fresh the next day.

"Give a small chore to the competent," he explains, "and it will be maximized; give a big task to the incompetent, and it will be diminished." Undeniably, he is one of the competent.

Retreating as a form of advancing

Freeing himself of duties, he had plans to

meditate and teach, to read and write. But the discerning had no problem in predicting that, barely 60 and with his stamina, he could not possibly retire like that. Chang P'ei-kêng, secretary-general of the Chinese-Tibetan Cultural Association of the Republic of China and a follower who is two years his senior, is of that opinion. "He knew too well," Chang observes, "that no matter what he did at Fo Kuang Shan he would still be an abbot. He needed urgently to peck through the shell. Leaving the abbotship was in fact leaving on a new journey in his life."

Hsing Yun's performance during the past decade has confirmed that view. He has emerged from his cocoon to create an all-round, global career in Buddhism as well as a radiant second spring in his own life. When asked to whom Fo Kuang Shan now belongs, his answer is: "Fo Kuang Shan is not owned by any one person. But it is yours to keep if you have it in your heart. ... I don't honestly feel as though Fo Kuang Shan is mine. Rather, I feel the world, the universe are mine to keep."

"For I can lay it all down," Hsing Yun

says."In so doing, I can pick it up again."

This Buddhist verse contains the gist of Hsing Yun's sentiments ten years after his abdication:

Transplanting green rice seedlings
all over the paddies with
[my] hands,
[I] lower [my] head to see the sky
in the water;
Purification of body and mind
being what the way should be,
Retreating turns out to be
a form of advancing.

Chapter 14
Like clouds and water[1]

The most well-known masters in *Biographies of Eminent Monks* are categorized in accordance with their cultivation, learning, preaching, asceticism, and so on. Hsing Yun will have to be ranked among the preaching masters.[2]

Buddha in his heart, the Way beneath his feet

With the Buddha in his heart and the Way

[1] In the original text, a bustling but not suffering *yün-shui sêng*. *Yün-shui,* clouds and waters, qualifying the homelessness of the monastics; *sêng*, a monastic.

[2] In the original text, *tu-hua sêng*, a monastic who preaches to deliver all sentient beings.

beneath his feet, he has endured the unendurable in spreading the Dharma for the deliverance of all sentient beings. Taking over the editing of Venerable Master Tung Ch'u's *Life* magazine in the early years, he often traveled on foot to Sanchung rather than spent one dollar for public transportation. Sometimes he would sit and watch the formatter and printer at work for hours on end without eating anything the whole day. The unthinkable happened when he, then 28, hit the road with followers to lecture on the Tripitaka across Taiwan. To preserve the tape recorder, a valuable item in those days, he set it on his own lap all the way eastward. Consequently, he suffered a case of arthritis that almost cost him his legs. Another time, on the train to Kaohsiung to spread the Dharma, he found himself penniless and without a ticket and had to hand over his fountain-pen in lieu of the fare.

Material wants, a norm then, were grueling enough, but more so was the insulation and inflexibility that shrouded society. Hsing Yun's resolve to spread the Dharma and deliver all sentient beings was to be tried again and again.

Public gatherings under martial law were always mistrusted. In the shade or in front of the stage, men from the national intelligence bureau would lurk, chewing over each word for suspected treason or breaking up the session on the pretext of a failure to preregister. The speaker, though, soon learned that opening with praise about the leader of the people and his government would ensure the absence of prospective disruptions.

Officials were equally suspicious of all campus activities, possibly an after-shock from the student movement that preceded the communist era on the mainland. Needless to say, Hsing Yun's Buddhist summer camps for postsecondary students in the 1950s were hounded, and attempts to speak on campus often barred. An already publicized engagement at National Taiwan Normal University was rescinded at the last minute without any explanation whatsoever. Many times he demanded to know why Catholics and Protestant preachers were admitted on school grounds but not the Buddhists. This demand was given nothing more than the cold shoulder.

Prisons, too, were out of bounds. As much as the Buddhists longed to reach out and bring peace to those within, political dissidents included, the conditions were not right. Similarly, the hope to preach to the armed forces and the police remained a dream.

The government largely held the button of the media, who did not appear any more accommodating. A day before *Gate of Faith*, the first national Buddhist telecast was set to go on the air in 1980, Hsing Yun learned that the visual of his five-minute prologue would be slashed, leaving just the audio – the reason being that monks were not allowed on screen. Trying to appeal his case with a cross-reference to monks portrayed in the popular soap operas, he was told to back off on the grounds that he was not an actor playing the role of a monk.

Political, economic, and social progress have increased with time and the master preacher has irrigated with his perseverance and patience the blossoms of Buddhism.

Today, Fo Kuang Shan and its branch temples are landmarks of Buddhist worship. Hsing Yun now takes the podium in the halls of government and other equally majestic venues. Twenty odd years since its inception, the Buddhist summer camps for postsecondary students have received into the arms of the Buddha tens of thousands of youthful intellectuals and, in the process, produced the most promising talent for Buddhism. Invitations and pleas from academia are endless. He has also taught a course on religion and life at Tung Hai University, established and chaired a research center in Indian culture at the Chinese Culture University, and is responsible for the popularization of Buddhist studies among the new generation of intellectuals in Taiwan.

Popularizing Buddhism in prisons and among the armed forces

Speaking on the Dharma behind prison walls is now routine for the monastics of Fo Kuang Shan. The department of legal affairs has conferred on Hsing Yun the official title of "educator of morality." He has spoken in almost every prison in Taiwan. "Prison is really the best place for practice," he often tells those serving sentences. "Take advantage of your time here to repent with the deepest sincerity. What freedom of mind it is to be able to regard your sentence as practice in solitude!" Once a timid young man came to see Hsing Yun. "Master, do you remember me?" he asked stuttering somewhat. "I was serving time five years ago when you came to speak. What you said turned my life around." Another time, he received a red packet on which was written: "An offering for the Master. In prostration, your disciple who has relinquished the wrong way for the right."

Spreading the Dharma among the armed forces, though relatively late in blooming, has been just as fruitful. The green light was not on until Hao Po-ts'un took office as chief of the general staff. Hsing Yun took the forces by storm when he toured the frontlines of Chinmen and Matsu in 1989 and was thereafter asked to speak by the ministry of national defense as well as the diehard department of central intelligence at a range of events.

With much growth in social diversification, freedom of expression, and the Buddhist populace, the media, too, have rushed to amend their policy in favor of Buddhist content and the appearance of monastics. All three television stations in Taiwan are more than glad to include Buddhist programs. Contrary to old times, when this monk literally bought air time for huge sums and the stations were thankless, they are hot in pursuit of him these days and more than willing to reimburse him handsomely for every three-minute appearance.

Never leaving for the day

Actually his preaching has attained new heights during the ten years since he left the abbotship.

"The freeway is my bed and the car, my cafeteria," as he likes to describe his travel style. He used to set off from Kaohsiung just before dawn and return from wherever when the stars dotted the sky. In the sweltering heat of July last year, he decided to go around Taiwan in three days. From Ilan, Hualien, Taitung,

Pingtung, Kaohsiung, Tainan, Changhua, Miaoli, Hsinchu, Taoyuan, to Taipei. He gave a total of 18 lectures and greeted 20,000 devotees. While the much younger members of the media touring with him were about to call it quits, the master was apologetic to the end. "I'm so sorry to have caused you much stress," he said to them. "I've been long accustomed to this. The body is busy but not the mind!"

Another time, he returned to Fo Kuang Shan from Taipei at one o'clock in the morning. He was there to conduct a memorial service commemorating the 29th anniversary of the passing of the late vice-president Chên Ch'êng at six a.m.. He returned to Taipei at noon, and then presided over a committee meeting for a fundraising concert and a discussion on vegetarianism and Ch'an. At midnight, he was at long last able to leave for the day. "It feels good to be off!" the master said, heaving a deep sigh. "Without any overtime compensation," his disciples chorused.

Never leaving for the day – that practically summarizes his daily life. Almost under no circumstances will he take time off for fear others would be let down. His right thigh bone was fractured from a fall in the bathroom in 1991. He was hospitalized and underwent surgery in which the bone was mounted with four steel pins. A lecture scheduled a week later for a literary society was canceled – only to be reconfirmed in three days. Newly discharged from the hospital, he took the podium in a wheelchair on that day and spoke for a full hour. Many were moved to tears at the sight of his paleness and frail health. "Even if he hadn't uttered a word," one was heard saying, "this is the very best lecture ever. What cultivation!"

Around the globe two and a half times yearly

Chasing the wind; racing the sun – that metaphorically describes his life as a roving monk who takes the Dharma to the ends of the world. Jetting around is only romantic and pleasurable to those who imagine it.

According to his diary, Hsing Yun is estimated to have traveled 160 kilometers each day and around the world two and a half times each year. In the summer of 1993 alone, he went to Russia, New Zealand, Australia, Hong Kong, England, Germany, Brazil, France, the United States, and Canada, across four continents in a single month. He is probably the most frequent flyer among Buddhist monastics. President Shih Yung-kuei of China Television, a long-time friend, once joked: "Looks like you don't need a passport any more!" And a couple of devotees gave the master two dozen pairs of reading glasses at one time, pledging that each would be kept at a different place for his convenience.

Although the sun has its daily recess, this wandering monk has not even the right to time differences. Adaptability must be instantaneous wherever he goes. Each year he averages 1,000 lectures; he conducts refuge ceremonies for some 80,000; he receives about 120 visiting groups and 1,000 guests; he writes about a million words and records 300 telecasts. "I seem to have some kind of microadjuster inside," he says of his own flexibility. "My mood and attention are automatically capable of tuning to changing time and space."

Let us tag along on one of his trips! The instant he sets foot in the airport, he is swamped by requests to say something or to have a photograph taken. Should a group show up for the latter, he holds his pose until everyone, especially the occasional over-zealous young female devotee, comes away with a satisfactory personal shot with the master. On board the aircraft, the crew as well as fellow passengers take turns sending hearty regards. Once on the ground, he is swamped again – virtually buried alive in leis and bouquets, blinded by the flashing of the cameras, and deafened by greetings. Security is understandably tight throughout. Then he is sped onto the next public speech, the next reception of guests, the next lecture, the next conference. Every moment is occupied, he does not seem to have a second in which to catch his breath. Finally when all is finished, he takes leave of each place – only to have the crowds of devotees swarm him again, though this time in the form of farewell.

Keeping busy is cultivation

Venerable Tzu Chuang remembers the record Hsing Yun set of stopping by 13 temples in Malaysia in one day. Guests were at the door first thing in the morning. Lectures went nonstop. And, devotees would not let the master return to his hotel alone. The venerable herself did not get to speak with him until two or three in the morning. There were crowds to welcome him, to see him off, to dine with him. He could barely find time to excuse himself to go to restroom. To ensure that joy be unto others, he ate one generous meal after another. Later he confessed that he deplores having to socialize, to waste time in that manner, and to show up in public eateries.

"Too often I just sleep with my robe on," he says. "And, waking up, I am lost as to where I am." Some blame it on what they perceive to be an oversized ambition. Those who know him better know that it is resolve:

> Let me borrow the past month,
> the past day

To pay back this month, this day;
Let me borrow the next month,
the next day
To make up for this month, this day.

No matter how eloquent he is, Hsing Yun is nearing 70 and weakening physically. More frequently he gets tired and needs a break. But there is so much to do and so little time. "It's easy for me to go away and practice in solitude," he says. "But so much preaching is waiting to be done. How can I take a recess? Disciples look up to me as their role model. Should I recede, they would all follow suit!"

Let us look at a breakdown of his daily schedule: speaking (lectures, classes, preaching, entertaining), 8 hours; writing, 4 hours; traveling, 4 hours; sleeping, 6 hours; eating, washing, and miscellaneous, 2 hours. Driven as he is, some might ask, how does he find time to practice? "Serving all sentient beings," he says, "satisfying the needs of all sentient beings, solving the problems of all sentient beings – keeping busy is cultivation. Anyone looking for leisure may find it in the grave."

On time management

Keeping busy as the norm, time management is of the essence. In fact, Hsing Yun is proud of his punctuality, which was inspired by a passage learned from a textbook at a nearby English school as a child: "Off to school in shirt-sleeves and shorts, [let us] always [be] on the dot." He always wakes up on time for the earliest morning engagement; he always leaves ample time for any engagement. Most inscrutable of all is the recording sessions for telecast, during which he keeps perfect timing of the 4-minute shooting, has never had a retake, and never needs to be edited. To the crew, it is like "he carries a timer in his sleeve."

He is especially clever with planning and takes great advantage of intervals. The exceedingly harsh training in the monasteries – in which he would figure out how to ready his clothes, belongings, and even bed each night to enable himself to complete his toilet in three minutes the next morning and to always be among the first three in line for the shrine – is the reason why, quite unruffled, he writes on planes, replies to faxed documents in vehicles, and chants the name of Amitabha Buddha as he drives by each power pole. With disciples rallying around, he is able to read documents, listen to reports, and give verbal instructions at the same time so as to make everyone happy.

The innumerable methods of practice always lead back to the path of the Bodhisattva. A decade of traveling has scattered lotus seeds far and wide and sown vast good causes and conditions.

In 1988 Hsing Yun, together with a volunteer medical group, traveled into the remote mountains and barren regions of northern Thailand in order to reach out to the illiterate and neglected. He went from traveling in a large vehicle to a small one, and then to a donkey, even a borrowed military helicopter at times. To those displaced descendants of the Dragon,[3] he gave sustenance and medical care to their bodies; and the Dharma to their anguished souls, so as to eliminate suffering and cultivate joy. Li Chien-yüan, daughter of general Li Wên-huan of northern Thailand's

[3] A general reference to people of Chinese descent.

third army, was in the audience. She later visited Fo Kuang Shan for three days and, on departing, became tearful. "Master," she said to Hsing Yun, "what you did for us in northern Thailand was like giving us another chance at life!"

Pearl of the Orient awash in Buddha's favor

The fruit of Hsing Yun's efforts is by far more visible in Hong Kong. The last British colony is understandably peppered with Christian churches, missionary schools, and hospitals. Indigenous faiths were once piteously undefined and best manifested in the immense following commanded by temples attributed to Huang Ta-hsien[4] and the like. The spread of Buddhism has been shouldered by a number of eminent masters. The endeavors of Masters Chüeh Kuang, Yung Hsing, Ch'ang Huai, and others, in hospitals, schools, and seniors' homes are exemplary. But somehow, the average person remains woefully alienated from

[4] A sage by the name of Huang.

Buddhism.

Hsing Yun first preached Buddhism in Hong Kong seven years ago. Things have improved year by year ever since. These days auditoriums are bursting at the seams. Officials at Hunghom Coliseum reserve three days annually for his Dharma lectures. The coliseum now proudly stands as "a pure lotus in the Fragrant Harbor." And, as always, his schedules are packed with requests for interviews from the media and the public.

The master from Taiwan has added his touch to eradicate the erroneous public concept that monastics merely take without giving to society. Each year he actively participates in local charities by way of alms-round fundraising for the government, Tung Wah Group Hospitals, Po Leung Kuk,[5] and other institutions for the developmentally challenged.

As time goes on, more Dharma lectures by local masters are dotting public events, more notables openly acknowledge

[5] An orphanage with a long history.

becoming Buddhists, and the society has learned to respect the sangha and the essence of Buddhism. The Pearl of the Orient is now awash in the favor of the Buddha.

Chiang Su-hui, Taiwan's information officer in Hong Kong and a resident for fifteen years, is sympathetic about the uncertainty in Hong Kong's future beyond 1997, and its people's quickened pursuit of spirituality. The timely entry of Hsing Yun in their lives and the stability and assurance he has given them are the reasons behind his soaring popularity among them.

One of the major gateways for import and export trade between China and the rest of the world, Hong Kong has the best of both worlds, East and West. Hsing Yun has become dedicated to the city. He won the people over when he took Xu Jiatun in.[6] With the mercurial worldwide emigration of the people of Hong Kong over the last few years, Hsing Yun's impact, too, mushrooms in every corner – England, the

[6] See details in chapter 15.

United States, Canada, Australia, and even South Africa. He is extremely grateful to the people in Hong Kong. He believes they have actually opened the way for the spread of the Dharma across all five continents.

A mere monastic

As events of the decade continue their flow, the monastic who merely wanted to unload duties at the temple to focus on quiet cultivation, teaching, study, and writing, has carved out a braver, newer world with remarkable causes and conditions.

The Dalai Lama once shared his sentiments toward his Nobel peace prize, saying: "I'm still a mere monastic. No more, no less." Hsing Yun gave the same reply when asked about his switch from being abbot to a roving monk.

Endurance is for the reciprocation of the Buddha's favor; labor is for the benefit of all sentient beings. Every step of his footprints leaves behind trails of lotuses; the rustle of his robe sweeps clean [the path to] the Pureland. Like Master Hsüan Tsang who, on his white steed, traversed 800 *li* of deep sand and vowed "rather to perish taking one step west than to survive taking one step east,"[7] Hsing Yun in his modern transport adds the latest chapter in the history of Buddhism.

[7] The west means destination and advance; the east, home and retreat.

Chapter 15

Heart for the isle, soul for the mainland

From the home base of Taiwan, Hsing Yun's preaching trips in the last ten years must have encompassed the world in its entirety. That is, save the land he left behind four decades ago. On the mainland, still under the communist ideology, religion is regarded as basically anti-government, incense-offering a superstition, and the preservation of a handful of monasteries and eminent masters but a diplomatic gesture. On the other hand, the nationalists, licking their wounds, had sworn to block all communicative channels with the mainland so much so that, for the longest time, not even the fast maturing Buddhist practice in Taiwan was able to find its way home. Not until the late 1970s did President Chiang Ching-kuo give the green light for family visits to the mainland, which in time activated economic and cultural exchange. These factors indirectly contributed to Hsing Yun's homecoming; they also constituted the position he would assume as the isle and the mainland started to nudge each other.

A cough drop, a condition

Conditions are such ineffable things. The condition that led to Hsing Yun's homecoming was one tiny cough drop. In 1986, Hsing Yun and T'ien-Liu Shih-lun, during the 60th birthday gala of Thailand's King Bhumibol Adulyadej, overheard the severe hacking cough of a lady seated in front of them. That was the wife of Zhao Puchu, chairman of the Buddhist Association of China. T'ien quietly pulled a cough drop from her own purse and slipped it over. It pacified Zhao's cough in an instant. For that, she was more than thankful.

Sharing the same roots, the encounter away from home touched off a spontaneous friendship between Zhao and Hsing Yun. That evening, Zhao Puchu delivered to Hsing Yun an autographed copy of his works.

Zhao, at 89 and ranked high in public office on the mainland, is an expert in Yüan opera and classical verses and one of the three foremost Chinese calligraphists of our time. Being a lifelong Buddhist, he has done his best to guard the Dharma through the worst of times. The last few years he has been especially dedicated to the revival and repair of the severely damaged monasteries. One of Zhao's recent accomplishments is the towering bronze statue of the Buddha overlooking Lantau Island in Hong Kong (which has made the illustrative front of the city's subway electronic pass and is viewed as its most updated cultural symbol).

Despite an age gap of twenty years, Zhao and Hsing Yun became bosom friends from then on. The pair agreed to meet again soon.

It happened two years later in California. Hsing Yun was on two major projects at Hsi Lai Temple: the 16th general conference of the World Fellowship of

Buddhists and the 7th general conference of the World Fellowship of Buddhist Youth. His heart for the isle and his soul for the mainland, so he took pains to bring both Buddhist organizations from Taiwan and mainland China under one roof, hoping that historical headaches over the Chinese representation[1] would subside once and for all.

To avoid political overtones, Hsing Yun stated plainly in the invitation that each delegation be representative of its organization, not its country. The only flags to be flown would be that of the United States representing the host nation, and that of the World Fellowship of Buddhists; no other flags would be allowed. Further, he suggested that the titles of The Buddhist Association of Beijing, China, and The Buddhist Association of Taipei, China, be adhered to.

The ensuing negotiations, verging on

[1] The delegation from the mainland withdrew in protest against the election of Taiwan representative T'ien-Liu Shih-lun as vice-chair during the 14th meeting in Sri Lanka. The Taiwan delegation was ousted altogether from the 15th gathering in Nepal as a result of pressure from Beijing.

breakup more than once, took a winding course indeed before settling down to a mutual acceptance of Hsing Yun's proposal. Setting aside their longlasting political deadlock, the twin Buddhist bodies were able to peer at each other across the same conference table at last.

The breakthrough, when proclaimed at the opening ceremony, won a standing ovation from more than 500 delegates from 80 Buddhist organizations in 30 countries. Representatives from Hong Kong and Southeast Asia were heard to tout the *Hsing Yun Model*.

What followed was an invitation from Zhao to Hsing Yun for a trip to the mainland.

A whirlwind tour

The host was urging; the guest was urged. This would be the first official visit by a Buddhist monastic to a country bound and shackled by materialist ideology for half a century. How it was to be justified, that would be the question. Lu K'êng, a journalist much respected on the mainland, Taiwan, and Hong Kong, returned to lay the groundwork. Finally in 1989, Hsing Yun led a Dharma Preaching and Family Visiting Group of International Buddhist Progress Society to the mainland. It started a whirlwind of Hsing Yun that swept across the land; it was also a knock on the door of the bonding between the isle and the mainland.

Academic consultants Charles W.H. Fu and T'ang Tê-kang, along with over 70 authors, journalists, and monastics, together with groups of devotees from the United States, Canada, and Singapore, formed a delegation of more than 200. Starting from Shanghai in the east, this group traveled to Tunhuang in the west, Beijing in the north, and Ch'êngtu in the south between March 27 and April 25.

The U.S.-based author Wang I-ling records the *highly formalized*[2] official reception for the international Buddhist leader and his much publicized tour: "He shook hands and dined with every

[2] In the diplomatic terminology of the Chinese government. *Kao kuei-kê* in the original text.

governor and mayor in every province and city he toured. No matter what time of day, droves of monastics and lay people greeted him at train stations and airports. The red carpet was unrolled, and the bell and drum sounded when he dropped by any temple to offer incense and pray to the Buddha. He went about in a motorcade so popular that officials on bikes, along with those on foot, were needed to lead the way through the overwhelming crowds at festivities at Lung-hua Temple in Shanghai."

Enraptured audiences followed at his heels as the master took them through the mind of Ch'an and the mind of the human. At the joint invitation of the universities of Beijing, Qinghua, and Renmin, he spoke at Beijing's national library and proved to be sensational.

Visiting Sichuan, the great monk from Taiwan was even on the lips of bustling shoppers .

"For years the nationalist government has been harping about pushing back," observed an amused reporter touring with him. "Today, the master has made it!"

Indeed, Hsing Yun was an unprecedented speaker from Taiwan who took the podium in the People's Hall. His coming restored faith and hope within mainland the Buddhist circle and turned the heads of its eminent masters.

A borrowed freshness

Freely Hsing Yun talked to leaders of the communist regime Li Xiannian and Yang Shangkun about concerns over the pillage of religion during the Cultural Revolution. He requested that a religious policy be put in place and that monasterial management be returned to monastics. His plea was sincere: "It matters little for you as communists not to believe in any religion, but you must understand religion."

To an appreciative Zhao Puchu, the visit was like "ten thousand *li* of fragrant blossoms bearing superlative fruits." To the deeply moved abbot Hsüeh Fan of Ch'i-hsia Temple, Nanjing, "his rousing of the Buddhist morale from its long hibernation is exactly the breath of fresh air that the Buddhist circle in China yearns to borrow."

Indeed, whoever met or heard him

was impressed by how precise and thorough, erudite and witty he was. Whatever he said, from words of praise and advice to teaching, officials, students of Buddhist colleges, and the public found impeccable.

Also, he left many generous gifts. To every monastic he ran into he gave a red packet of good affinity; to many monasteries he gave works of his own and sets of the *Fo Kuang Encyclopedia*; to Ch'i-hsia Temple a jade Buddha and two new cars; to the Gallery of Modern Literature, a handsome donation; to the Buddhist Association of China, a generous sum and a tour bus; to Chiangtu and Haian, his hometown and his master's, monetary gifts; and to other charities, transportation vehicles and ambulances.

Professor Wang Yao of Tunhuang Research Institute and Central Institute of National Minorities in Beijing called Hsing Yun "the embodiment of altruism." "It's been one hearty embrace between the master and the people of the land," Wang noted. He saw Hsing Yun's visit as the signaling to a tormented, mortified nation that its innate spirit is alive and well on the international stage.

Dear, dear home

Finally, he alighted on the soil of his hometown, Chiangtu.

The eyewitness account of publisher Lu K'êng of Hong Kong's monthly magazine *People* are as follows: "It was the first time this journalist of 51 years saw a city empty itself onto the streets to salute someone. Two or three rows of people lined both sides of the main street; people were straining to see from buildings; people were perching in trees; people were clapping and cheering. With all this as a backdrop, he handed his mother a bouquet and grabbed her hand.

'I'm home!' he told her, and could say no more.

'It's good to have you back!' she echoed. 'It's good to have you back!'

The shimmer of their tears would never, ever suffice to reflect what it had meant to be without each other. Mother and son then greeted the crowds from the balcony. A band of monastics delivered a trilling *Ode to Mother*; T'ang Tê-kang and I recited congratulatory verses for the reunion.

'This is Li Kuo-shên!' In plain Yangchou dialect the popular religious leader reintroduced himself to his townsfolk."

'At long last Yangchou has come up with a truly fine human being!' murmured a teary elder.

Hsing Yun, turning to depart, was caught by a well-groomed mother, who raised her baby to him. He bent to touch the youngster's cheek with his own. Two dozen cameras must have captured the shot. ..."

Despite her pride over brother Kuo-shen's achievements, sister Su-hua, who now resides in Kuanghsi province with her family, could not help being wrecked by how long they had been apart. "I've turned grey," she said, as she strolled along the shaded path in Yühua T'ai (Terrace of Rain-soaked Blossom) Park in Nanjing, "and he's grown old, too. He's but a child in my memory!" She could not fight back tears each time she relived their reunion.

On his return to Ch'i-hsia Temple the principal and teachers of the vinaya college, who had disciplined the fledgling Hsing Yun, received him with utmost ceremony. From the seat of the guest of honor Hsing Yun rose to thank Ch'i-hsia for its nourishment of the Dharma and benefit of grace. Weeping as he spoke, he shared a poignant moment with a muted gathering of disciples and devotees. "May the radiance of Ch'i-hsia light up the future of Buddhism in China," later he gave a lecture to the young monastics.

Back in Chiao-shan Temple, Chên-chiang, he rejoined those masters from whom he had learned to pray and chant, and amused everyone with candid confessions of childhood follies and an occasional escape or two.

Far-reaching consequences

With Hsing Yun on board the yacht Emei along the Yangtze, professor of religious studies Charles W.H. Fu of Temple

University wrote about the revitalization of Chinese Buddhism and noted a revelation about the trip:

"First, it indirectly indicates the stirring of Chinese Buddhism in response to external aid and timely conditions. Buddhist morale in the country has reached new heights as a result. The lift that Hsing Yun gave the Buddhist circle there, which is too subjugated politically and economically to have bounced back on its own strength, was exactly what it needed.

Second, it helps resume Buddhist cultural interflow [between the country and the rest of the world]. While Buddhists from outside are dumbfounded by the magnificent stone-sculptures of Tatsu,[3] Sichuan, ancient monasteries, and other relics, the Chinese Buddhist circle is being updated, through the gifts of publications, as part of the new progress of modern Buddhism.

Third, it helps resume Buddhist

[3] Images of the Buddha sculpted from cliffs which are masterworks dated from the T'ang dynasty.

scholarly exchange [between the country and the rest of the world]. Hsing Yun's seminar with research fellows of the Chinese Institute of Social Sciences was the only one of its kind ever. Together they probed the extent of religious modernization, and the interrelationship between religion and socio-economic developments. In the meantime, he urged scholars to overcome the prejudice and ignorance that "religion is superstition."

Fourth, it transcends the political reality between Taiwan and the mainland. While the two continue to lock horns over timeless political differences, a religious unification seemed the least disputable, and Buddhist bodies can serve as the ideal go-between."

Needless to say, political enthusiasts in the media both in Taiwan and Hong Kong seized this opportunity to expound from different angles. They questioned the legality of his visit to the mainland because of his status of central advisory committee member;[4] they speculated that he was playing messenger for the government of Taiwan; they predicted that he would be bought by the communist rulers; they chided him for trying to buy his way through the mainland.

The Xu Jiatun Incident

All such speculations were evanescent bubbles in contrast to the mountainous wave that was to thrash against the shore a year later - the Xu Jiatun Incident.

On their return to Los Angeles, Hsing Yun and company stopped over in Hong Kong to dine with Xu, then heading the branch office of the New China News Agency in Hong Kong.[5] Tracing back his intentions for the occasion, Xu, who is now settled in the United States, is open and frank: "I regard the master as an eminent Buddhist figure, a high official in the

[4] His trip, actions, and speeches were later ratified by the ruling party.

[5] A position some regarded as authoritative as the governor of Hong Kong.

nationalist government, and a relatively significant target of diplomatic assimilation."

Chiangsu is hometown to both Xu and Hsing Yun. The former relates with fondness their first get-together: "Like old friends, we started to chat with the same accent." Hsing Yun then courteously booked their next appointment at Hsi Lai Temple, which Xu cheerily confirmed. Just prior to the June 4 disaster, a thank-you note reiterating the promised meeting reached Xu, who was somewhat tickled: "Hsing Yun's conspiratory letter is here!"

In the aftermath of the Tiananmen rampage, the reformists were subdued while the hard-liners pushed on with house-cleansing, and Xu, who had publicly sympathized with the student movement and never curbed supportive demonstrations staged by his staff, was naturally blacklisted for future retaliation. Lamenting over the absence of refuge within the system, he ultimately decided to take time off the following May and flew to the United States, where he would cash in on the rain-check that Hsing Yun had for him. Xu was received under the roof of Hsi Lai Temple.

Xu's disappearance shook many on the mainland, in Hong Kong, and the United States. After all, Hong Kong had come to cherish and respect the man who had been at the helm of the city's branch office of the New China News Agency for seven years. On the other hand, the 50-year veteran communist party member was the highest ranking official to flee since the flights of Wang Ming to the then-Soviet Union in the 1950s and Lin Biao to Mongolia in the 1970s. The enigma of his whereabouts must have caused more than a few sleepless nights.

Initially no one was quite aware of Xu at the temple. Not until a fortnight later when Hsing Yun accompanied him on an excursion to San Diego and Las Vegas. In the Ghost Town on the way, they were spotted by tourists from Hong Kong and, before they knew it, pictures were in the papers. Thereafter the temple was bombarded with phone calls day and night asking about Xu.

At that, Hsing Yun consulted his guest: "Monastics don't lie. Since you're here with us, I can't tell people otherwise. Neither will evading the calls solve anything. We have to say something."

Xu thus gave consent for a press conference in which Hsing Yun and Lu K'êng would announce, on his behalf, his four personal principles. They are, namely, no political asylum, no violation of national security, no interviews with the media, and no contact with exiled members of the June 4 movement.

Buddha gate opens for those who suffer

When all was straightened out [about Xu], questions about Hsing Yun were left unanswered. How could a monk, supposedly above and beyond the three realms, get caught up in a political maelstrom? What was he after? Let bygones be bygones. Hsing Yun has no regrets. For the Buddha gate is one of compassion and shall always open for those who suffer. "I've never treated Mr. Xu as a political personage," he says. "Just someone in need."

Hsing Yun, taking his stand and refusing to be embroiled in the strife of politics, declined requests for the gathering at Hsi Lai Temple of exiled members of the June 4 movement and for Buddhist services to be conducted to deliver victims of the Tiananmen killings. But the communist government could not forget easily. When Xu was officially expelled from the party the following year, he was also accused of involvement with subversive elements.[6] That was about as guilty as Hsing Yun would be projected. In the ensuing streak of events, he was banned from the mainland. The good will from his family visit and preaching tour vanished overnight. The Buddhist circle in the mainland held its tongue; some hastened to draw the line.

The visitation ban lasted two years until Jiang Zemin annulled it. Hsing Yun was allowed home again to see his mother, though not without the strictest *protection*[7] – a sign of sustained distrust on the part of

[6] According to the communist government, Buddhist monastic Hsing Yun of Taiwan and subversive journalist Lu K'êng.

[7] Called *full-time accompaniment* in the protocol of the communist government.

the authorities.

Surprisingly enough, the most emphatic affirmation and support for Hsing Yun was from Hong Kong, itself playing a dubious role in the China issue. The master came just after Jiang Zemin and before Li Teng-hui in a public poll for the most newsworthy people.

Xu has since lived in recluse in the United States. Often he ponders how much Hsing Yun has done for him: "For all the time I've been, the master has consistently respected my privacy while attending to all my needs as far as personal health and daily life."

Looking back, Hsing Yun's virtue and gallantry were undeniable to many. Some, however, cannot endorse how he was pulled into political muddy water. The subsequent rift with the communist government would considerably slow down the momentum from his first preaching tour and almost terminate all efforts to reinvigorate Chinese Buddhism.

Tangible exchange

So far, Hsing Yun has enjoyed attention in China like no other. His *Taiwan Experience* will always be helpful should Chinese Buddhism be allowed to pick up where it left off. Hence the communist government remains lukewarm toward him. As for Hsing Yun, it is clear to him that, despite opening the doorway superficially to the outside world, the mainland has little room for religious development. There, Buddhism is still revolving around aesthetic gardens and ancient relics, not yet to be practiced as a faith. For a thousand years or more Buddhism has been an undertow in Chinese culture but, to blossom again, it will just have to wait longer for causes and conditions to mature. Before that happens, he must spread as many Bodhi seeds as he possibly can.

In the current context of tangible exchange, free issues of *Universal Gate* and *Awakening the World* are distributed regularly to the mainland even though these might never reach the intended readers. The dozen or so letters each month requesting financial assistance for the sangha and monasteries are all answered. A joint effort between Hsing Yun and P'an Hsiao-jui provides annual scholarships for 20 students from the mainland to study in the United States and 20 local Buddhist college students. His publications are widely reprinted; *Universal Gate* is considered a gem in many monasteries.

Hsing Yun's latest project is the publishing of *Anthology of Buddhist Scholarly Essays*, edited by Fo Kuang Shan's consultant Chi Kuang-yü. The anthology's dual topics are, namely, the problems and future of Chinese Buddhism. Contributing authors are invited from the academia in China. The publication, to be produced in Taiwan and distributed in the mainland, is destined to be instrumental in the scholarly exchange between both Buddhist circles.

Tending to a future cause

So long as the mainland carries on with its economic advancement and political moderation, Hsing Yun foresees plenty of space for communication. "All conscientious Chinese people want a unified China," he asserts. "It's not as if one side is swallowing up the other but a peaceful, equal form of unification."

"Prior to unification, attainment of the following must be complete: first, mutual strengthening of the economy; second, cultural dialogue; third, respect for religion; and fourth, political democracy. China isn't the exclusive property of a few. The country is the convergence of the majority."

On being labeled as unionist, he says: "No partisan politics for me," he replies. "Only this heart for Taiwan and this soul for China."

As a monastic, Hsing Yun is not about to budge from the principle that "politics are politics and religion is religion," but hopes that both governments, with graciousness, shall tend to the future of the Chinese people.

Part V

Buddha's Light held high

At International Buddhist Association
of Queensland, Australia

With California Secretary of State March Fong Eu
(second from left) and friends at the site of
Hsi Lai Temple, Hacienda Heights, Ca

With President Clarence Seignoret of
the Commonwealth of Dominica
at the B.L.I.A. inauguration,
Hsi Lai Temple, 1992

With President Diosdado Macapagal of the Philippines, et. al., 1963

Congratulating the inception of Tzu Chi Hospital,
Hualien, Taiwan

Chatting with archbishop Lo Kuang

Visiting the temple of Dhammakaya Foundation for the casting ceremony of its golden Buddha, Thailand, 1994

Visiting the Ajanta in India

Chapter 16
The Dharma coming west

Four decades ago Buddha's Light branched off from the mainland. Hsing Yun rode the crest of Taiwan's economic boom and in doing so took Buddha's Light to all the corners of the world. From Southeast Asia in the 1950s, Japan and Korea in the 1960s, Europe and the Americas in the 1970s and 1980s, to Africa in the 1990s, the globalization of Chinese Buddhism has been historical and its maturation phenomenal.

And, the making of Hsi Lai Temple is the most momentous of all.

Largest in the Western hemisphere

Hsi Lai Temple is some 20 miles to the east of Los Angeles and 20 minutes by car from Monterey Park, otherwise known as *Little Taipei*. Breezes of late May are still kind and gentle, and morning over the largest and most dynamic city on the west coast is beckoning. Just under an hour by freeway from the Los Angeles International Airport, the road lightly tilts and turns and, before one knows it, a blinding patch of light on a lushly treed slope meets the eye. How the golden walls and glittering roofs have lit up what would have been another mundane landscape! High up the colossal mountain gate the inscription which its founder holographed, *Fo Kuang Shan Hsi Lai Ssŭ*, looks upon each and every who passes through.

Officially registered in the name of International Buddhist Progress Society [I.B.P.S.], Hsi Lai Temple (Ssŭ) is a milestone that marks the Dharma coming to the Western world. In addition, it is a major platform on which traditional Buddhism plays out its social role in modern society. The temple perches atop a 15-acre property in Hacienda Heights. The sprawling 102,432-square meter structure was designed by U.S.-based architect Yang Tsu-ming. Ground-breaking was in 1986 and completion, November 1988. To symbolize endless continuity of the Dharma lineage and Dharma water, Hsing Yun had expressly requested from India the five-grain bricks, from the Ganges its sacred sand, and from Fo Kuang Shan its soil, for the foundation of the Main Shrine.

The palatial temple made the pages of *Life* magazine, which called it "the largest temple in the Western hemisphere" and "the Forbidden City in America," and became the subject of a feature in *Reader's Digest* the following April.

Indeed, Hsi Lai Temple carries the torch of Fo Kuang Shan as a spiritual and cultural center in America, a learning ground of Buddhism for Westerners, and the convergence of cultures - East and West. Daily, devotees and visitors of all nationalities stroll the grounds; lamas from India and bhiksus from Spain sojourn at the guests' house; and exchanges in diverse languages and dialects reverberate beneath the Buddha's feet.

Marvelous showcase of Eastern culture

With its direct descendancy from Fo Kuang Shan, Hsi Lai Temple becomes an inevitable west coast stopover for political and social moguls from Taiwan. Former chairperson Hao Po-ts'un of the executive council, legislator K'ang Ning-hsiang, general Chiang Wei-kuo, presidential political advisor Li Huan, and former Kaohsiung mayor Yü-Chên Yüeh-ying are among a few. Once Hsing Yun told Chang Ch'ing-yen, former head of the Los Angeles office of the Coordination Council for North American Affairs: "Please feel free to utilize the facility for hospitality and entertainment purposes!" More important, the temple, above and beyond the tension between the isle and the mainland, provides a buffer zone and has hosted stays of China's ambassador to the United States, Zhu Qizhen; [former head of the Hong Kong office of the New China News Agency,] Xu Jiatun; [leader of the June 4 Tiananmen student movement,] Wuer Kaixi; and one of Taiwan's most vocal political dissidents, P'êng Ming-min. Local notables, too, frequent the temple with pleasure. California's Secretary of State Dr. March Fong Eu, in particular, marvels at such a fine presence in her home state.

Today Hsi Lai Temple showcases Eastern culture and is the headquarters for the spread of Buddhism in the West. But it was in no way spared the daunting struggle typical of any pioneering effort.

The seed was sown when Hsing Yun first came to America as a guest of its bicentennial celebrations some twenty years ago. The country's cultural diversity and receptiveness struck him irrevocably. Further, the need of a spiritual anchorage for the fast increasing number of immigrants of Chinese heritage was more than obvious. But most of all, Hsing Yun pondered, in contrast to the heavily armed and intrusive ways in which Christianity penetrated China in the last century, could Buddhism now be taught peacefully in the West?

The mind having moved and thought having risen, and at the urging of eager devotees, he dispatched Venerable Tzu Chuang, who was accompanied by the

English-speaking Venerable Yi Hang. With US$50,000, a remarkable sum then, the two would delve into the possibility of building a temple in America. Venerable Tzu Chuang, as it turned out, was utterly taken aback by the prices she heard, US$70,000 - 80,000 for a single house. She was ready to head home when the master, however, flew over and joined the quest. Together, they eventually came upon a church building for sale. While disciples ruminated over the notion of having to convert a church into a Buddhist temple, the master immediately snapped up the deal. To him, a building originated for religious purposes would only make things easier, not harder. A US$20,000 down payment was given and the loan application was approved. That was the beginning of perpetual hope for Chinese Buddhism in America.

The monastics repaired the walls and painted images of the Buddha. The first chanting session drew devotees from a great distance and the ensuing gatherings filled the temple each time. Next came Pai-t'a (White Pagoda) Temple in Maywood, whose subsequent success laid the causes and conditions for a grander facility.

The resistance of Hacienda Heights

Hsing Yun's longtime follower Chang-Yao Hung-ying was a major driving force behind the vision. Her US$300,000-donation, together with others, helped purchase a hilly property in Hacienda Heights. Somehow, the application for the state of California's approval to launch construction touched off an uproar within the local community, an affluent, conservative, and predominantly white suburb of retirees. The resistance of Hacienda Heights was bitter. Residents fretted about everything from the annihilation of the natural landscape, disturbances from the chanting and festivities, negative impact of the monastic attire on the young, to the safety of their own household pets (didn't the Chinese all love dog meat?).

Subsequent legal proceedings took the form of six public hearings and over 100 explanatory sessions, thorough revision in terms of construction area, height, and colors to accord with the proposals of the Hacienda Heights Improvement Association, and the promise to redirect some future funds for charity in the community.

It was all a matter of fear, not legality. Fear from the distrust of a different culture. The process was tough – unknowing young hooligans lobbing an occasional rock or spitting a coarse word or two. But Hsing Yun – from his discernment and tolerance – was patient, and he waited for things to take a better turn. Community representatives were invited over to chat and to tour the site. The master, too, would show his sense of community by means of leading disciples and devotees in many an environmental cleanup. Slowly but surely, the locals were won over. In one of the public hearings, a Protestant minister literally pleaded on behalf of Hsi Lai Temple: "My wife is Vietnamese. She hasn't passed a day without crying about missing home since coming to America. For all her longing I hope there's a place of solace."

Home for the Buddhist body and mind

Hsi Lai Temple came into being after a decade of struggle. Well-wishers both within the Buddhist circle and without were genuinely congratulatory. To that end, a message from U.S. congressman Matthew G. Martinez ran thus: "The majestic Hsi Lai Temple will not only benefit its devotees and the local community with endless activities but also bridge the gap between cultures and thoughts of the East and West." The executive president Venerable H. Ratanasara of American Buddhist Congress added: "[Hsi Lai Temple] is destined to be the lighthouse for the spread of Buddhism ... a supreme glory for the Dharma in the Western hemisphere."

When the temple, on its completion, hosted the 16th general conference of the World Fellowship of Buddhists, the first ever held outside Asia, it also set the stage for a globalized Buddhism.

Over the next ten years, Hsi Lai

Temple has evolved into an international and multifaceted center of cultural exchange. In temple activities – especially the Dharma functions of the [monthly] Great Compassion Repentance, the Eight Precepts retreat, and the Amitabha Buddha seven-day retreat, along with a range of Buddhist lectures – the Buddhist populace in America finds an anchorage for its spirit and stability for its body and mind. In the counseling provided by the monastics, the immigrants, strangers in this strange land, find ready solutions to their daily problems as well as help for their emotional and psychological frustrations. Sociologically speaking, therefore, this is where social interaction takes place and where social identification can be found.

Every lunar New Year, devotees of Chinese heritage (with roots in the mainland, Taiwan, and Hong Kong), Vietnamese, Cambodian, and other heritages come from all over to pay homage to the Buddha. Many drive two or three hours for the occasion. When the temple's 200 parking spots are filled, others are forced to leave their cars much further down, they have to walk uphill. An incredulous bystander once described the spectacle: "One closely behind another, they're like a line of focused, homecoming ants."

Visitors are welcome to stay and are treated with the utmost hospitality. A new immigrant was able to stay at the guest house until he found a job and settled into his own residence.

To enrich life at large, the Hsi Lai cultural training center offers classes in floral arrangement, vegetarian cooking, T'aichi, Chinese zither, calligraphy, and Dharma meetings for women. To lend dual-income devotee families a hand, daycare for children is being considered. An ideal weekend for neighboring families is learning a craft or two, making plenty of friends, and savoring the vegetarian cuisine at Hsi Lai Temple.

Those traveling from far and near

To serve Westerners who have traveled from far and near seeking the joys of the

Dharma, Hsi Lai Temple sponsors Buddhist camps and study sessions in English, hosts dinners for community residents, and ensures that simultaneous interpretation is in place for all regular Dharma functions. In fact, Western devotees made up as much as one fifth of the 300 who participated in the refuge ceremony, during which the sweet dew was sprinkled and devotees took refuge in the Triple Gems last year. Numbers are certainly on the increase. The distrust and rejection a decade ago have given way to congeniality and enthusiasm. Annual visitors from educational, religious, and professional bodies average 18,000 individuals in 200 groups, three fourths of which are from America, and the rest from Europe and other continents. For all of them, comprehensive guided tours in English are provided.

Last year, a total of 5 large-scale and 33 smaller conferences, which opted to take advantage of the spacious location, were held at the temple.

A California state council meeting in Sacramento was inaugurated by a Buddhist purification ceremony in which Hsing

Yun's presence was requested.

Mondays and Thursdays on Channel 53, telecasts of weekly features and updates revolve around the topic *Buddha's Light Coming West*. In the meantime, efforts by individual devotees are mounting in the translation of Buddhist literature for the benefit of the English-speaking community. Vice-chancellor Wayne Huang of City College, Los Angeles, has just published two major texts in English translation, the *Diamond Sutra* and the *Heart Sutra*.

To date, Hsi Lai Temple's devotees have surpassed 20,000 – as verified in the temple's computerized statistics.

The five-year-old Hsi Lai University, temporarily accommodated in the temple, is a small and specialized institution of higher learning with distinguished faculty. Classes are conducted in English. Students pursue bachelor's degrees in Buddhism and master's degrees in religious studies. In the words of vice-president Venerable Tzu Hui: "The most vernal of the Ivy League schools are 100 - 200 years old. It takes at least 50 years for any institution of higher learning to sprout. Hsi Lai University has a long,

long way to go. But it will cope."

French cyclist Bénédicte Storme, originally intending to spend ten years traveling around the world, stopped at the mountain gate two years ago and has parked there since. Though she was raised as a Catholic, she has taken both the Five Precepts and Bodhisattva Precepts at Hsi Lai Temple and studies at its university. "I used to be so frightened of the unknown future," she says, recounting the impact of Buddhism on herself, "and twice I saw my own life imperiled. But I'm a Buddhist now and no longer fearful. For I know that the Buddha resides in my heart, not [just] in the temple."

Karl Uth, a Buddhist of German descent, is set to publish German translations of the master's writings in his home country. He has expended countless hours of work to complete this task. These days, he is planning on early retirement to devote more energy to his faith. Moreover, Uth is resolved to donate a scenic family property back home for the site of a temple to be erected in three years. It will be a new base for the spread of Buddhism in Germany.

A global network

Like the master, Hsi Lai Temple has never failed to keep its word. Chanting is always discreet and the temple grounds immaculate. Donations of funds and books are made to area schools on a regular basis. Emergency relief was expediently organized in the aftermath of the disastrous quake in Los Angeles. Conference facilities and services are provided free to educational and cultural organizations. Even real estate prices in Hacienda Heights remain stable despite the general economic slump. The notion that "it's safe to be around Fo Kuang Shan" is prevalent within the Chinese community.

The small step that Hsi Lai Temple has taken is one gigantic advancement in the evolving history of Buddhism. Patterned upon this temple, other branches – about half out of the total of 100 – have sprung up like vernal bamboo shoots after the rain: 12 in Asia; 13 in the United States and Canada; others in London, Berlin, Paris, and

Switzerland; International Buddhist Associations in Queensland, Australia, North Island and South Island in New Zealand; I.B.P.S. do Brasil and a meditation center in Paraguay, South America. Venerable Hui Li, the first Buddhist monastic in history to spread the Dharma in South Africa, currently undertakes planning and construction of I.B.P.S., South Africa. To backtrack a little, last September Hsing Yun conducted the historical ordination of ten African Buddhist monastics in South Africa. Many of them hold doctorates and other academic credentials. For Chinese Buddhism, that was the epochal spreading of the light to the vast African continent.

Hsing Yun, with much humility, attributes the quickened pace of globalization to several facilitating causes. First, emigration resulting from relaxed government policies in Taiwan since the mid-1970s has resulted in the most well-educated and affluent immigrants to date. Second, from Hong Kong, where concern over uncertainties after 1997 intensifies, there has been a continuous outpour of emigrants to the British Commonwealth countries. Third, the influx of refugees from

Indo-China countries has never quite diminished. All of them of Chinese ancestry and offspring of the mother faith of Buddhism, they need Buddhism as a haven for their minds. Conversely, it has been with their support that Buddhism is able to thrive.

Dreamer and doer

Both a dreamer and doer, Hsing Yun acknowledges the long and winding road ahead of him. Historically in America alone, Buddhism did not reach beyond devotees of Eastern descent until the Parliament of the World's Religions in Chicago, 1893 – barely a century ago. And [in Europe,] the first Buddhist organization, Buddhist Preaching Society of Germany, was not formed until 1903 in Leipzig, Germany. Looking back on China, Buddhism, which was first introduced from India, took 400 years of adaptation and harmonization with Chinese thought and culture before evolving into the "Chinese version of Buddhism." Likewise, it might be hundreds of years before Buddhism will take root and exert any influence elsewhere. Therefore, the grooming of those who are to be instrumental in helping globalize the Buddhist faith will be essential.

Presently among the monastics pursuing higher learning abroad are Venerable Yi Fa, who is expected to be the first bhiksuni with a doctorate from Yale University, and Venerable Hui Kai, a Ph.D. candidate in religion from Temple University. Six years of spreading the Dharma in America, like he did elsewhere, has assured Venerable Hui Kai that, to open others' minds to the Buddhist teachings, one must take into account the background history, culture, customs, habits, and circumstances. Therefore, he has actively delved into all aspects of Western culture – religion, philosophy, sociology, and their interrelations – as well as religions such as Christianity and Hinduism.

Knowing what the master wants him to do, Venerable Hui Kai makes it a point to take up residence in a predominantly white suburban neighborhood, befriends Christian ministers, and speaks often at neighboring institutions. Closely he follows the daily news, in order to gain a picture of the American mentality pertinent to the economy, education, family [values], gun-control, drugs, and other areas. In the process, he reflects on what the Dharma can do to help alleviate the problems of America.

Sharon Silver, an ardent admirer of the Chinese culture and an elementary school teacher, went to Fo Kuang Shan more than ten years ago. Every school year she invites her good friend Venerable Hui Kai to speak to her class about the meaning of Buddhism. At the end, students are taught to meditate for five minutes. And their teacher is astounded again and again to see kids, who otherwise can barely settle down longer than a minute, sitting quite still the whole time. From the Dharma these school children learn the Buddhist etiquette in the American classroom: rising before each class and joining their palms to greet their teacher. They even learn to greet and thank their monastic mentor in Chinese. Last year, their welcoming song virtually took his breath away. It was *Fo Kuang Buddhists in the Four Seas* - sung in Chinese, of course.

Integration of Buddhism and Western culture

Ch'an, meditation, therapy for the body and mind – they are getting more popular than ever in the West. Yet, when compared to Japanese Zen, introduced to Western society by Dr. D. T. Suzuki whose scholarly works were extensively translated into English, or the spread of Tibetan and Thai Buddhism, the coming of Chinese Buddhism to the West has been a fairly late development. Looking ahead, one may ponder on what Buddhism will be like 500 years from now, and which school will be the major source of influence.

On congratulating the completion of Hsi Lai Temple, the Dalai Lama also addressed the same questions: "Rising interests in Buddhism in recent years have led to the rise of Buddhist places of worship in the West. We must be aware that, like the integration of Tibetan Buddhism and Tibetan culture or that of Chinese Buddhism and Chinese culture, Western Buddhism will have to integrate with Western culture. Integration of Buddhism with the existing culture hastens societal acceptance. It also facilitates practice. So long as the fundamental doctrine remains intact, such an integration is only beneficial to and supportive of the normal development of Buddhism.

"While we practice, we should learn to respect other religions. This is especially vital for those of us who are new in our faith. Let us remember that personal inner cultivation and progress far exceed the superficial in importance."

Three decades of international efforts

Hsing Yun started breaking through international boundaries much earlier than most would have realized. In an article for *Awakening the World,* he wrote about plans to preach to the world and proposed training for English-speaking preachers of the Dharma. He was only thirty then. During the next two decades he traveled to India, Thailand, Malaysia, Singapore, the Philippines, Hong Kong, and Japan, while laying the groundwork for the globalization of Buddhism. Once, in a refuge ceremony in

Malaysia, offerings by devotees took three hours to complete. Another time, 3,000 people jammed the 2,000 seat Dewan Tengku Abdul Rahman and those outside almost took down the door to hear him speak. "What happened this evening," quipped Penang's chief minister Tan Sri Dr. Koh Thu Koon at the opening speech, "reaffirms my resolution to put up an indoor stadium with a 10,000 - person capacity, so that when Master Hsing Yun preaches in the city again, no one will be locked out."

Buddhist devotees in Islamic Indonesia, vowing to remain vegetarian for three months, ultimately moved the government to lift the ban for the public preaching of Buddhism so that Hsing Yun was able to speak to a historical gathering of over 1,000 Buddhist devotees.

Last year in San Francisco, the master's lecture on the *Heart Sutra,* with simultaneous translation by Venerable Hui Qun, amazed his American audience. Journalist Lu K'êng observed: "In engineering humanistic Buddhism, founding Buddha's Light International Association, and organizing international events, you're the master of social movement. What we have not appreciated more is your wonderful erudition in Buddhism studies."

The globalization of Buddhism has united Buddhists worldwide. It also comes as a form of religious diplomacy, with disciples and devotees stationed at various branch temples as a type of informal diplomacy. Even Fo Kuang Shan's branch temples surpass Taiwan's foreign consulates in number. The language experts of Fo Kuang Shan include over 100 of those conversant in English, over 60 in Japanese, over 40 in Cantonese, and others in German, French, Spanish, Portuguese, Tibetan, Thai, and Malaysian. "I'm afraid that Fo Kuang Shan's pool of foreign language experts," Chiang Hsiao-wu, former consul to Japan, once lamented, "is more diversified than ours."

Fo Kuang Shan also has this special hold on the overseas Chinese communities. In Paris, most residents of Chinese descent are concentrated in the 13th district. A lot of them are in the restaurant business. To have a gathering of a hundred or so people is never easy. But some 2,000 turned up when Master Hsing Yun was there to conduct the refuge ceremony.

Bodhi seeds from the East

Two thousand years ago, the Buddha spent some four decades in propagating Buddhism across the five regions of India. Today, the one who has carried on with the selfsame spirit in disseminating Bodhi seeds from the East to the rest of the world is master Hsing Yun. He truly is able to "let the Buddha's light shine through the great chiliocosm of three kinds of thousands of chiliocosms, and the Dharma water flow across all five continents."

Chapter 17

Buddha's Light International Association

What separates a human from a Buddha?

Buddha is a Sanskrit word for the enlightened one.

Some 2,500 years ago, Sakyamuni Buddha attained enlightenment while meditating on the diamond throne beneath a Bodhi tree and gazing into the starlit skies. He was awakened to the good roots and good nature in all living beings, which are merely veiled by the five desires[1] and three poisons.[2] For the ensuing forty-five

[1] Wealth, sex, food and drink, fame, and sleep.

[2] Greed, anger, and ignorance.

years, the Buddha spoke on the Dharma in an effort to bring the deluded back to their true nature. For all living beings are Future Buddhas. Thereafter, Buddhism was introduced to China, Japan, and Korea in the north and Sri Lanka, Thailand, and others in the south – sprinkling the dew of the Dharma along its path, and delivering those to be drown in the sea of suffering.

Some 2,500 years later, Hsing Yun, expending a lifetime to uphold the Buddha's teachings and to transform humanistic Buddhism into a reality, has come to realize that the sangha alone cannot revitalize Buddhism, and that Buddhism shall only be empowered by an integrated lay community. This become his goal, after relieving himself of the abbotship of Fo Kuang Shan.

Correct knowledge and correct view

A Fo Kuang Buddhist can be a member of the sangha, a student, a teacher, a staff member, a devotee, or basically someone sharing a good affinity with Fo Kuang Shan.

Hsing Yun had the notion in the early 1970s. The term is not meant to attract attention to the birth of another school. It stands for a consensus, a certain set of principles, the possession of correct knowledge and correct view, and the qualitative conditions of a Buddhist.

The next decade saw Taiwan with an unprecedented economic growth, diversification in society, and universality in education. Parallel to these is the dawning of Buddhism as the fruition of decades of cultivation and efforts within and without the circle. For the first time, the lay community is seen to comprise of academics, political leaders, and forerunners in business.

Yet, there is a lack of cohesion and unification in the now enthusiastic Buddhist community, as observed by a Buddhist scholar Chêng Chên-huang. There is not any leader or institution to organize the devotees. Hsing Yun can not agree more. The number of monasteries and monastics is limited, but the resources of the masses can be infinite. Therefore, Hsing Yun believes that efforts to spread the benefits of the Dharma must be sustained by the vast number of devotees.

As the community of Fo Kuang Buddhists expanded over three decades, the branch temples continued to act as the axle of the Buddhist practice and refinement, while judiciously playing their roles in social education alongside public and interpersonal relations, and ensuring that religion and life are interwoven at all times. Finally at the end of the long insulation, Taiwan's society saw the light of day with the introduction of democratic policy by President Chiang Ching-kuo. The lifting of martial law and permission for public organizations meant that causes and conditions were perfect for the continuation of the spirit and principle of Fo Kuang Shan. Under Hsing Yun, the birth of another Buddhist organization was naturally imminent.

Alliance of the sangha and devotees

Buddha's Light International Association (B.L.I.A.), R.O.C. was formed on February 3,

1991, in Taipei.

It was another pioneering feat in the history of Buddhism.

Why such timing? How would the organization be woven into the fabric of the fate of Buddhism and society at large? In essence, it is a manifestation of Hsing Yun's long-standing concern for the continuation of social evolvement, his deep sentiments for a society remiss of order, value, and faith, and his optimism for the Dharma-abiding joint forces of the sangha and lay community to help people to delve into the Canon, uphold the Five Precepts, and shepherd society back to purity and serenity.

At the launching of B.L.I.A., R.O.C., he was specific about goals:

"People used to think that Buddhism was mainly for monastics, not for lay people. The coming of B.L.I.A., R.O.C. shall presage a transition from Buddhism for the sangha alone to Buddhism for everyone, a shift from the temple to society, to every household. The inertia, monotony, and solitary cultivation associated with

Buddhism shall no longer be. The coming of B.L.I.A., R.O.C. shall reenergize Buddhism sufficiently for its altruistic function.

"In the past, people used to think that there were many Buddhists in Taiwan only. However, because of the establishment of B.L.I.A., R.O.C., it's possible to spread Buddhist teachings to every corner of the world. In the past, devotees would always be devotees only no matter how well they practiced. On the other hand, a devotee crossing the threshold of monasticism would promptly assume the status of a teacher. The coming of B.L.I.A., R.O.C. shall enable qualified devotees to join the sangha to preach the Dharma and to purify minds, correct social trends, and contribute to the happiness and prosperity of society and the nation."

That is,

- from the sangha to the lay community
- from the monastery to society
- from self-cultivation to altruism
- from a stationary state to active state
- from [the status of] disciple to [that of] teacher

· from Taiwan to the rest of the world

Those who understand Buddhism know how much vision and courage is required to promote such ideals. In the traditional Buddhist circle, monastics are considered superior and lay people inferior. For the founding of B.L.I.A., R.O.C. to entail the inclusion of lay people in "shouldering the family task of the Tathagata" could easily have been misinterpreted as the decline of monastic sovereignty or subjugation of the sangha. But it was never Hsing Yun's way to bow to the pressure of convention or to promote class distinction. That those who have renounced their homes and those who practice from home, the unworldly and worldly, should share equal importance and join hands in prodding Buddhism to prosperity is all he believes in.

The mushrooming effect

Built on the solidity of Fo Kuang Shan, B.L.I.A., R.O.C. actually began with a membership of over 3,000 from branches under four district associations in the north, central, south, and east of Taiwan. In addition, there are lateral branches like Tainan's Buddha's Light subchapter for teachers, Tathagata subchapter set up within the immigration department, and Pao-kuang (Precious Light) subchapter organized by finance and business professionals.

The whole mushrooming effect has been phenomenal. Hsing Yun once sanctioned the establishment of a record 15 subchapters in one day. Membership is categorized into individual, group, and preliminary together with family and associate. The list of benefits runs on and on: Buddhist studies, career and general counseling, social activities, consultation on weddings and funerals, and more. And, whatever the place and whichever the chapters, the familiarity of the trademark golden vest embroidered with the nine-petalled lotus invariably breeds kindred warmth.

The inception of Buddha's Light International Association a year later – May 16, 1992 – at Hsi Lai Temple, Los Angeles, was a prompt reply to devotees overseas regarding the immediate headway gained by the parent association. It was also an evidence of strength in the context of an international organization.

The impact

Some 4,000 members representing 51 districts from 30 countries on 5 continents and international dignitaries convened for the opening of Buddha's Light International Association. Amid the ruins of racial and sectarian barriers stood the monument of a globalized Buddhism, a milestone for the onward march into the next century. During the inauguration ceremony of B.L.I.A., Sir Clarence Seignoret, President of the Commonwealth of Dominica, Dr. March Fong Eu, Secretary of the State of California, Mr. Jung-chi Chung, Chairperson of Social Workers' Association, and Ven. Sharma Rinpoche of Tibet came to congratulate this auspicious event. To commemorate the occasion, Monterey Park Mayor Samuel Kiang expressly proclaimed May 16 the city's Buddha's Light Day.

The festive gala was a display of historical union for the Buddhist sangha and devotees from countries and regions such as China, Japan, Korea, India, and Tibet, and divisions and schools like the north and south, the exoteric and esoteric. Nishihara Yuichi, president of B.L.I.A., Tokyo, was elated to have befriended 4,000 fellow Buddhists in a day.

Prior to the opening, a distraught Los Angeles was faced with racial differences apparently too stupendous to solve. Riots in the inner city both rocked the world and intimidated would-be visitors. It was against such a backdrop that Hsing Yun scheduled the auspicious event. There and then he rallied Buddhists of all races and from everywhere in "joy and harmony," in true openness and mutual acceptance. Nothing could have said more about the peace and tolerance of the Buddhist doctrine.

Up to the end of 1994, the world organization – founded solely by the Chinese Buddhists – boasted 1 head association,[3] 79 chapters,[4] and 17 preliminary chapters.

3. A country with more than 4 chapters is eligible for the establishment of a head association.

4. A chapter has 10 subchapters, and a subchapter has 100 members or more.

The omnipresent Fo Kuang Buddhists

B.L.I.A.'s golden vest worn against skin colors of every kind is living proof of the omnipresence of the Fo Kuang Buddhists; so is its five-color, striped flag, symbolizing the ultimate transcendence "across ten directions, throughout three junctures," which now flies in 51 countries and regions on all five continents – North America's Canada and the United States; Central and South Americas' the Commonwealth of Dominica, Brazil, Paraguay, Argentina, and Costa Rica; Europe's France (Paris), England (London), Switzerland (Zurich), Germany (Berlin), Russia (St. Petersburg), and Holland; South Africa; Australia and New Zealand; Asia's Taiwan, Japan, Hong Kong, Macao, Malaysia, the Philippines, Indonesia, Thailand, Singapore, Sri Lanka, Sikkim, and India.

The question about this explosion and magnetism is *why*. Legislator P'an Wei-kang, a member of the board of directors of B.L.I.A., R.O.C. and a veteran of board meetings, marvels at the earnest sharing and delightful harmony that typify the association's meetings as opposed to others, which tend to resemble battle grounds. Vice-president Chang Nai-pin of the Los Angeles chapter, who founded a social service hotline in Taiwan, speaks the mind of the Chinese community in America: "The presence of B.L.I.A. calms the anxiety of drifting, uncovers the infinite treasure of our mind, and links together the hearts of every Chinese around the globe."

Hsing Yun, well-known for his organizational capabilities, has devised for B.L.I.A. an ingenious developmental strategy which works both ways. On the one hand, influential public figures invited to chair the local chapters help recruit local members. On the other, both regular and special functions are implemented to absorb the individuals. For instance, to cater to the needs of the members of the Chinese community in Germany, most of whom are in the restaurant business and often too wrapped up with their own livelihood to socialize, Venerable Man Che of I.B.P.S., Berlin has come up with a form of happy hour, which really runs from midnight to two in the morning every Tuesday. Participants are able to leave behind the discomfort of kitchen grease and noise of the workplace for a hearty chat, a Dharma session, or a philosophical exchange. President Ting Chêng-kuo of the Berlin chapter was among the many thankful attendees of these get-togethers. Further, 2,000 took refuge when the master conducted the ceremony in Paris. Afterwards they became B.L.I.A. members.

Awash in the Dharma rain together

While membership is approaching a million, more and more Buddhists of other races and origins are seen to join.

Fred Webb, one of three vicepresidents of the Los Angeles chapter, has for two years been most diligent in his service and devout in his faith.

The 30 or so English-speaking members who make up the Hsi Lai subchapter convene and practice Fridays at the home of president Al Duffy, and attend the English Sunday program together. Duffy, who is of Scottish descent, has received the Five Precepts and is proud to be Buddhist. Often taking time to volunteer at Hsi Lai, he greets whoever he meets the Buddhist way – lowering his head, joining his palms, and, with his American accent, saying: "Ni hao, Ê-mi-t'o Fo!"[5] A visit to Fo Kuang Shan impressed him so much that he is planning on moving to Hsi Lai Temple in two years' time. The 30-year veteran in marketing is readying himself for more active participation in the spread of the Dharma among the English-speaking masses.

Not just another religious body, Buddha's Light International Association is also a cultural bridge leading from Taiwan to the rest of the world. A case in point was the second annual convention held in Taipei's Lin-k'ou Stadium, where 30,000 representatives from around the world assembled, President Li Teng-hui attended and spoke, and the international visitors were invited on an excursion to see first-hand the present Taiwan – overall another sparkling public-relation event.

Looking into the future, Hsing Yun

[5] "Hello! Amitabha Buddha!"

hopes that eventually there will be 100 more national head associations and the whole world shall bask in the Buddha's Light and all humankind be freshened by the Dharma rain.

Integration and coexistence

The theme of its second annual convention was virtually brimming over with the richness of B.L.I.A.'s universal character – integration and coexistence. It originated from the Buddhist saying of universal kindness [and] common sympathy.

Hsing Yun's elaboration was this: "When I came to Taiwan four decades ago, I was called a monk from the mainland; after four decades, I'm still called a monk from mainland. Then, I returned to the mainland after an absence of four decades, only to be called the master from Taiwan. After years of traveling in America, Europe, and Australia, however, I don't see the bridge of my nose rising or my eyes turning blue; nor has anybody called me American or Australian. I can't help asking where I belong.

"It is all self-interest and intolerance, I've come to realize, that brew conflicts among nations and bias between races. So long as the planet Earth doesn't desert me, I'll just be an earthling. For there's only humankind. So let's treat male and female, old and young as one; let's treat rich and poor, noble and ignoble as one; let's treat all cultures and races as one. Let not Buddhists help Buddhists alone; let not the Chinese help the Chinese alone. Let's share the same existence on earth."

The concept of integration and coexistence gives those who live in this turbulent age a break and a home. On the occasion of the opening of the Paris chapter, president Chiang Chi-ming of the third subchapter was quite beside himself trying to account for his struggle: "I'm Chinese-Cambodian. I fled to France when the communists took over my country. In the first place, China wouldn't acknowledge me as Chinese. Back home, Cambodia wouldn't acknowledge me as Cambodian. Out here, France won't acknowledge me as Frenchman."

"For the longest time I was pained and

listless. That is, until what the master said struck me. I finally got it! I need to grieve no more. From this day on, I'm going to be an open-minded, compassionate, joyful, and generous earthling."

Affinities of beauty

Its tolerance and selflessness enable B.L.I.A. to extend its touch as far as Moscow in the upper north to mountain city of Ladakh 15,000 feet above sea-level. Venerable Sanghasena, president of Ladakh's Buddhist association, recounts what it feels like to be part of B.L.I.A.: "Through eight years of my term, my repute, my influence, and everything else had no way of reaching beyond Ladakh. Now, as vice-president of B.L.I.A.'s Ladakh chapter, I am able to contact with Buddhists the world over."

In addition to providing devotees with everything ranging from a spiritual haven to study and discussion groups, lectures and cultural trips, meditation classes and visits, the association opens windows in their lives. Fêng Tê-jung, who works in the department of economy and has just taken over the presidency of the Pao-kuang subchapter from his wife Kuo Li-fên, is equally animated: "From the home base of Taiwan, I can bond and walk with the rest of the world. How global net-working maximizes the space and scope of life for me!"

Behind B.L.I.A.'s charitable undertakings is an all-embracing notion: all living beings belong together. Its various branches in the United States lost no time in providing emergency relief for the recent disasters such as the flood in the midwest and the fire in Los Angeles. The winter before last, the Los Angeles chapter donated 300 packs of everyday necessaries to the homeless taken in by the First African Methodist Episcopal Church in south-central Los Angeles. The sight of the cringing, tired men as they received warmth and help from the Chinese Buddhists so moved the thankful Reverend Murray of the church that he called it "a flight across the gigantic racial and religious gap, and the transformation of love into a beautiful affinity."

Such potency of resolve

On a personal basis, Hsing Yun literally laid down the abbotship of Fo Kuang Shan to ride the crest of another set of causes and conditions, which swept him onto an even more commanding stage. Indeed, one has to give so as to get.[6]

Watching him traveling from one point to another and establishing one B.L.I.A. branch after another, one has to wonder how he has toiled: adapting incessantly, racing against time, and having to bear the unbearable. Once engine problems on a flight from New York to Sao Paulo, Brazil, took him 26 hours instead of the scheduled 11. Another time, practically everybody in the group succumbed to acute mountain sickness due to the high altitude air of Ladakh, whose temperatures range from 37 degrees Celsius in summer to subzero degrees in winter and whose

[6] *Shê-tê* in the original text. The two characters are usually used together to mean willing to give. They are also separated here to illustrate the process of giving which often results in getting.

annual rainfall averages 92 millimeters. While others were allowed to slow down somewhat, Hsing Yun still had to conducts ceremonies and meet with guests despite a splitting headache, swollen cheeks, and shortness of breath.

Such potency of resolve propelled the three-year-old B.L.I.A., R.O.C. into making the shortlist of most outstanding organizations in Taiwan for two consecutive years. In 1994 it came first in close to 2,000 candidates. Further, it is already the world's fourth largest private organization. Most of all, it is in the process of applying for nonpolitical group membership in the United Nations. While the government in Taiwan is yet to regain entry into the U.N., what may happen next is for B.L.I.A. to break out of that diplomatic deadlock.

Of wheels, of wings

The big brother of the Buddhist circle, the Chinese Buddhist Association, pales miserably before the rising star and readily slips from memory. Some speculate that B.L.I.A. is Hsing Yun's declaration of independence after years under the Chinese Buddhist Association and even a challenge to the latter. He has never formally responded to such a view except that "the founding of B.L.I.A. is to the Chinese Buddhist Association like the implementation of a courier service to the freeway system, which is all-good."

In reality, the two *are* different. the Chinese Buddhist Association is primarily of and by the sangha, and B.L.I.A., of and by devotees – many of whom are members of the social and intellectual elite with a much higher and more progressive attitude toward their faith than traditional Buddhists. And Hsing Yun sees to it that devotees play the lead and monastics take the back seat, that is, lend support and guidance to the former.

The concept of humanistic Buddhism according to Hsing Yun is the map of a globalized and living Buddhism with collaboration of monastic-run temples and devotee-run Buddha's Light International Association. Or, in laying the foundation for grander, more lasting progress, the sangha is the cement and devotees, the sand and stones. Hsing Yun wants to see the two collaborate, like the wheels of a cart or the wings of a bird.

A century ago, British colonists sailed the four seas and, through military conquest, built an empire where "the sun would never set" – its flag rising wherever the sun rises. A century later, a Chinese monk emulating the compassion, wisdom, vows, and practice of the four great Bodhisattvas[7] sowed seeds of the Dharma all over the world. With peace and tolerance, he founded Buddha's Light International Association and, thereby, let the Buddha's Light shine and Dharma water flow wherever the sun rises.

[7] Avalokitesvara, Manjusri, Ksitigarbha, and Samantabhadra. Other lists exist.

Chapter 18

Holding space in an embrace

A retrospective look at human civilization reveals religion as another entity entailing a variation of forms and visages that is evolving with the ever-changeable cultural milieu and social structure. For instance, Christianity is split into Catholicism and Protestantism, the Western church branching extensively from the Roman communion – sometimes with bloodshed. In fact, history is rife with records of warring religions and the deep scars which they have left. All in all, it seems that religion has yet to come up with a cure for the prejudice and selfishness of humankind, who apparently has yet to learn to be compassionate and tolerant.

Many doors to cultivation

How exactly did Buddhism, as old as any other, evolve?

Sakyamuni Buddha related, as early as 2,500 years ago, various methods of cultivation in accordance with the varied natural capacities of all living beings. After his passing away, disciples interpreted his teachings based on their own understanding and compiled a whole range of works. These were studied at length by generations of eminent masters, who, depending on personal interests and the source materials available to them, begot respective viewpoints of the Buddha's teachings. Hence various schools now exist.

The wandering masters took the Dharma south to Cambodia, Burma, Thailand, and Sri Lanka, and north to China, Japan, Korea, and Vietnam. This resulted in Theravada Buddhism and Mahayana Buddhism respectively. In the process, the Buddhist faith interacted with each and every set of historical, cultural, and social conditions further bringing about finer divisions such as the 50 or so schools in

Japan.

Buddhism in China, introduced during the reign of emperor Ming of the Eastern Han dynasty [58 - 75], underwent intermingling and harmonizing with the existing religions, Confucianism and Taoism, and ultimately blossomed into eight primary schools, each with its own practice and emphases. This verse conveys the big picture:

> Esotericism for the rich,
> Ch'an for the poor,
> Pureland for the convenience of all,
> Yogacara for the patient,
> San-lun[1] for emptiness,
> Hua-yen for orthodoxy,
> Vinaya for cultivation,
> And Tien-t'ai for structure of doctrine.

In other words, the T'ien-tai school emphasizes teaching and its organization; the Hua-yen, Yogacara, and San-lun schools in textual study; and the Vinaya, Ch'an, Esoteric, and Pureland schools in practice.

[1] *Chia-hsiang* in the original text, who founded the San-lun school during the reign of emperor An of the Eastern Chin dynasty (397 - 419).

The Esoteric school is otherwise known as Tibetan Buddhism due to its prevalence there. The Esoteric cultivation requires the guidance of masters. To them devotees make a practice of generous offerings, which only the more affluent can sustain. The Ch'an practitioners with their straw sandals and chipped alms-bowls aspire to enlightenment by way of simplicity, scantiness, and the emancipation from desires. And, regardless of intellect, gender, or location, those who chant the Buddha's name with utmost dedication shall attain rebirth in the Pureland. Hence the method of convenience.

Unlike other religions, each of the Buddhist schools picked its path through independent, spontaneous growth rather than mutual, contrived contention. In China, all eight schools together took center stage to further enhance the cultural pageantry of the Sui and T'ang dynasties. Although fickle imperial favoritism sparked mortal persecution of the sangha more than once,[2] never has harmony and respect been tarnished between Buddhism and other religions, or among the Buddhist schools themselves.

One master, one way

Through history, some of the eight schools of Mahayana Buddhism faded while others emerged more vibrant than ever. The evolution of Buddhism as an integral force in world history hit a snag when the southern, northern, and Tibetan divisions drifted apart due to manifold geographical and cultural factors, and barriers went up. Visionaries from different time periods called for the unified preaching of all eight schools, the harmony of the Exoteric and Esoteric,[3] and the dual practice of Ch'an and Pureland. Then, along came Hsing Yun, who would make those dreams a reality.

Hsing Yun's conviction is such that,

[2] Textual mention of the four most catastrophic cases in Chinese history in which enraged monarchs ordered the annihilation of texts, images, and the sangha, or monastics were forced to renounce their vows. The incidents took place, namely, in the 7th year (446) of the reign of emperor T'ai-wu of Northern Wei; the 2nd year (573) of the reign of emperor Wu of Northern Chou; the 5th year (845) of the reign of emperor Wu-tzung of T'ang; and the 2nd year (955) of the reign of emperor Shih-tzung of Later Chou.

[3] The twofold categorization of Buddhism according to practice. The Exoteric division or *Hsien-tzung*, comprises seven of the eight schools except the Esoteric school or *Mi-tzung*, which stands in its own division.

under founder Sakyamuni Buddha, there is only one master and one way for all, that all should be mutually caring and supportive, nondiscriminating and collaborative. This, to his mind, is what the healthful strengthening and growth of modern Buddhism must rely on.

Efforts in the last ten years, especially, have pointed toward bonding within the Buddhist circle. A feat worthy of celebration was the friendship between Hsing Yun and the Dalai Lama.

Admittedly, Tibet has been cautious about any relations with Taiwan because of political and cultural drawbacks. The exiled Dalai Lama has not once set foot on the island of Taiwan. The coming of Hsi Lai Temple soon turned all that around, however. This base in the West was like a key for the Tibetan sangha and devotees to get better acquainted with Buddhism in Taiwan. In July, 1989, the Dalai Lama and his entourage finally visited with Hsing Yun at Hsi Lai Temple.

For three hours they chatted. The Dalai Lama gave a speech afterwards. The following day, his 55th birthday, Hsing

Yun, along with almost 1,000 guests, attended the festivities. The Dalai Lama requested that Hsing Yun be seated with him during dinner so that they could pick up where they left off the day before. Many were excited because of the encounter, deemed legendary to all.

In five days the two eminent masters convened four times to lay down a specific agenda: scholarships at Hsi Lai University for the Tibetan sangha, and student-exchange between Buddhist colleges in India, Tibet and Taiwan. As a result of this, Venerable Yi Hua is currently studying at International University, India.

The Exoteric and Esoteric joining forces

The meeting was no coincidence. It was the product of years of painstaking cultivation and sowing of good seeds for the alliance of Exotericism and Esotericism.

Early in 1985, Hsing Yun initiated the Chinese -Tibetan Cultural Association of the Republic of China and the subsequent joint Dharma function of the two traditions for the preservation of the nation held in Taipei, which drew combined Chinese and Tibetan devotees of 10,000. That was the cornerstone of collaboration.

The next year, Fo Kuang Shan hosted the World Sutric and Tantric Buddhist Conference to discuss harmony in relationship to the evolution of global cultures. Three hundred participants from 19 countries and regions were there, including lamas and scholars from Nepal and India.

"Modern Buddhism is no longer regional or divisional," Hsing Yun stated, "Buddhist development should be a harmonization of Mahayana and Theravada, of the lineage both north and south, of the sangha and the lay community, of all four orders,[4] and of orthodoxy and modernity. But more crucial than the others is harmony between the Exoteric and Esoteric traditions."

Lamenting over the state of affairs in Tibetan Buddhism was clearly audible

4. Bhiksus (monks), bhiksunis (nuns), upasakas (male devotees), and upasikas (female devotees).

as the head of the Tibetan Sa-skya school spoke: "Buddhism, above all else vital to Tibet, has been devastated by the communists. But I'm exalted to see it back on its feet in Taiwan."

A whole string of activities paved the way to the later historical get-together of Hsing Yun and the Dalai Lama. The next few years saw Esoteric monastics ordained at Hsi Lai Temple or furthering their studies at Fo Kuang Shan, lamas and rinpoches spreading the Dharma in Taiwan. Hsing Yun's vision of harmony between the Exoteric and Esoteric finally took form.

Mahayana and Theravada under one roof

Whether Exoteric and Esoteric, or the Mahayana and Theravada, Hsing Yun wants to see all of them united. For the differing schools of teachings resemble flowers of differing hues and shades which, bunched together, form a delightful bouquet. "After all," he asserts, "there's but one Sakyamuni Buddha!" His book of travels, *Traces of Wandering in the Seas and*

Skies, indicates that he visited the Thai monarch and head monastic around 1961. And his visit has been reciprocated more than a few times by visiting Buddhist dignitaries from that country. From these ongoing contacts Hsing Yun is aware of the fact that not only is the status of female monastics deprecated in Theravada Buddhism, but there is also no ordination for bhiksunis. In view of this, he once proposed at length that the sangha of bhiksunis be restored.

A remarkable number of Theravada participants came to the month-long Triple Platform Ordination in 1988 at Hsi Lai Temple. In the process, the wall of regionalism that has separated the south and north for more than 1,000 years was broken down. Those invited to pass on the precepts included eminent masters from the southern and northern schools. And, among the 200 or so preceptees were monastics of the Theravada tradition as well as disciples of the Tibetan Esoteric school. Many of them were monastics of high seniority seeking to repeat their vows and intellectuals with superior academic credentials devoting themselves to Buddhism.

Three languages – Mandarin, the Taiwanese dialect, and English – were employed for the explication of the precepts, which were passed on irrespective of gender or school. So overwhelming was the number of participants, nations, and schools that the success of the event was unprecedented in the history of Buddhism.

At the end of the preceptoral period, preceptees took with them lessons learned from a thorough exchange among themselves as regards traditions, concepts, ceremonies, discipline, and doctrine - the most inclusive and globalized experience possible so far in Buddhism.

Last spring, Hsing Yun was off to Thailand's Dhammakaya Foundation, a brother temple, for the casting ceremony of its golden Buddha. He was driven through streets strewn with flowers and lined with 100,000 persons who were there to greet him – an unprecedented honor for a Mahayana monastic in a Theravada country. White Pagoda Temple in Los Angeles, which was the forerunner of Hsi Lai Temple, has been turned over to the Dhammakaya International Society of California to serve as the base of Thai Buddhism in America.

Others closely associated with Fo Kuang Shan include Tōdai Temple in Nara, Japan, the Japanese Buddhist visiting group, the Nichiren school, and the Ts'ao-tung school. Venerable Jung Woo of Tong-do Sa (Temple), Korea, heads the Asian liaison committee of B.L.I.A.

Dual practice of Ch'an and Pureland

For the harmony of Exotericism and Esotericism, the inclusion of the Mahayana and Theravada, and the collaboration of all eight schools, Hsing Yun's resolution has never faltered. He even chooses to view in a positive light the criticism of sectarianism from Taiwan's Buddhist circle, maintaining that it is an indication of prosperity and a sign of versatility. Like the four legendary mountains in China coexisting over time, he says, it is from the school of Sakyamuni Buddha that all Buddhists invariably descend.

Despite the similar dominance of Ch'an and Pureland in Taiwan, Hsing Yun, being the 48th patriarch of the Lin-chi school of Ch'an, will not be confined to a certain school. In creating the first chanting sessions back in Ilan, he also boosted the Pureland method of aspiring for rebirth in the Ultimate Bliss by way of calling on Amitabha Buddha's name. Furthermore, he is credited for the popularity of meditation these days, as it is a regular feature in all branch temples of Fo Kuang Shan. Its new meditation hall is the largest, best equipped in Taiwan with the most vigorous discipline. The meditation facility of the Taipei Temple close to Sungshan train station, serves the hard-pressed city folks as a convenient location for practice.

Revering the masters, prodding the newcomers

To the venerables and masters in Taiwan, Hsing Yun is indiscriminately cordial and courteous. Among these, Master Ching Kung was invited to the Buddhist college to speak on the study of Yogacara, Master Liao

Chung on the *Sandhi-nirmocana Sutra,* Master Tung Ch'u on the Chinese monasterial system, and Master Yin Shun on the Dharma, along with Nan Huai-chin to conduct seven-day meditation retreats.

Universal Gate magazine, though headquartered at Fo Kuang Shan, reports monthly on temples all over Taiwan and is in numerous ways a communication center for the Buddhist circle.

To the up and coming generations of monastics, Hsing Yun is especially supportive. He prodded the formation of the Chinese Buddhist Youth Association, and helped fund the founding of Venerable Chêng Yen's Ching-ssŭ Vihara. Since then, each time he lectured in Hualien where the latter is located, he would open with this line: "What a wonderful place Hualien is! The landscape is so lovely, and the air so fresh. Above all, Hualien is where the Buddhist Compassion Relief Tzu Chi Foundation[5] is!"

5. One of the most acclaimed Buddhist charitable organizations in Taiwan. Its founder is Reverend Chêng Yen.

His advice for young monastics is to break the stubborn habit of older generations in not ever communicating among themselves. He urges dialogue and teamwork irrespective of differing thoughts, and the common goal of bringing Buddhism onto new heights. Over time, he has enlisted plenty of backing from them, who often resonate his call by joining him on his lecture tours.

The beauty of religious accord

What does it mean to hold space in one embrace and gauge the worlds as numerous as the sands of the Ganges?

Hsing Yun upholds harmony both within and without Buddhism. He once analogized the human quest for the true, the good, and the beautiful with journeying toward a certain destination. The yearning being the same, it is only the ways that are different. We can choose to bike, drive, ride, fly, or sail to get there, different religions really lead to the same end.

Once in the early years, a band of some 80 Dominican priests and nuns came to Fo Kuang Shan with the purpose of learning about the Dharma; so did a bishop from the Vatican a couple of years back. Hsing Yun and archbishop Lo Kuang once held a brilliant exchange on religion, philosophy, life, and faith. The two masters, both compassionate and wise, came to the agreement that religions must be tolerant of one another. For there are always differences to be had amidst similarities, and similarities to be sought amidst differences. In their concern for the times and commitment to purify minds, the respect and affirmation they had for each other was beautiful to behold.

Later, at the request of the archbishop, Hsing Yun spoke on the wondrous use of Ch'an at Fu Jen Catholic University.

Sharing their concern for the chaotic society, Hsing Yun joined archbishop Lo Kuang, Protestant minister Reverend Chou Lien-hua, and vice secretary-general Chang Ch'êng-ch'i of the Taoist Association, in an in-depth discourse on the reconstruction of values to prevent social disintegration. The gathering was conducted by *Global View Monthly* for the religious leaders.

On the completion of the Taipei Temple in February 1994, a 49-day lecture series, titled *The Running Water of Life*, featured such animated speakers from other religions as Father Ting Sung-yun of the Catholic institute of Kuang-ch'i Shê, and Shih Yung-kuei, a Moslem. The event was in every way a display of the beauty of religious accord.

Still another time, Chung Jung-chi called for a rally of leaders from various religious schools: Islam, Protestantism, Catholicism, and others. Hsing Yun hosted the event with a discussion on vegetarianism and Ch'an.

Last year, he donated the royalties from his writings to six needy organizations, namely, Taipei Relief Foundation for Women, Sunshine Foundation, Hsin-lu Cultural Foundation, Christian Ch'ên-hsi Society, Yi-kuang Society for Volunteers, and Shan-mu Society for Catholic Nuns. Like the mandara flowers on all living beings, his own all-inclusive showering graciousness is expressed: "To give is not just about asking society to give alms to Buddhism. We as Buddhists must give alms, too!"

Tolerance for folk religions

What about all those mystical folk religions out there?

Hsing Yun could not have phrased it better: "Correct belief surpasses superstitious belief; superstitious belief surpasses nonbelief; and nonbelief surpasses evil belief."

Beliefs, like learning, are widely varied in depth and sophistication. But, so long as they are committed to doing good, Hsing Yun has every reason to believe that they should all be valued.

"I remember back home in Yangchou," he recounts, "no police patrol would be in sight in tens of *li*, or a court of justice in hundreds. So what could be done when people got into a dispute?"

"What happened was that the parties concerned would go and pray at the temples of the earth gods, and all would be solved. For the townsfolk were unwavering believers of the law of causality and harbored a perfect willingness to be tried before the deities."

Hsing Yun for his own orthodoxy has never ventured to set himself apart from the others. Quite the contrary, he remains affirmative about the positive effects which deities such as Ma-chu and the earth gods have given the common folk, and takes a stance of tolerance and respect toward folk religions. For sure he does not tolerate the charlatans whose practice does nothing but jeopardizes social well-being under the quise of supernatural power. They belong to what Hsing Yun describes as *evil belief*.

Buddhism is in no way superstitious; nor is Hsing Yun superstitious. Many, speculating on the sophistication of his personal practice, are tempted to badger him with questions about divination, physiognomy, and geomancy, or with prying curiosity about the supernatural powers he might or might not possess.

These are his least favorite topics. Instructions in the *Sutra of the Buddha's Exhortation Left After His Passing* for the Buddhist practice run as this: "Do not engage in divination; do not practice astrology." For none of these are in accord with the causes and conditions, correct livelihood , and the rules and principles. One of his pet sayings is: "When joy is in the heart, everyday is a good day and every place a good place."

Ahead of his time

History is to be rid of the fatalism of contending humans and their nature or, plainly, humans at war. Neither World Wars sufficed to awaken the innate good in us, it seems. The end of another century looms, wails of carnage and destruction have not ceased. This must be the moment, if no other, for him to lead us out of darkness. The visionary and gallant Hsing Yun has expended half a lifetime patching and repairing Buddhism, bonding with other religions, tapping social resources, and creating a diversified and all-encompassing religious model. Ahead of his time, Hsing Yun sheds a light on peaceful coexistence among human beings. And he does so in a superlative style.

Part VI

Returning on wings of his vows

Sitting with friends and
Venerable Tzu Hui, Australia, 1991
(Courtesy of Liao Hui-mei)

Launching a basketball match – his favorite sport (Courtesy of Huang Ming-wei)

Desk-bound (Courtesy of Chen Chih-min)

Being honored for outstanding socio-cultural achievements

Breaking ground for Fo Kuang University, 1993

With disciples

At his 60th birthday,
Fo Kuang Shan, 1987

With other sentient beings

Sitting for a portrait
(Courtesy of Tseng Yao-chih)

Chapter 19

Heart of a child

Once somebody asked him what the reality of life is.

"Life," he replied, "is half in the Buddha's world and half in the devil's world; it is half advancing and half retreating."

At the end of close to seventy winters and summers, he believes, he is able to "be free in accordance with the heart, settled in accordance with the environment, acting in accordance with joy [for others], and living in accordance with conditions" because he has mastered this *half-and-half* principle.

Just the right dose of unworldly and worldly sentiments

Quintessentially above and beyond the three realms while still roving amidst the defilements of the world, Hsing Yun is, to outsiders, as enigmatic as he is familiar. Not unnaturally, many itch for a look into his personal life and his private feelings. In regard to the latter, it must be said that, all along, he has been the master of his own heart and has managed just the right dose of unworldly and worldly sentiments.

Callow as he was in those early days, he missed being around his mother and siblings and being home. But, having entered the monkhood, the austere discipline and his master's expectations had, over time, kept him away much more than he might have wanted. In that way, Hsing Yun was able to sublimate his personal emotions with the help of religious practice. Then, on the eve of his flight from the mainland, he chose to bid farewell and reveal his plans to spread the Dharma in Taiwan to his master rather than to his mother. His family had not the slightest inkling of where he had drifted during the next four decades.

In Taiwan, the pursuit of settling the sangha and sacrificing for the Dharma dispelled much of his private longings. However, thoughts of loved ones would invade the stillest of nights. And, ever since reconnecting with them a few years back, he has taken upon himself the responsibility to care for them – 100 or more relatives in all – as though he were repaying some mountainous debt of forty years. Needless to say, he was willing to bend in any good way he could to bring pleasure to his mother, who was stunned by the thousand or so monastics inhabiting Fo Kuang Shan.

"Are they all under you?" she asked him.

"Yes," he replied, "but I alone am under you!"

He made every effort to be with her on her birthday the past two years. Back in Yü-hua (Rain-soaked Blossom) Vihara, Nanjing, the master was but the son of a regular family once again. He would let the congee cool off before she consumed it, or sit by her bedside and reminisce with her. A master of international repute would then become the humblest listener.

A tree, about to fall down, finds the wind unceasing as ever; a child, readied to repay his parents, finds them no longer around. While he treasures every chance to be filial to his mother, he is filled with regret for Master Chih K'ai. For it took him years to fully comprehend the profound caring beneath the sternness of the master, who was killed in the Cultural Revolution. On his homecoming five years ago, a stricken Hsing Yun broke down completely at the graveside of Master Chih K'ai and, on subsequent visits, makes it a point to go and chant a sutra there.

Repay a drop of water with a gushing spring

For Hsing Yun to harbor perpetual thoughts of his biological mother and ancestral master is a matter of course; just as he bears in mind whoever has helped or supported him. To them he is sure to repay every single drop received with a gushing spring.

It was a time of extreme turmoil when

he graduated from Chiao-shan Buddhist College and became principal at White Pagoda Primary School in 1947. To evade the bandits, guerrillas, and soldiers, he was compelled to go into hiding with his teaching staff for days. There was a loyal worker at the school who would bring them food daily despite the extreme perils. Never has Hsing Yun forgotten him. On his first homecoming five years ago, he made a point of reestablishing contact. Finally, he tracked down the family. Braving a heavy downpour one day and bearing gifts and good will, he visited them. "Even though the man [who had helped us] is no longer with us," he told his disciples later, "his son is, and I'm no less grateful. That's why I've every reason to go on taking care of his offspring."

Another person to whom he shall forever be thankful is the late Sun-Chang Ch'ing-yang. From the time he came to Taiwan all alone to the founding of Fo Kuang Shan, Madam Sun treated him like one of her own and protected the Dharma with all her might. During her last days, Hsing Yun took time out to be with her whenever he could and, when he could not, would make sure that his disciples would take his place. On her passing away, he conducted her funeral and undertook to execute her will with utter meticulousness. Chang Fo-ch'ien, a writer, described the memorial service presided over by Hsing Yun for Madam Sun as the most impressive and solemn one he had ever seen.

His teachers – Masters Yüan Chan, Hsüeh Fan, Ho Ch'ên, and Hui Chuang – he had flown to America as an expression of his gratitude. When Master Shêng P'u fell ill last year, he made sure that his Chinese language teacher be amply provided for and properly treated.

Although tradition has it that monastics see everything as empty and act like withered wood, it is not quite Hsing Yun's way. When it is time to be warm and tender, his warmth and tenderness surpass most.

More than a few embarrassing moments

Many wonder about the private world of his inner feelings. Those who have known

Hsing Yun since the early days or those who have chanced upon pictures back then cannot get over how distinguished the young monk looked: his 180-centimeter stature and his piercing eyes, his grandeur and his eloquence. Thus superiorly endowed, was he ever subject to temptation as such? Or, was he ever touched in any way?

Seasoned as he is today, Hsing Yun has no qualms about telling how, when he was a twenty-something monasterial director at Ta-chüeh Temple, overly doting parents were seized by the wishful thought of adopting him and several, with the happiness of their daughters in mind, would try to dissuade him from the monkhood. And, admittedly, more than a few young women devotees were seen to frequent the two temples, Lei-yin and Shou-shan, out of a special regard for the smashing young monk rather than for the Buddha – a confession from the now mellow bunch.

Su Hsiu-ch'in, a longtime follower in Kaohsiung, recalls how she and others used to share the purest admiration for the splendor of the master's Dharma appearance, and draw the line between feelings for the Dharma and feelings of love.

Still, the media would, from time to time, publish what they deemed to be clues to the secret life of a master monastic. Somehow, these no longer bother him nearly as much as they used to, and he dismisses them as sheer unfounded gossips.

One of the more drastic cases was that of a woman in her seventies who was obsessed with what she considered an entwinement with the master through seven lifetimes. One day, she dropped by Fo Kuang Shan demanding to see the master as usual. But this time round, she was with two handsome young men. Along the way the trio ran into the master, who was giving visitors a tour of the premises. The next instant, she was ordering the young men to get down on their knees, saying: "This is your father! Address him right now!" The young men, visibly embarrassed, had to comply but returned later to apologize for their mother's obsession. Hsing Yun had no problem whatsoever with the episode. What the bystanders thought was another question.

An equally obsessive high school teacher used to approach the podium with copies of books midway through Hsing Yun's lectures. When asked about her intent, her reply was a illusive "I want to pluck that cloud from the sky." Once Hsing Yun was waiting by the elevator when she emerged from nowhere to adjust his collar for him. The few who saw this were flabbergasted and Hsing Yun was rendered utterly helpless. Who could have thought something like this would happen to him?

Still another time, one of Fo Kuang Shan's most ardent supporters suddenly announced her dissociation for the most ludicrous of reasons: the master was taking a fifth concubine, or so she had heard. It turned out that the sower of the vicious rumor was a former teacher at the nursery who was dismissed for her misconduct. And the master, for all his innocence, had not even the slightest inkling of who she was.

Faithful for half a century

Half a century since his tonsure, Hsing Yun has abided by the monastic precepts throughout, and his conscience is clear in the face of temptation and distortion of any form. To Buddhism he has been faithful in that he never allowed any affection to carry him away. For deep down, his is a boundless world of sentiment, and his love is not for one but for all.

"All elders under heaven are my folks," he says, "all children my own, and all people my family."

"Monastics, too, have an endless love about them. Only it is more endless, more wonderful, and more sublime."

"A sublime sentiment becomes compassion, which asks for no return. A sentiment asking for no return is wisdom."

For his love many seek to repay him with love and respect, and they do not hesitate to let him know that. On the master's 68th birthday in 1993, devotees from every corner of Taiwan came to Fo Kuang Shan and gave him a three-evening gala salute.

Love for all creatures

He loves all creatures large and small. Pigeons have been his favorite companions since he was young, and for years they would stop by and feed on his window sill at Fo Kuang Shan. Should he be away at times he would see to it that they were treated to grain and water just the same.

Hsiao-chün, a stray puppy who took shelter at the Buddhist college, displayed the Buddha nature by attending every lecture with amazing concentration. Hsiao-chün would always rise on the approach of Hsing Yun but, as he advanced in years, slowed down visibly. One day, Hsing Yun was speaking with students in the corridor when he spotted Hsiao-chün struggling to get up again. Out of consideration for the aging dog, the master simply slipped into an office without having to inconvenience him any further.

Lai-fa, another puppy, was barely a month old when he was taken to Fo Kuang Shan. His home for the ensuing six or seven years would be Hsing Yun's door. There it stood guard whether the master was entertaining or out lecturing. Then, one day, Lai-fa was gone. Hsing Yun missed him a bit. A few months later, someone brought along another puppy which, strangely enough, resembled Lai-fa in color, disposition, and even movement. Everyone called it Lai-fa, Jr. Hsing Yun cared for junior the same way he did senior until junior died of old age. A chanting service was held in his memory.

Simple, simplicity

Visitors at Fo Kuang Shan marvel at how a temple can be so magnificent, so modern, and so worldly – all at the same time. What meets the eye is for the joy and convenience of everyone. It is an extension of goodwill and, most of all, a reflection of the *advancing* aspect of Hsing Yun's life. Yet watching him conduct himself daily, one also comes to realize the existence of a *retreating* aspect.

Regarding clothing, his favorite line is: "Simplicity is basic for a monastic." He alternates between a couple of robes all the year round, adding thermal wear or a knit sweater underneath when the temperature plunges. A 3- or 4-centimeter, centipede-like pattern on his left shoe turns out to be a tear which he neatly sewed himself. Both shoes are in fact quite battered in the sole, showing the linen padding already. When asked why they are not replaced, he says: "They've been like this for a while. I guess they can't get any worse, can they?"

The way he eats sometimes is another wonder. He will run in holding a bowl of steaming plain noodles, cool it before the air-conditioner, devour it, and dash off again to his next commitment. Decades, one can say, have been rushed through in such a way.

Dining with him is both a pleasure and a pressure. While the host keeps helping his guests with sumptuous amounts of food, he himself merely touches a couple of the dishes closest to him. He never replenishes his bowl by taking from more than one dish, and finishes fast.

Little known is the fact that Hsing Yun takes after his father who was skilled in vegetarian cooking. In the long list of his personal creations, peanut tofu, tomato noodles, imperial bean noodles, and arhat soup are among Fo Kuang Shan's most requested dishes and their preparation is required of all the cooking staff. Whenever the temple was swamped with visitors in the early days, Hsing Yun could be seen in his apron helping out with the fried noodles. He has not done much of that lately but, last year in Hong Kong, I was thrilled to have feasted on an ethereal dish he made for everyone: twisted fritters and tender pea shoots. The plate was emptied in no time.

His favorite food is really no more than plain noodles sprinkled with soy sauce and sesame oil, or rice soaked in water and served with fermented bean curd from Ilan. His taste buds have become most adaptable as he ranges from one place to another and are perfectly at home with anything from Japanese and Korean pickled vegetables to American bread. The only things from which he refrains are fruit, tonic food, and vitamins.

Everywhere is his home

"Even heaven and earth feel small when the heart is full, but a bed feels spacious when the heart is free." As spacious as Fo Kuang Shan is, for years his quarters consisted only of a cubicle in the corridor of Chüan-têng Chamber until he moved into the Founder's Quarters, which Venerable Hsin Ping built in his honor two years ago.

Not having a permanent home, the roving monk is just as comfortable aboard a trans-Pacific jet as he is in a car on the freeway, and is certainly restful in both. What really bothers him is extravagance. Once on a lecture tour, the Korean master who was his host reserved for him the presidential suite in a five-star hotel. He did no more than sit in one of the chairs and, pull up a corner of the bedding, curling up for the night. Totally unaccustomed to luxury, he could not bear to spoil the impeccable setting.

Like many who have seen the worst of times, Hsing Yun learned to be frugal the hard way, and fame has not changed that. There is this anecdote which his disciples love to tell. Each time the master is abroad preaching, he has at hand a bunch of U.S. dollars for the purpose of establishing good affinities. At the same time, all the tissue paper he uses on the plane, restaurants, or washrooms, he uses once, then folds neatly and keeps in his pocket, thinking none should be squandered. Once on his return, an attendant helping him unpack found as many as 70 or more pieces of tissue paper in his pocket. "The master left home with U.S. dollars," he declared, quite amused, "and returned with tissue paper!"

Vimalakirti once said: "With the Dharma joy, I no longer relish worldly joys." Hsing Yun, too, rarely buys for himself, and the last time he did so, he had to borrow money from Venerable Tzu Hui to get a larger wrist-watch while in transit in Japan only because his eyesight is failing.

A disciple was moved beyond words when she saw, one day, the master pull out a NT$1,000 note with utmost caution and hand it over to someone, saying: "Respect it, and there will be more!"

Relinquishing, he views the five desires and six defilements as illusions; receiving, he views the great chiliocosm of three kinds of thousands of chiliocosms and all living beings as his wealth.

Hard on himself, easy on others

Hard he has always been on himself but not so on others. As always, offerings from devotees are completely channeled to the temple to facilitate a multitude of projects. "I know not if it's a positive or negative aspect of my character," he remarked, "but I am not able to keep any money. I tend to look for every chance to part with it." With his stipend, for instance, he loves bringing everyone a little something each time he comes home from a trip. That is, along with his care and appreciation.

His heaviest *investment* as such is on the young. All the disciples currently studying abroad are financed by Fo Kuang Shan. On top of that, Hsing Yun visits them whenever he can and leaves them extra funds from his own pocket.

He met Venerables Chi Ch'ün and Hsiu Yung from Hsiamên Buddhist College in Hong Kong the summer before last. They had a cordial exchange. Hsing Yun gave them a handsome collection of texts, including the *Fo Kuang Encyclopedia* and *Hsing Yun's Lecture Series*, and urged them to return home to work hard for Buddhism on the mainland. Parting, they prostrated to thank him. Hsing Yun hastened to help them up and handed over a red packet, which he had just received from a devotee some ten minutes before. The pair left with tears in their eyes. Monetary matters may be mundane but, when given out of sincerity become a universal sustenance.

Indeed, as a monastic, he lives a simple and frugal life. "I've never held the key to my room," he notes, "nor are any of my letters ever hidden, or my whereabouts unknown."

The world is as large as the heart that can hold it

Verily, the world is as large as the heart that can hold it. In the same way, how much we can achieve depends on how much we can tolerate. The reason Hsing Yun is capable of creating the most expansive Buddhist body worldwide hinges on the broadness of his mind, which enables him to break through monastic conformity.

Author Lin Ch'ing-hsüan and director

Liu Wei-pin were doing a documentary on location at Fo Kuang Shan years ago when Liu was suddenly smitten with the idea of shooting from the top of the offering table before the Buddha. At such innovation and professionalism, Hsing Yun's approval was just as prompt. Lin also recalls his stupefaction in watching a game of basketball by the sangha at Fo Kuang Shan – led by the master himself.

Hsing Yun once said that what holds the most indelible place in his heart is not the majestic structures of Fo Kuang Shan but the basketball court in Tung Shan. The sports enthusiast that he is almost faced expulsion when he resorted to building his own hoop because the Buddhist college curriculum then did not include physical education. Since that time he yearned for a basketball court, especially when he came to have his own temple. He used to have the time of his life playing in the evenings with the disciples, the only pity being the occasional interruption in which he had to quit halfway and hurry off to greet visitors – still sweating from the game.

An advocate for basketball among the

sangha, he hopes that, with more exercise comes better health for them. Also, basketball is representative of

- fairness, justice, openness, personal progress, valiance, speed
- group spirit, glory for all, collaboration
- honesty, humility, obedience, kindness
- love for the opponents without whom there could not be a game in the first place

The basketball court is really where, between master and disciples, the Dharma – not just the ball – is passed on, and bonding – not just competition – is completed. Despite being *banned* from the sport after fracturing his leg, he still does his three-pointers, though from a wheelchair. For 27 years, those at Fo Kuang Shan have all turned out to play in the annual basketball tournament celebrating the master's birthday!

Heart of a child

Those around him tell of a personable and fun-loving character. Author Yao Cho-ch'i spent a month with Hsing Yun on his homecoming in 1989. Yao remembers how the master bought a panda hand-puppet at the entrance to the Ming tombs in Beijing and became very dextrous handling it with three fingers. He would hide it in his sleeve and pull it out to greet whoever passed by, winning laughs and hearts.

A good number of those traveling with him at the time were lay devotees for whom the abrupt switch to vegetarianism was somewhat taxing, especially in view of the meaty cuisine along the way. Finally in Xian, seven of them could no longer refrain and, at the direction of the local guide, were about to sneak out for a feast of mutton when they bumped right into the master.

"Why," he laughed, "going somewhere for a bite?"

They had little choice but to tell the truth.

"Watch out," the master added. "It's probably safer to have the chef at the hotel prepare it for you."

The next day, a full course nonvegetarian meal was laid out before them – including mutton. Everyone had a pretty good idea where it all came from.

Another time in Japan, at the close of the B.L.I.A. executive meeting, he amused himself – and others – holding his cane at his chest as though it were a rifle to salute everyone at the hotel entrance.

Not bothering anyone

To be a monastic of exceptional calibre in an age of professionalism must be extra trying. But, that is exactly what Hsing Yun is, exceptional, and what he has achieved is professionalism.

His meticulousness makes him an infallible host, who makes sure that all lights are on and the roads are clear before a tour commences, seats are in order, air-conditioning functioning, and tea ample before a meeting begins, so that guests shall feel at home.

After three years alongside Hsing Yun on the television program *Hsing Yun's Dharma Words*, producer Ch'ên T'ai has only this to say: "Top-notch!" Ch'ên recalls the master having no misgivings whatsoever about going to great lengths for a perfect shot. Once, after three or four hours under seven 5,000V spotlights, he stayed composed and smiling as ever. Not his disciples though, they were ready to cry foul: "The master is going to be roasted!"

Although nearing age 70, Hsing Yun is nonetheless young at heart and receptive, and forever an impeccable role model to disciples and followers. In the way he walks, pulls the door, or opens a drawer, he causes no disturbance. He takes care of his own chores, like shaving his own head, laundering his own clothes, and cleaning up after himself at each bath – even in the hotels. As the saying goes: "Rather move the water of one thousand rivers, but not disturb the heart of the practitioner."

He is most attentive to the thoughts of the young and the needs of disciples and followers, and rarely negates them. Never commanding, his words for anyone acting out of line are: "If I were in your place, I might try another approach – it may bring better results." Truly that is what it means by "criticism, should not be too harsh, it must be acceptable; instructions, should not be too demanding, they must be feasible."

Unlike the stereotypical greying monk lost in meditation, Hsing Yun raves over fun. "Joy," he often tells those who are down, "is the indoor sunshine." He refuses to be persuaded that anything is unsolvable.

"Joy," he adds, coming up with the smartest analogy, "is like perfume. Spray it on others a bit more generously and we're sure to catch a few drops ourselves."

"When one rule is understood, all else shall be clear." Over time he has gained a certain fluidity and sophistication. "Failing in work is acceptable," he often says, "but not in getting along with others." And only when time, space, and human relationships are pursued to perfection can all be happy.

Reading up on life

His credentials, though informal, stem from a lifetime of self-study. Text after text have gone from his side and his desk to the various collections of Fo Kuang Shan's dozen or so cultural departments and eight libraries. He relishes the few pages read before bedtime no matter how long the day has been, and his reading materials include the biographies of the eminent masters, the classics, martial arts fiction, science fiction, journals, and newspapers.

Books are his gifts to disciples and friends, and he speaks often of reading as a source of happiness. It must not result in defilement but joy, he says, and must accord with one's nature and inclinations. The force of learning should underlie professionalism, not paper qualifications. Most of all, the truly learned should be a thorough reader of the texts of life and humanity.

Many are curious about the worldliness with which he was reared in monkhood. The reason is he is the best listener there is. Visitors, friends, devotees, and disciples he heeds with patience and humbleness, and he learns from them. He once called himself a sponge soaking up information and retaining it, or a computer storing select views and ideas and turning them into his own.

Acceptability and feasibility

T'ang poet Tu Fu once said: "One who reads thousands of texts pens with utmost spontaneity and eloquence." Hsing Yun is one of the most prolific authors among the monastics in Taiwan. He took years to train himself. He will not forget the lean years in which, instead of finding pen and paper to jot down his thoughts, he could only keep them close to his heart. He used to make mental drafts while at meals or in line for the shrine and still does the same while on the road. Perhaps that is one reason for the spontaneity and compactness of his writing.

Understandably, Hsing Yun's style is easy and popular. He does not hesitate to pick up diction evolved with the changing times and incorporate it into his writing. Critiqued as "seasoned and essential, simple and lasting," his format is lively and his language unpretentious, but his intent is profound. His own favorite author is Kumarajiva , a brilliant translator of some of the most chanted sutras. Hsing Yun's principle in writing is that it should be simply understandable, readily accepted, and easily incorporated into life.

A living treasure-trove

Followers have long realized that the master is a living treasure-trove. A recent discovery is his calligraphy. The Dharma sayings in brush and ink rendered in his spare time – if any – he gives devotees in appreciation of their dedication. He is humble about his own ancestral background, which was nowhere near academic, and about his lack of practice, which he says has consisted of no more than writing up posters and couplets for lecture halls. That he is able to make gifts of his calligraphy is, first and foremost, a surprise to himself.

Hsing Yun has dedication of character - one of forgetting both the world and the self, and treating oneself and others as one. This permeates his calligraphy, which has become increasingly sought-after among collectors. Some of these now fetch hundreds and thousands of dollars, as in the recent fundraising art auctions for Fo Kuang University. At the same time, he does not think twice about rendering a piece expressly for a twelve-year-old who pledges NT$100.

Living is joy, dying is not necessarily grief

Despite basking in the Dharma for half a century, Hsing Yun, like all others, is merely sojourning in a physical body which is subject to the changes of birth, aging, infirmity, and death. Principled in the joy for others as he is, he hardly ever mentions his health conditions. The fact is that diabetes is affecting his vision and memory somewhat, even his skin. Disciples and followers lose no time to ask him to slow down, and some have offered herbal medications and other prescriptions. Li Wu-yen, a follower of thirty years and a radiologist, has gone down on his knees more than a few times pleading that the master should take his medical check up.

"There's but one human," he answered with that lightness of his, "one life, and one heart."

Others have not been as casual about the master's race against time. "The position can be replaced but not the person or the prestige." They speculate, what would happen to Fo Kuang Shan should he pass away?

To that, his answer is ready. "I've no fear for death," he says, "for death is a matter of course. Not that we who have our religion won't die. No, it's just that, in the face of death, we know that it is not the end but the beginning of another existence."

"I often use the analogy of death as moving home or changing into a new garment. Life and death, death and life, are really two in one, one in two. Living is certainly joy; dying is not necessarily grief."

"Fret not for Fo Kuang Shan when I'm gone. Hasn't it fared well since I left the abbotship? It's been established to be in accordance with the Dharma and it is systemized under healthy leadership. This is a pure, harmonious, and joyful sangha. There's no need to draw any connection between the fate of Fo Kuang Shan and mine."

Free to follow conditions

Irrespective of others' admiration, or concerns or doubts, Hsing Yun's self-evaluation is this - lifting the weighty as though it were light; following the conditions of freedom through one life. Ch'an master Chih Hsien of Hsiangyen (Fragrant Rock) depicted the same in a verse:

> Devoid of marks and traces anywhere,
> Splendor rules beyond sights and sounds.

Thus Hsing Yun wrote in his diary:

> I embrace the vow of compassion
> to deliver all beings,
> I float like an untied boat
> in the Dharma sea;
>
> Ask me what merits have I
> over a lifetime,
> They are the Buddha's Light
> across the land.

Indeed that is how he views his

whole existence.

As he puts it this way, everyone is the architect of his/her own fate. A Buddhist who has undertaken to revive his own faith and who lives out his life, marches on – never turning back. He is an ordinary monk who is quite an extraordinary leader while leading a sincere and pious life.

Chapter 20

Buddhist path only

Viewed from afar, Hsing Yun is a vigorous monastic who weaves his way in and out between the Buddha gate and the secular world, and everywhere in between. He is a marvelous discerner who ranges over the past, present, and future; an erudite man of letters who writes and speaks with the utmost eloquence; a peaceful character of infinite affinities who befriends all levels of beings. He is a dynamic business magnate of international repute who originates and handles mega corporate planning and financing. The thought of such a versatile monastic might make one wonder if there is any other like him. Or, even, if he has gone somewhat too far.

A scrutiny of his past – his thoughts, sayings, and deeds – reveals a life that has been principled in Buddhahood and little else. Bearing the surname of Shih,[1] Hsing Yun is committed to vitalizing his religion and, moreover, to delivering the world by means of the Dharma.

As the study of life, the teachings of the Buddha is about the truth of all matters and things within the universe. Methods of interpretation and dissemination may vary to agree with changing times and circumstances. But, the doctrine and spirit are the essence and never quite depart from the Buddhist ancestry. Hence in advocating humanistic Buddhism, Hsing Yun aspires to transform traditional Buddhism into a fine new tool for the resolution of contemporary issues.

[1] As in Shih-chia Mo-ni, the Chinese transliteration of Sakyamuni Buddha. Hence the surname Shih for all Chinese monastics.

The Dharma, environmentally friendly for the mind

The 20th century spirals, both visibly and audibly, into a maelstrom of natural disasters, human hostilities, deceit and plunder. All living beings find themselves seeking to catch their breaths or trying to survive in constant fear, uncertainty, and restlessness. Environmental preservation of the physical world is crucial on a planet stricken with problems of landfill, air pollution, sewage, and unrelenting land exploitation. Social issues concern a society afflicted with problems of politics, crime, and poor relationships. Spiritually there is a general mentality plagued by loneliness, emptiness, and confusion.

Hsing Yun has indeed come up with a rational and legitimate resolution which is steeped in the spirit of humanistic Mahayana Buddhism. How to live with family and be with relatives; how to love spouses and care for friends; how to relate to society; how to handle the resources of everyday life; and how to tackle matters of finance, religion, health, medicine, politics, society, and the world at large.

Apart from its manifestations in education, culture, and charitable causes, Hsing Yun's humanistic Buddhism also assumes many other forms. For example, teaching by qualified speakers from both the sangha and lay community; consultation for those seeking guidance and advice in careers, family, and other relationships; emergency relief; shelter for the aged, infirm, and disabled; and others.

Believers are many, but practitioners are few, so says Lian Chen, head of the supervisory council in Taiwan. He is aware of much greater enthusiasm for material donations to gather merits than in spiritual cultivation for the elevation of the mind and betterment of society. Hsing Yun agrees, and he looks forward to a more rooted understanding – not blind adherence – of the Dharma and a much broader adaptation of its values by all.

Laying the groundwork

When many rave over the coming of a

brand new epoch in Buddhism, one of unprecedented influence, esteem, and promise, Hsing Yun is at once elated and wary. For beneath the surface prosperity of the Buddhist faith, a range of structural issues remain unsolved.

For years Hsing Yun, [a monastic] whose life is pledged to the Triple Gems, has called for a progressively solidified groundwork: the establishment of a modern system; the betterment of the quality of the sangha; the expansion of Buddhist enterprises; and the promotion of humanistic Buddhism.

In fact, the absence of a unified system in Buddhism worries him greatly. The state of affairs in Taiwan, in particular, resembles loose sand. On the one hand, the increasingly affluent society has little problem supporting a proportionately growing sangha. On the other, even monastics relatively superficial in cultivation and knowledge are now able to round up a bunch of devotees, put up their temples, conduct Dharma functions, take their own disciples, confer precepts, and enjoy their share of sustenance.

For chronic lawlessness, however, Fo Kuang Shan provides a cure in its comprehensive systemization covering all possible areas: personnel, finance, monasterial administration, preaching, Dharma functions, tonsure, precepts, and many more.

A far cry from any form of monasterial renaissance, the systematic rules and disciplines in Hsing Yun's mind are modern and convenient. They are instrumental in the unification and evolvement of Buddhism as a whole.

A lame-duck law

Just what has kept a unified system from prevailing in the Buddhist circle of Taiwan? A lame-duck law. The supervisory regulation for monasteries implemented by the nationalist government as far back as 1929 is mandatory only for Buddhism and Taoism, no other religions – not even the occult. Alive and well to this day, its consequences are grave. With the abbot playing second fiddle to the monasterial supervisor, too often either the sangha is overpowered by lay people or the two groups lock horns constantly. In some cases, devotees are empowered to meddle with the monasterial operation. Or, the abbot's inability to stipulate and reinforce the acceptance of disciples and the conferment of precepts lead to a further decline in standards. And, last, the absence of a defined term for abbotship often results in individual monopoly of monasterial properties.

On many an occasion Hsing Yun has made public pleas for fairer, healthier circumstances under which all religions may be enabled to grow. He insists that both the congregation and monastery be integral parts of Buddhism at large, not pertaining to an individual following or private ownership; that administrative supervision by lay people be abolished, making way for professional management by the sangha and ending the strife between the two once and for all; that abbots be required to have been trained in orthodox Buddhist colleges and to hold legitimate and professional credentials; and that terms for abbotship be clearly defined to facilitate proper succession.

Pleas for Buddhist education

To elevate the quality of the sangha, Buddhist education is the key.

Taiwan's situation is such that Fu Jen Catholic University has its full-scale religious department and curriculum and that the Protestant Tung Hai University has its own legitimate school chapel. Not the Buddhist colleges. Their graduates can't enjoy the same status as the others. Worse, the occasional cries for their abolition are still heard in the same government that gives the others full endorsement.

Even the communist regime of the mainland runs a centralized operation despite its intrinsic atheism. All Buddhist colleges are funded by, and directly under the government, and their faculties salaried like their counterparts in the teachers' colleges. In America, all theologic institutions enjoy unreserved recognition. And, universities in Japan both national and private are known to conduct the most developed religious studies.

Somehow, in Taiwan alone, the Buddhist college seems orphaned within the educational system. After three decades of efforts in Buddhist education, Hsing Yun is still fighting for a legitimate status for Buddhist education by calling for official registration of all Buddhist colleges, the general acceptance of official guidelines from the ministry of education, official recognition of student credentials, and official permission to publicly recruit students.

Hsing Yun's proposals for the promotion of Buddhist education are that:

- the elementary, middle, and university levels should be clearly defined
- eligible teachers are certified by examination
- the curriculum is standardized
- the facilities are standardized
- educational administrators are trained and recognized
- the leadership is centralized
- outstanding graduates are sent for higher learning
- intercollegiate activities such as lectures and contests are conducted
- student credentials are recognized
- positions such as preachers, abbots, and

directors are assumed by Buddhist college graduates only

- joint examinations are devised for Buddhist student bodies in postsecondary institutions to enable eligible examinees to serve in the Buddhist circle in the future and
- scholarships, grants, and loans are obtained within the Buddhist circle

Powerful are those nations who are forerunners in education and vice versa. By the same token, as much as religion is accountable for educating society, how can it purify minds and revise trends if the qualifications of its people are questionable?

The question of self-sufficiency

Tradition has it that so long as monastics carry on their efforts in chanting sutras and conducting Dharma functions, they can make a decent living and the temple will thrive. Or, as the saying goes, "clouds of incense gathering above,[2] vegetarian feasts

[2] As in a service.

are consumed all about." Not much of that has really changed. Monastics are still competing for devotees or soliciting donations for the purpose of monasterial upkeep – a sign of materialistic dependence and, for sure, one of the reasons why Buddhism is yet to command society's respect.

The agri-Ch'an livelihood which Ch'an master Huai Hai of the T'ang dynasty led and advocated was committed to self-sufficiency by way of day-to-day toil and productivity; Master T'ai Hsü at the turn of the century went to the extent of urging that factories be set up and run by monastics not only for self-sufficiency but also to benefit society. Along that line, the conviction of Hsing Yun, who was reared in orthodoxy [like the two masters], is such that the Buddhist circle should be as productivity- and business-oriented as the Catholic and Protestant circles so acclaimed for their medical and educational undertakings. The Buddhist circle in Japan, too, has ventured into the retail and hotel businesses, and society appears to have little problem with that. He urges that Taiwan's

Buddhist circle should quit regarding business enterprises as taboo, and that it must be economically resourceful to better serve society and benefit all living beings.

As for Hsing Yun himself, his business schemes have spanned the longest time, from Chih-kuang, a school of commerce founded with fellow monastics Wu I and Nan T'ing some 30 years ago, P'u-mên High School at Fo Kuang Shan 18 years ago, Hsi Lai University [in 1990], the newly launched and feverishly pursued project of Fo Kuang University, a whole range of ongoing enterprises like Fo Kuang television and radio stations, to the construction of a Buddhist daily and a mass communications center.

Fo Kuang University is Hsing Yun's ultimate dream which is about to come true. The institution of higher learning is destined to be another milestone in Buddhist enterprises at large. On a sprawling 56-square-hectare property overlooking the sea in Linmei (Beautiful Woods), Chiaohsi (Rocky Brook) in the county of Ilan, the ground-breaking ceremony was held in October, 1993. Initially, it is scheduled to begin with seven departments – Chinese, philosophy, mass communications, business management, foreign languages and literature, fine art, and drama – and to accept applications for its graduate school in 1995.

Hsing Yun's mental picture of Fo Kuang University is one of a diversified, superfine, and natural institute which harmonizes life and the humanities. The University is to be a shining model of education. Its first chancellor is Dr. Kung P'êng-ch'êng, a young scholar of Chinese literature.

In the meantime, efficacious fund-raising through public donations and auctions of all forms has amassed a remarkable foundation for the institution, and so far has evidenced a most wondrous connection between Buddhism and society at large. No other puts it better than Hsing Yun himself: "Who owns Fo Kuang University? Certainly not myself or Fo Kuang Shan. This is an institution that belongs to society. Indeed, Fo Kuang University belongs to everyone!"

Riding the universal crest

More often than not, his concerns for and projections of the state of affairs around him, when articulated, either annoy a privileged few or simply fall on deaf ears. But Hsing Yun knows too well that the home, one's own base, is where everything begins.

So this branded liberal in the Buddhist circle has vowed to create a monasterial institution of modern character named Fo Kuang Shan, whose system is healthy and viable, and whose operation is organized and smooth. Its Buddhist colleges have to this day generated over 1,000 graduates, all vibrant new blood in the monastic lineage. What is more, in recent years other Buddhist bodies have been seen to pattern themselves upon that of Fo Kuang Shan in the network establishment of educational, medical, charitable, and cultural enterprises.

Hsing Yun is never overly excited or afraid but basically hangs on to the principle of Buddhahood – and Buddhahood only – and rides the universal crest of undertaking. Problems still abound, and perfection is yet to be attained. Indeed, the fruit of Buddhahood takes more, much more, than a mere lifetime to mature. Hsing Yun has great faith that the undertaking shall continue through succeeding generations, and someday soon Chinese Buddhism shall sport a sparkling new look.

Chapter 21

No regrets whatsoever

Out of the clear, cool nocturnal blue above southern Taiwan rains gold and silver and loose diamonds – fireworks! Among the shadows of trees and groves, ornate lanterns sway to and fro. Applause and cheering rise and fall ... and rise again.

That is the Dharma function of the lanterns of peace featured each lunar New Year at Fo Kuang Shan from the 1st to the 15th of the first moon. Then, on the 1st day of the second moon, also the anniversary of Hsing Yun's renunciation, devotees converge again for the annual general meeting. It happens year after year without fail. In that month alone, hundreds of thousands of them from all over would head toward the Great Welcoming Buddha, the Main Shrine, or, plainly, home – sweet home.

From the rubble of postwar poverty Taiwan rose like a phoenix from the cauldron of epochal vicissitudes. The legend of Hsing Yun was wrought from a like foundation. But then again, Hsing Yun's is much, much more than a fabulous tale. For he inherited no lineal prominence and earned no formal credentials; nor was he ever anywhere close to being a child prodigy. Still as a child, he lost a parent; became a novice, he faced infinite chaos; was a loner, yet he survived.

His odyssey is an inspiration to those of us who seek the extraordinary despite our own ordinariness. He is like a borrowed light for the revelation of our inner nature as well as for projecting into our future.

Focus, then strive on

Focus, then strive on ... to the end.

That is the synopsis of his career and

the characteristic of his life, and that brings him success.

Choosing monkhood over home at the tender age of twelve, the child was driven to implore his mother and thereafter to dare a decade of tribulations in monastic training by the sole realization of what honor meant.

Again picking a winding path to Taiwan in 1949, the young monk found himself a total stranger in a strange land with little means and no knowledge of the language. He was hungry; he was cold; he was sick; he was jailed; he was wronged; he was battered; he saw many around him succumb to similar circumstances. What kept him going, somehow, was the pact with Master Chih Yung to fend for their faith in the mainland while carrying the Buddha's light across the strait, and the overall commitment to the renaissance of Chinese Buddhism. So he took four years to learn to live under someone else's roof, twelve years to learn to lay the groundwork for the future; and years and years to learn to build Fo Kuang Shan.

All the time, when things and people

around him changed, the life choice of living his faith did not.

Like the economic progress of Taiwan and the maturation of its social conditions, Hsing Yun's diligence, too, has born bountiful fruits. His first-generation disciples, torch in hand, have taken their positions in an astounding global network, and the second generation is ready and waiting. The mammoth body of Buddhist enterprises known collectively as Fo Kuang Shan embraces close to 100 branch temples worldwide, together with 180 peripheral establishments such as Buddhist colleges, high schools, kindergartens, nurseries, publishing houses, hospitals, and seniors' homes.

Forever and ever handing down the light

No one can ever doubt Hsing Yun's achievement in rearing the young for the Buddhist faith. Whether viewed from the standpoint of modern education or that of orthodox formality, that Fo Kuang Shan commands a total of over 1,100 monastics is a record in the history of Buddhism. For it is Hsing Yun's quintessential conviction that, in handing down the light, it is to be forever ... and ever.

To make sure that development of all forms be strong and lasting, Hsing Yun harmonizes the orthodox monastery with the modern institution to come up with a versatile system – in terms of administration, economy, finance, personnel, education, and welfare – capable of marching with the times. The overall scheme is such that all those who head the 100 or so branches abide by the system as the core of a network built upon monastic fellowship. A mighty mechanism, it is also a fair and open, tight and smooth operation.

Thematically, Fo Kuang Shan embodies the spirit of Mahayana Buddhism, which Hsing Yun seeks to manifest in the forms of humanistic Buddhism and realistic Buddhism. Employing modern preaching methods, he seeks to spread such concepts as life preceding death and Buddhism as a religion of blessedness. In the meantime, Taiwan's economic boom, social diversity, and educational progress together have formed fertile ground for the growth of humanistic Buddhism. Presently, Fo Kuang Shan's devotees number over one million, along with hundreds of thousands worldwide. Overall, Buddhism has become a popular faith among the rich, the famous, the intellectual, as well as the common folk.

True that Fo Kuang Shan is Hsing Yun's brain-child. But "the Dharma is to be relied on, not the preacher." And, the system must be adhered to. He decided to pass the baton of abbotship on to Venerable Hsin Ping a decade ago to make sure that Fo Kuang Shan's growth would never cease.

Lay down in order to pick up once more

One has to "lay down in order to pick up once more." As if broken free from some cocoon, Hsing Yun went on to preach across all boundaries and, eventually, founded Buddha's Light International Association. Destined to be a major player in the future of Buddhism, B.L.I.A.'s 100 or so chapters are already seen to be injecting much new strength.

Hsing Yun is frank about his inward journey: "All my life I have deplored, most of all, broken promises. To me, honor is of the essence. Reality is such that, regardless of how much you've gone through, all that people care about seems no more than the result. I just set my goal and thereafter refuse to be shaken or to change my mind no matter how bitterly trying it is along the way. The knottiest problems can be solved, just like that.

"Indeed, the determined always has hundreds of thousands of solutions, and the undetermined, hundreds of thousands of obstacles."

Hsing Yun's philosophy is that irrespective of our role upon the stage called life, we should always play it as though we were the protagonist.

A thoroughfare to modernity

The *Diamond Sutra* states: "All things going, they resemble dreams and illusions, bubbles and shadows, dew and lightning. That is how things should be viewed."

It means that whatever is seen and heard is but empty and unreal. But on the other hand, for the worldly to appreciate Master Hsing Yun, it would be hard not to trace and analyze his career and contributions in the light of history and of a projection into the future.

A lifetime's bustling has aged him markedly. His first and foremost achievement is that, in bringing orthodox Chinese Buddhism to Taiwan, he has transformed a desert deprived of the Dharma rain into a Pureland abloom with Bodhi growth. On top of that, he has opened up for Buddhism a thoroughfare to modernity. Under Hsing Yun, "the doctrine remains orthodox while the format is contemporary; thinking remains unworldly while undertakings are worldly; living remains conservative while preaching is progressive." As more and more become drawn to Buddhism now than any day in history's past, some even reckon that he is singularly responsible for Buddhism's comeback in Taiwan, if nowhere else.

Second, he has reared generation after generation of talent for the perpetuation of the Dharma lineage. Especially noteworthy is that he has been way ahead of his time – and certainly above his peers – in acknowledging the [equal] giftedness and competence of the bhiksunis and in promoting them to positions [historically beyond their reach]. For the Buddhist convention has it that the bhiksus always come before the bhiksunis. The latter are subjugated to the extent that in Thai, Sri Lankan, and Tibetan Buddhism, no bhiksuni precepts are conferred. Not in Taiwan, which has produced a constellation of brilliant bhiksunis, like Venerables Hsiao Yun, Chêng Yen, and many others, together with Hsing Yun's first-generation disciples, Venerables Tzu Chuang, Tzu Hui, Tzu Jung, Tzu Chia, and Tzu I. In fact, Fo Kuang Shan's bhiksu and bhiksuni population is a record 3:7 proportion. Added to that is Venerables Tzu Hui's vice-presidency in the World Fellowship of Buddhists under the auspices of Hsing Yun. Traditionally the domain of representatives from the Theravada tradition and out of bounds to women, the tight-knit executive circle has been broken through.

In the hearty words of Venerable Chao Hui, "he has genuinely attained the equality among all living beings as taught by the Buddha."

Third, he has established an order for the coexistence and mutual respect between the sangha and devotees. Contrary to the traditional monastic superiority regardless of personal dedication or practice, which tends to alienate the lay community more than anything else, Hsing Yun stresses a Fo Kuang Shan free from class distinction.

"As a nation can't be without people," he says, "a temple can't be without devotees. Nothing invigorates Buddhism more than the joining of forces between the sangha and the lay community."

Newly elected is an outstanding group of lay preachers and teachers of the Dharma in Buddha's Light International Association, which is the consummate affirmation of the role of the lay community in Buddhism.

The master and his circumstances

Even beyond the realm of religion, Hsing Yun has never stopped giving, directly and indirectly.

Back in Taiwan, the four million Buddhists there are justifiably a major source of stability, and their faith provides regulation amidst the nation's political, economic, and social strife. In addition, himself a monastic originally from the mainland, he has demolished the barrier of regionalism by leading a majority of indigenous devotees in Taiwan. In truth, the breakdown of regionalism is giving Buddhism in Taiwan a fresh outlook.

Overseas, the intricate web of organizations under Fo Kuang Shan and Buddha's Light International Association executes its function in diplomacy with flying colors. From the chateau in France, the grassland of Australia, to the desert of South Africa, Hsing Yun and his disciples and followers have replaced the century-old impression of a pent-up nation with a glittering new image of a vibrant people –

the Chinese of today.

"Look on the farthest side, and do whatever is closest at hand; contemplate on the most doubtful, and strive wherever things are toughest" – such is how Hsing Yun's undertakings are principled.

If his religious leadership were a product of Taiwan's social evolvement and himself a heroic figure made by circumstance, Hsing Yun, in dispatching the messages of Buddhism across the world, would still be a master who has carved out his own set of circumstances.

Hsing Yun, the name and its meaning

If slander is a twin to acclaim, now and again he finds himself in the whirlpool of controversy. Whatever the case, indeed, in no other life story is such a kaleidoscope of views reflected but Hsing Yun's. While some are agog with expectation on the temple grounds, waiting to catch a glimpse of his towering stature, others snort at how devoid of spirituality those concrete Buddha images are; while the repentant ones weep at the delivery of the Dharma, others are dismayed at his presence in the national political arena; while most donate in earnest to gather merits for themselves and loved ones, others attempt to profit under the shingle of Fo Kuang Shan; while many pay homage and offer incense, others scrutinize each book of merits and wonder how much he must have pocketed.

The ultimate irony is how harsh people tend to be on the subject of their hero-worship, which they happen to have created themselves. But, is that the intent of the hero himself?

"Who am I?" Hsing Yun asks. "Only a regular monk! Only a rural person!"

Criticism or praise, they are to him as fleeting as swans across the sky and snow on the ground, for he has long formed his own definition of life.

Once on the road, this weather forecast from the radio came through: "Satellite pictures of the clouds[1] indicate ..."

[1] *Wei-hsing yun-t'u* in the original text. Venerable Tzu Jung was hit by the words *hsing* (star, as in *wei-hsing* or satellite) and *yun* (cloud, as in *yun-t'u* or picture of clouds) in the weather report. Hence her question.

At that, Venerable Tzu Jung was struck with a question: "Master, first the grand master named you Chin Chüeh. Then you named yourself Hsing Yun. Pray tell us what transpired!"

"I remember learning to use the dictionary in the monastery when I stumbled upon the term hsing-yun-t'uan (masses of stars and clouds)," Hsing Yun replied. "I read on and its definition ran like this: Huge, old, and without bound, there was a union of countless cloud-like stars before the universe took form. How I admired that state! While I vowed to bring light to those in the dark, I reckoned I would always be above and beyond care and bondage. So I took the Dharma name *Hsing Yun*."

On a portrait which Li Zijian painted of him, Hsing Yun had written a verse, which is in essence a summary of his life:

> Ask him who he was, [he'd say]
> Atop the mountain of
> Fo Kuang he lived,
> Which, since twenty-seven
> years he founded.
> On the Dharma he spoke
> through forty falls,

A thousand disciples he taught,
or more,
The light he brought o'er
five continents.
Countless roles he would assume, and
A purified world's companion he'd be.

Paving the way for the next 500 years

Against the backdrop of an unsettling age, Hsing Yun, with his broad-mindedness, insight, flair, and resolve, has emerged from ordinariness to attain extraordinariness.

In an article titled *The Next 500 Years in Buddhism,* U.S.-based historian and author T'ang Tê-kang delivers an almost conclusive evaluation of Hsing Yun:

"In teaching the major religions of the world, I make sure that students bear in mind the old Chinese proverb: 'Every 500 years a king shall rise.' For learning world history that way is a breeze.

"As regards the dates of various religious founders, that of Jesus is the easiest to remember. Five hundred years before him came Sakyamuni Buddha (563 - 483 B.C.E.), Lao Tzu, and Confucius. Pushing altogether 1,000 years back, that would be the time of Moses, founder of Judaism."

"It was Mohammed (570 - 630?), founder of Islam, who came 500 years after Jesus. Altogether 1,000 years later came Martin Luther (1483 - 1546), founder of Protestantism. Now, as the clock ticks toward the end of another 500 years since the religious reform [in Christianity] of 1520, apparently the next epochal leadership in religion is again anticipated."

"A circumspective look at the world's cultural, philosophical, political, and economic developments today reveals that Buddhism is where a new life-force generates. ... For Buddhism today is not only sweeping across Southeast Asia but also penetrating the five continents. So potent is its impact and so excellent are its conditions that it has long surpassed the Christian reform [of the 16th century]."

"With the four young dragons[2] emerging at the Pacific Rim and China rising feverishly to catch up, the enormous

[2] Taiwan, Hong Kong, Singapore, and Korea, the first three being of the Chinese descent and the last of relative descent.

middle class that results is asking for a religion of their own – a Buddhism which is adaptable to modern circumstances, and one which is home-oriented instead of monastery-oriented as in orthodoxy. Hence a Buddhist reform is in the works, and a reformer is here."

"The new state of Buddhism is such that, at long last, the Mahayana and Theravada along with the ten schools are to join forces, and together they shall take China and the rest of the world by storm. Now, in paving the way for Buddhism in the next 500 years, just who is capable of shouldering the task bestowed from heaven? Apart from Venerable Master Hsing Yun, founder of Fo Kuang Shan, I honestly can't think of anyone else."

Once a monk, always a monk

Like his mother giving her son away to the masses, Hsing Yun, too, has long given himself to all living beings. Was he ever sorry that he had but made that one choice over a lifetime? Or, if he could start from the very beginning, how would he have spent this life?

"The greatest blessing in this life of mine has been attaining monkhood," he remarks. "I pledge to be a monk in my next life, and in the many, many lives to come."

Emperor Shun-chih of the Ch'ing dynasty once penned poetry to honor monkhood. It ran like this:

> As rare as gold and white jade are;
> The rarest of all is to wear the cassock.

Monkhood to Hsing Yun has been a task for a man of fortitude and courage, not what mere generals and ministers could have tackled.

Should he return in the next life he would still have no regrets.

Appendix 1

Chronology of Venerable Master Hsing Yun

1927 Born on the 22nd day of the 7th month of the lunar calendar in Chiangtu, Chiangsu province, [China]. Named Li Kuo-shên. Father Li Ch'êng-pao, mother Liu Yü-ying. Third of four children, with older brother and sister and a younger brother.

1931 Became vegetarian alongside maternal grandmother, a Buddhist.

1934 Entered rural school.

1937 Father missing on a business trip to Nanjing.

1939 Midway to Nanjing in quest of his father with mother, took the tonsure under Venerable Master Chih K'ai at Ch'i-hsia Temple. Given the Dharma names Wu Ch'ê and Chin Chüeh. Became a disciple of the 48th generation of the Lin-chi division in Ch'an Buddhism.

1941 Ordained at Ch'i-hsia Temple.

1944 Studied at T'ien-ning Temple, Ch'ang-chou.

1945 Transferred to Chiao-shan Buddhist College.

1947 Arrived in Ta-chüeh Temple, Pai-t'a Mountain. Became principal of White Pagoda Elementary School. Founded monthly *Raging Billows* with schoolmate Master Chih Yung. Was arrested by the communists.

1948 Became director of Hua-tsang Temple, Nanjing. Edited *Splendid Light* supplement of newspaper *Hsü Pao*.

1949 Arrived in Keelung, Taiwan, with monastic relief group. Arrested with Master Tz'u Hang and others on allegations of subversive activities and incarcerated for 23 days.

1950 Took shelter at Yüan-kuang Temple, Chungli, under Master Miao Kuo. Also stood guard in the mountains around Fa-yün Temple, Miaoli, where he authored *Singing in Silence*, his first work.

1951 Took charge of academic affairs in a Buddhist seminar conducted by

Venerable Ta Hsing. Edited *Life Monthly* and learned Japanese.

1952 Elected an executive of the Chinese Buddhist Association. Raised funds for emergency relief of the flood in Hualien.

1953 Spoke on the Dharma at Lei-yin Temple, Ilan, on the invitation of Li Chüeh-ho. Published *Discourse on Avalokitesvara's Universal Gate Chapter.*

1954 Stationed at Lei-yin Temple and started preaching in rural areas and prisons. Venerables Tzu Chuang, Tzu Hui, and Tzu Jung took refuge in the Triple Gems.

1955 Preached around Taiwan while promoting the reprint of the Buddhist Canon. Suffered severe arthritis in the legs. Published *Biography of Sakyamuni Buddha,* the first-ever hardback Buddhist text.

1956 Completed the lecture hall for the Ilan chanting group . Founded the first kindergarten, Tz'u-ai, and tutored in arts and sciences, Kuang-hua. Preached in prisons.

1957 Published *National Master Yü Lin*. Founded and became chief editor of *Awakening the World*, a magazine which was published three times a month.

1958 Conducted the Dharma function for the preservation of the nation held by the Chinese Buddhist Association in Taipei. Venerable Hsin Ping was tonsured.

1959 Supported the Tibetan Buddhist movement against communist suppression. Organized the first float parade in celebration of the Buddha's birthday. Established a Buddhist cultural service in Sanchung, Taipei. Published *Biography of Sakyamuni Buddha's Ten Great Disciples*.

1960 Published the *Enlightenment Sutra*.

1961 Became publisher of *Buddhism Today*. Led the Ilan youth choir and cut the first six Buddhist records in Taiwan.

1962 Took over the publishing of *Awakening the World*.

1963 Organized a Buddhist visiting group alongside Venerable Pai Shêng and toured India, Thailand, Malaysia, Singapore, the Philippines, Japan, and Hong Kong. Met with king Bhumibol Adulyadej of Thailand, President Diosdado Macapagal of the Philippines, etc. Petitioned for the release of 700 arrested Chinese, and rescued two fishing vessels in Kaohsiung.

1964 Completion of Shou-shan Temple, Kaohsiung, followed by the founding of Shou-shan Buddhist College. Established a school of commerce named Chih-kuang together with Venerables Wu I and Nan T'ing. Published a book of travels and a range of bilingual Buddhist texts in Chinese and English.

1965 Published a series of lectures titled *Awakening the World*.

1967 Construction began for Fo Kuang Shan. Shou-shan Buddhist College renamed Tung-fang Buddhist College. Took over a Christian mission service, which was turned into a home for the aged and poor.

1969 Held the first Buddhist summer

camp for postsecondary students. Founded the first Buddhist Sunday school for children. Built Pilgrim's Lodge at Fo Kuang Shan.

1970 Founded Ta-tz'u Nursery. Established pilgrims' group.

1971 Completion of the Great Compassion Shrine, followed by the blessing of the Buddha's image. Founded P'u-mên Vihara, Taipei, which later became P'u-mên Temple. Elected president of Sino-Japanese Buddhist Association.

1972 Introduced the constitution of Fo Kuang Shan's Committee of Religious Affairs .

1973 Chiang Ching-Kuo, head of the executive council, visited Fo Kuang Shan for the first time. Basketball court at Tung Shan officially opened. Founded Fo Kuang Shan Ts'ung-lin College which was renamed Chinese Buddhist Research Institute.

1974 Ground-breaking of Fu-shan temple, Changhua.

1975 Foundation laid for the Great

Welcoming Buddha and the Main Shrine. Conducted a three-day lecture at the National Arts Hall, which was the first-ever Buddhist lecture held in the halls of government.

1976 Attended the U.S. bicentennial festivities and preached the Dharma for the first time in the country. Ran Buddhist summer camp for seniors and started an English Buddhist center. Was founding publisher of *Fo Kuang Scholarly Journal*. Launched a clinic at Shou-shan Temple, Kaohsiung, and P'u-mên Hospital.

1977 Lectured at Chung-shan Hall, Taipei. Founded P'u-mên High School. Established the editing and publishing center for the Fo Kuang Buddhist Canon. Chinese Buddhist Research Institute and University of Oriental Studies, U.S.A. became sister schools. Ten Thousand Buddhas Triple Platform Ordination, deemed a preceptoral model.

1978 After becoming president of R.O.C., Chiang Ching-Kuo visited Fo Kuang Shan again. Held Dharma function for the preservation of the nation in Dr. Sun Yat-sen Memorial Hall. Raised funds for the establishment of a Chinese Buddhist Youth Association. Received honorary Ph.D. from University of Oriental Studies. Became first president of International Buddhist Progress Society. Raised funds for the establishment of Hsi Lai Temple.

1979 In view of severe diplomatic ties between Taiwan and the United States, held Buddhist concert at Dr. Sun Yat-sen Memorial Hall to raise funds for a national foundation of self-sufficiency. Launched *Universal Gate* magazine. First Buddhist program *Sweet Dew* televised. Led pilgrimage to India. Held first Buddhist summer camp for children. *National Master Yü Lin* adapted for the stage at the National Arts Hall.

1980 Produced the first set of Buddhist bookmarks and calendar. Became director of Chinese Culture University's Indian Research Institute. Telecast of the program *Gate of Faith.*

1981 Held Buddhist summer camp for mothers. Taught Buddhist philosophy at Tung Hai University.

1982 Became brother temples with Tong-do Sa, Korea. Conducted the 5th International Buddhist Scholars' Conference.

1983 Honored by the ministries of legal affairs and education for outstanding educational achievements.

1984 Met the Dalai Lama. Established a mobile clinic to offer free medical care. Founded the first Buddhist city college at P'u-hsien Temple, Kaohsiung.

1985 Held World Buddhist Youth Scholars' Conference. Passed the abbotship of Fo Kuang Shan onto Venerable Hsin Ping. Practiced in isolation at Hsi Lai Temple, Los Angeles. Served as executive officer of the Chinese-Tibetan Cultural Association of the Republic of China. *The Platform Sutra of the Sixth Patriarch* televised; as well as *Venerable Master Hsing Yun's Lecture Series,* which was honored by the department of information.

1986 World Sutric and Tantric Buddhist Conference held at Fo Kuang Shan. Took office as advisor of nationalist party affairs. Launched new annual lecture series at Kaohsiung Chung-chêng Cultural Center.

1987 Became founding president of the American Buddhist Youth Association. Visited Chinese Buddhist Temple, Sarnath, India. *Hsing Yun's Ch'an Talk* televised.

1988 Inauguration of Hsi Lai Temple, where the 16th World Fellowship of Buddhists conference and the 7th World Fellowship of Buddhist Youth conference were held. Conducted purifying service for the opening of the California state and Los Angeles municipal meetings. Preached in Hong Kong for the first time at the City Hall. Held the first alms-round fundraising event for the Fo Kuang Shan Cultural and Educational Foundation. Traveled to northern Thailand with medical team and preached there. The *Fo Kuang Encyclopedia* honored by the department of information.

1989 Held International Ch'an Conference at Fo Kuang Shan. On his first homecoming in four decades, paid homage to ancestral stupas in Ch'i-hsia and visited his mother in Chiangtu. The Dalai Lama was a guest at Hsi Lai Temple. *Hsing Yun's Ch'an Talk* honored by the department of information. Spoke on the Dharma to the armed forces and their respective academies.

1990 Invited to attend the inauguration of U.S. President George Bush. Received his mother at Fo Kuang Shan and Xu Jiatun, head of the New China News Agency in Hong Kong, at Hsi Lai Temple. Began an annual three-day lecture at Hunghom Coliseum, Hong Kong. Went on preaching tour in England, Holland, Belgium, France, Switzerland, Austria, Yugoslavia, and Italy. Plans for the construction of International Buddhist Association of Australia under way on a 36-acre property donated by the city of Sydney, Australia.

1991 Hsi Lai University, temporarily

housed in the temple, opened. Founded Buddha's Light International Association, R.O.C., and raised funds for floods on the mainland. Hospitalized for a broken right thigh. *Hsing Yun Dharma Words* televised. Established a branch temple in a chateau outside Paris and began the spread of the Dharma in Europe.

1992 Buddha's Light International Association established and its first meeting held at Hsi Lai Temple. Devotee Chang Sheng-Kai donated his own residence for the establishment of the first branch temple in South America, I.B.P.S. do Brasil. Was requested to put up a temple in Johannesburg, South Africa by Dr. Hennie Senekal – the first step in the spread of the Dharma in Africa. For the second year honored by the ministry of education for outstanding educational undertakings. Fo Kuang Shan Cultural and Educational Foundation also honored.

1993 *National Master Yü Lin* televised on CTS. Second B.L.I.A. world conference held in Taipei. Registration of Fo Kuang University officially approved by the ministry of education, followed by ground-breaking ceremony in Linmei, Chiaohsi, in Ilan county. Buddha's Light International Association named the most outstanding social organization in Taiwan.

1994 Extensive fundraising for Fo Kuang University through art auctions. Taipei Temple inaugurated. Received city key to and honorary citizenship of Austin, Texas. Third B.L.I.A. world conference held in Vancouver, Canada. Fo Kuang Shan provided emergency relief for the massive floods in August at the request of President Li Teng-hui. *Hsing Yun Says* opened on TTV. *Diary of Hsing Yun* published in 20 volumes. Ten monastics of African descent tonsured. Held honorary presidency of World Fellowship of Buddhists and presidency of B.L.I.A.

Fo Kuang Shan Distribution of Branch Temples in Taiwan, 1996

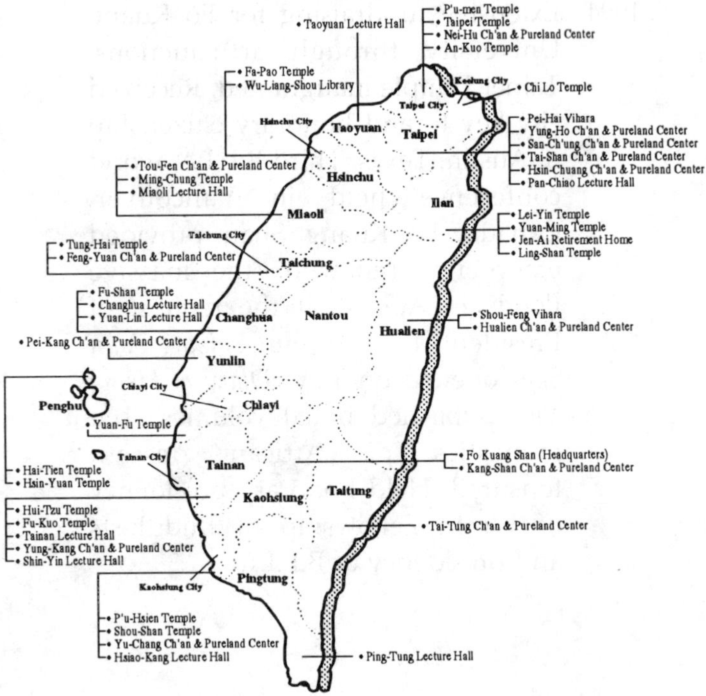

Sweden
Norway
Netherlands
Belgium
London
Europe
Denmark
Germany
France
Switzerland
Yugoslavia
Moscow
Ulyanovsk
Asia
Korea
Japan
Sarnath
Buddhagaya
Sikkim
Ladakh
Nepal
Bhutan
Delhi
Bangladesh
Andhra Pradesh
Burma
Maharashtra
Bangalore
Madras
Sri Lanka
Thailand
Chinmen
R.O.C.
Hong Kong & Macao
Vietnam
Philippines
Guam
Malaysia
Brunei
Singapore
Indonesia
Africa
Congo
Newcastle
Bloemfontein
Lesotho
Pretoria
Johannesburg
Durban
Cape Town
Australia
Queensland
Perth
Victoria
Sydney
Canberra
North Island, New Zealand
South Island, New Zealand

Fo Kuang Shan Global Distribution of Branch Temples, 1996

I.B.P.S. -- International Buddhist Progress Society

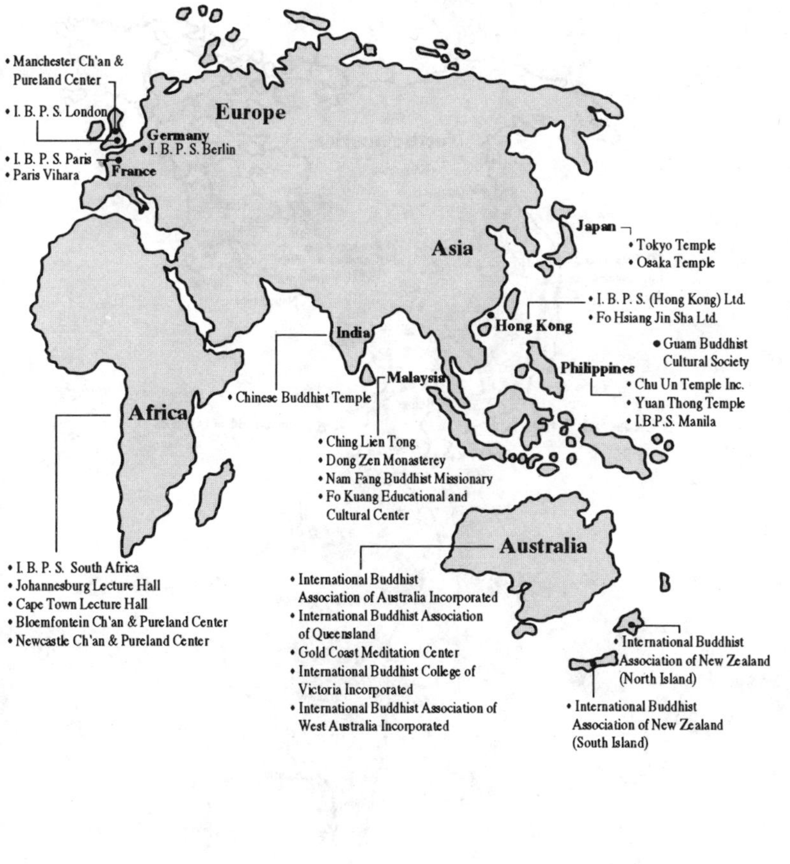

Europe
Asia
Africa
Australia
• Manchester Ch'an & Pureland Center
• I. B. P. S. London
Germany
• I. B. P. S. Berlin
• I. B. P. S. Paris
• Paris Vihara
France
Japan
• Tokyo Temple
• Osaka Temple
• I. B. P. S. (Hong Kong) Ltd.
• Fo Hsiang Jin Sha Ltd.
Hong Kong
India
• Chinese Buddhist Temple
Malaysia
• Ching Lien Tong
• Dong Zen Monasterey
• Nam Fang Buddhist Missionary
• Fo Kuang Educational and Cultural Center
• Guam Buddhist Cultural Society
Philippines
• Chu Un Temple Inc.
• Yuan Thong Temple
• I.B.P.S. Manila
• I. B. P. S. South Africa
• Johannesburg Lecture Hall
• Cape Town Lecture Hall
• Bloemfontein Ch'an & Pureland Center
• Newcastle Ch'an & Pureland Center
• International Buddhist Association of Australia Incorporated
• International Buddhist Association of Queensland
• Gold Coast Meditation Center
• International Buddhist College of Victoria Incorporated
• International Buddhist Association of West Australia Incorporated
• International Buddhist Association of New Zealand (North Island)
• International Buddhist Association of New Zealand (South Island)

Buddha's Light International Association Global Distribution of Chapters, 1996